Taste and the TV Chef

Taste and the TV Chef

How Storytelling Can Save the Planet

Gilly Smith

Bristol, UK / Chicago, USA

First published in the UK in 2020 by
Intellect, The Mill, Parnall Road, Fishponds, Bristol, BS16 3JG, UK

First published in the USA in 2020 by
Intellect, The University of Chicago Press, 1427 E. 60th Street,
Chicago, IL 60637, USA

A catalogue record for this book is available from
the British Library.

Copy editor: Newgen KnowledgeWorks
Cover designer: Clare Whiting
Cover photos: Brooke Lark, Unsplash, Steve Edwards at etch. and Shutterstock
Production manager: Laura Christopher
Typesetter: Newgen KnowledgeWorks

Print ISBN 9781789383058
ePDF ISBN 9781789383065
ePUB ISBN 9781789383072

Printed and bound by Hobbs

To find out about all our publications,
please visit our website.
There you can subscribe to our e-newsletter,
browse or download our current catalogue,
and buy any titles that are in print.

www.intellectbooks.com

This is a peer-reviewed publication.

FSC
www.fsc.org
MIX
Paper from
responsible sources
FSC® C020438

For Pat Llewellyn, whose story this is.

(1962–2017)

Contents

Acknowledgements

My thanks to all the producers and academics who gave me so much of their time as I researched this book over the last seven years. In particular, I'd like to thank Pat Llewellyn, Jo Hook, Zoe Collins, Nick Thorogood, Jo Ralling and Amanda Murphy from the TV camp, and Dr Louise Fitzgerald and Dr Jess Moriarty from the academic, without whom this book would have been a very different beast. My thanks to Amanda Martin, mother of two small children and struggling novelist who transcribed all my interviews.

Interviews with British television producers and (international) academics were held in person or by Skype or phone, and some (Pat Llewellyn, Zoe Collins, Nick Thorogood, Amanda Murphy, Signe Rousseau) over a period of years. Dr Louise Fitzgerald was my academic Jiminy Cricket and I am but the Morecambe to her Wise. As a journalist in television (as well as print, radio and podcast) first and as an academic second, I straddle both worlds, and Louise was my scholarly coach, prodding me to rethink Nigella within fourth-wave feminism and pulling apart the producers' business-focussed answers to reveal their impact on society.

Thank you too to the gang of 'editors', friends and colleagues who read through the manuscript as it morphed from academic to mainstream, bubbling with voices from the front line of the food revolution: Dr Jess Moriarty, Dr Liz Maudslay, Rob Steen, Lyn Weaden and Jed Novick.

Introduction

'Tell me what you eat, and I will tell you what you are', wrote the epicurean Parisian lawyer and food philosopher, Anthelme Brillat-Savarin, in 1825. Since he threw down his gauntlet, Brillat-Savarin's words have been spun into one of the most famous epithets of all time: 'we are what we eat'. But more than shape and size, we are what food itself has come to represent in society. Our diet is a signifier of who we are, what we would like to be and, perhaps more importantly, what other people think we are. It defines our peer group, divides the rich and the poor, the first world and the developing world and, increasingly, the billion bottoms and the bottom billions. A lesser-known quote of Brillat-Savarin is perhaps even more timely: 'The destiny of nations depends on how they nourish themselves.'

How we nourish ourselves has changed fundamentally in the last 30 years, about the time-span of my career in television, radio, print and podcasting, telling stories about food. Back in the early 1990s, when I was a young researcher on *Food File* (1992–96), Channel 4's first TV series about the politics of food, the films we made about high-welfare farming practices, mobile abattoirs and diets from the Mediterranean that could change our lives in the UK were groundbreaking for British television. While Derek Cooper on Radio 4's investigative food series *The Food Programme* (1979–present) was quietly prodding at the deeper questions around what we ate, British food culture was largely about fuelling up. Pret a Manger, Eat. and Yo! Sushi had yet to revolutionise our lunchtimes, and unfeasibly exotic foods were years away from being a regular Friday night out. Popping out for a bite from our offices even in multicultural Camden High Street would usually mean a tuna sandwich from M&S, although the Portuguese café downstairs did a mean *nata* even then. Location lunches in middle England were a smorgasbord of Hula Hoops and Diet Coke; dinner was a pizza accompanied by a raffia-bound bottle of house red.

In terms of a take-out, the high street in 1990s Britain was stuck in the 1970s, although a smattering of immigrant delis was beginning to give the sandwich a fragrant makeover. But the seeds of change were beginning to grow new ideas on the book shelves. Among our consultants on *Food File* were Geoffrey Canon, co-author with Caroline Walker of *Food Scandal: What's Wrong with the British Diet and How to Put It Right* (1985), and Tim Lang, who would go on to advise Jamie Oliver and become Professor of Food Policy at City University London's Centre for Food Policy. Lang was also one of the 37 leading food academics and scientists to write the 2019 *EAT-Lancet* report on how to feed the 10 billion people likely to live on the planet by 2050. (Spoiler alert: there's not a lot of meat in its conclusions.) It was a feisty time for food, and it would take a whole new turn when a young researcher called Pat Llewellyn, who would go on to discover Jamie Oliver, took her seat in that office above Camden High Street.

It would be another ten years before we met in 2005 – I moved to another TV job while Pat discovered a wild-haired environmentalist cook called Hugh Fearnley-Whittingstall and tried him out as a guest presenter, but we shared an unusually foodie childhood only 40 minutes away from each other. Mine was in Abergavenny, before it became the food Mecca of the UK, with my parents' love of food playing out on a plate of pigs' brains on toast or a milky tripe and onions. There always seemed to be a hock simmering away on the stove, fresh from my father's regular trip to the abattoir. I still find offal a challenge. While my brother and I were dispatched to boarding schools, they would dedicate every Saturday to a recipe from their growing Cordon Bleu part work spending the entire day shopping for the ingredients and the evening prepping, cooking and feasting, mostly just the two of them, sometimes for lucky friends. During the school holidays, the four of us would put aside the seething tensions of our family life and chop and chat as if the Galloping Gourmet himself were in the room.

Meanwhile, Pat's parents ran a hotel further down the A40. 'I think my mum and dad probably brought the first duck a l'orange to Newcastle Emlyn!' Llewellyn told me as we chatted about the smells and tastes in our family kitchens. My chats with her began as I researched a biography of Jamie Oliver in 2006, and continued well into the work on this book. We'll meet her co-architects of Lifestyle TV, Mark Thompson, Peter Bazalgette and Jane Root, later; when they all told me that it was their similarly anachronistic foodie childhoods that inspired their interest in Food TV, I realised just how much my parents' curries, inspired by living in the Far East when I was a small child and perfected over the rest of their lives, had influenced mine.

It was with the second edition of my Jamie Oliver biography, *The Jamie Oliver Effect: The Man, the Food, the Revolution* (2008), with a further three chapters dissecting the intention behind and impact of his campaigning (as seen on Channel 4's *Jamie's Fowl Dinners* [2008] and *Jamie's Ministry of Food* [2008]), that I began to ponder the influence of television in changing the way we live. By the mid-2000s, food was becoming serious. The issue of peak oil, as told in David Guggenheim's 2006 film *The Inconvenient Truth*, showed us that wasting precious oil reserves by buying shrink-wrapped groceries really could bring about the end of civilisation as we know it. The success of the film in getting people to come together in the Transition Town movement all over the world had me scratching my head and making more notes. It also had me signing up for my local Transition Town's food group to envisage a post-oil future. As austerity struck in 2008 with the fall of the banks, and the food conversation changed again, my new role as senior lecturer in Broadcast Media and Broadcast Journalism at the University of Brighton had me teaching my students *why* to tell stories, as well as how.

The journey of this book stretches from that second edition of *The Jamie Oliver Effect*, through Transition Town and into the lecture halls, not just of my own university, but around the world to conferences where I would listen to academics deconstruct television shows and discuss narratives around storytelling. It occurred to me that there were some important people who had yet to be invited to the debate about what I was beginning to realise was one of the most important media feats of all time: the power of TV to change the way we eat, and therefore who we are. I would set about talking to the people behind the camera and put their arguments directly to media academics for the very first time.

The book was born in one of those conferences at the University of Sussex on the influence of Pierre Bourdieu, the French philosopher who *owned* the academic discourse on 'taste'. As I doodled idly, the words appeared on my notepad: *Taste and the TV Chef*. It rolled off the tongue and could, I thought, explain Bourdieu to my students, bite-size. That was in 2012, and this book has bucked and bitten and spat out much of the academic theories that weighed down its chapters in its first iterations. As I left academia and went back into journalism in 2016, the heat was turned up under the issue of food as the triple whammy of obesity, climate change and Brexit questioned our disintegrating relationship with the need to nourish ourselves and the earth itself. The book began to morph into a deeper and more urgent question about how food as lifestyle, the most influential narrative ever created on television, could help us achieve net-zero carbon emissions by 2025, and what we can learn from the gamechangers in TV storytelling that can change the way we live. As the Earth burns and the rains flood the winter of 2019/2020 and we stumble blindly into a post-Brexit future, the story is changing too fast for old-fashioned publishing, and I can only hope that by the time this book hits the shelves, it will be laughably out of date.

The early twenty-first century is a mash-up of contradictions: an unprecedented era of apathy and activism, self-loathing and narcissism, slow food and junk culture is hurtling us into an uncertain future of climate change. As the National Health Service buckles under the news, reported by Butland et al. in 2007, that by 2050, obesity is predicted to affect 60 per cent of adult men, 50 per cent of adult women and 25 per cent of children, a new dialectic around our relationship with food is emerging.

Our relationship with food is deeply paradoxical: even if a new generation which has been brought up surrounded by TV Food and on the high street has not been taught to cook at school or at home, eating well and interestingly is a familiar part of daily life for many. And yet the world is divided into those who eat too much and those who have barely enough to stay alive; food waste and food banks are the yin and the yang of the last 20 years of food. The Food Foundation's 2019 *Children's Future Food Inquiry* reports that 25 per cent of children in the UK are suffering from food insecurity, yet in the NHS *Health Survey for England 2017*, 28.7 per cent of adults in England were classed as obese and a further 35.6 per cent as overweight. Information about calories, sugar, fat and salt is easily accessible with apps scanning QR codes to read levels on ingredients, and while governments engage in spats with campaigners like Jamie Oliver about their role in forcing regulations on the food and drink industry, information is everywhere.

As I write, the rows between food journalists and farmers, scientists and academics, activists and politicians are reaching fever pitch as the role of ruminants and the rise of veganism in a healthy society divide opinion about their threat to life and livelihoods. The one thing they seem to agree on is the net-zero, highly nutritious oyster: who would have thought that this lowly bivalve could offer a glimmer of hope for a carbon neutral world? Never has it been so important to dissect what this all means for the future of the planet. As we enter the geological era scientists call 'the Anthropocene', there's incontrovertible proof that human activity is having an irreversible impact on the planet, forcing the extinction of millions of species as we destroy their habitats for our junk-food habit. But changing the way we eat really can save the human race. An increasingly persuasive body of research can now plot a clear trajectory between the industrialisation of food culture, obesity and climate change. Activist storytelling such as *Cowspiracy* (2014), *Fed Up* (2014), *The End of the Line* (2009), *The Age of Stupid* (2009), *GMO OMG* (2013), *Food, Inc.* (2008), *A Place at the Table* (2012), *Four Horsemen* (2012), *That Sugar Film* (2014) and Anthony Bourdain's *Wasted! The Story of Food Waste* (2017) are among the many films to have brought information previously only available in the boardrooms of multinational food companies and lobbyists to a new kind of diner. Available to watch on YouTube, the viewing experience is democratising the world of food politics: being a foodie, which was once about aspiration and *cultural capital*, that passport to a higher social status, is now about taking responsibility for the provenance of food, where it's going and how it gets there. From the water and energy used to produce it, to the carbon footprint it leaves behind, from the ethics of animal welfare, to our attitude towards waste, how we eat and the choices we make about what we put in our fridges and on our tables have the most powerful impact on the health of Planet Earth. *Fed Up*, which is by the filmmakers behind *The Inconvenient Truth*, made the same claims about sugar in 2014. Ninety-five per cent of Americans will be obese within two decades, while private profit is placed ahead of national health in the American government's agenda. As stated in *Fed Up*, 'Years from now, we're gonna say, "I can't believe we let them get away with that." '

The Internet has created a super-highway of open access and revolutionary spirit which is blasting open the doors of perception, while viral campaigns name and shame industry heads and politicians who favour the interests of the food industry over public health. A new media meritocracy is emerging as the story-telling landscape changes. From social media to the increasing space available to independent filmmakers on the Internet, and the new channels of communication open on campaigning websites (Anna Lappé's Realfoodmedia.org, for example), there are real opportunities to harness the successes of the past and to use our screens to change the world. As filmmaker Ross Ashcroft says in *Four Horsemen*, his 2012 call to arms, 'We need people who speak the truth in the face of collective delusion. To understand something is to be liberated from it.'

Who would have thought that the humble, playful, delightful factual entertainment genre of Lifestyle TV could have transformed British food culture since the early 1990s from the bland, cold comfort food of meat and two veg to a feast of flavours and a cornucopia of culinary styles? Who could have known that Britain was ready for Jamie Oliver and Nigella to cleanse our palate with a heady mix of aspiration, sex appeal and cool Britannia? The answers that British TV producers gave me for this book could provide the answer for audiences all over the world: lifestyle, using the makeover formula of social aspiration to create a promise – a myth – of a better life, has a simple message: cook well, impress your friends and you too can have it all, from the girl-next-door, as Jamie did, to a candlelit dinner party like Nigella's, with an extra bowl of ice cream before bed.

The complexities of the politics of modern food seem at odds with the simpler notion of delicious, delightful eating with friends 20 years on, but perhaps there is an argument for stripping it back to that ubiquitous hashtag, the currency of Instagram. For me, the answer to how to eat is #lessbutbetter. For TV's storytellers, it's an international message for a global village, and with the proliferation of screens offering new opportunities for storytelling based on the simple narrative of keeping up with the Joneses, it's time to galvanise all of our skills to change the international conversation and save the planet. The Intergovernmental Panel on Climate Change (IPCC), the United Nations body for assessing the science related to climate change, reported in August 2019 that it will be impossible to keep global temperatures at safe levels unless we fundamentally transform the way the world produces food and manages land. Vast swathes of forest are decimated to plant soy or corn to feed factory farmed animals. Peatlands, important stores of carbon and one of the most valuable ecosystems on Earth, have been lost due to land management driven by an intensive agriculture industry in mega farms designed to maximise output while minimising costs. 'The impact of intensive agriculture which has helped the world's population soar from 1.9 billion a century ago to 7.7 billion', wrote Robin McKie in *The Guardian* in August 2019, 'has also increased soil erosion and reduced amounts of organic material in the ground.' The IPCC report, quoted by McKie, warns: 'Climate change exacerbates land degradation through increases in rainfall intensity, flooding, drought frequency and severity, heat stress, wind, sea-level rise and wave action.' It's a global crisis, but one which we still have time to change. Just.

The relentless quest for growth is one of the most powerful narratives of the 20th and 21st centuries, and illustrates what can happen when the stories are written by the wrong guys. In 2007, I was part of my local Transition Town movement, planning for a local food system to counter the most pressing danger of the time, peak oil, which threatened food security and with it, social stability. As we looked for answers, I watched environmental campaigner and chair of the UK Sustainable Development Commission, Jonathon Porritt, warn then Department for Environment, Food and Rural Affairs (DEFRA) secretary, David Miliband, of having 'an astonishing view of economic growth at all costs', of encouraging a 'Buzz Lightyear' approach of 'To Infinity and Beyond'. It was the age of expansionism, said Porritt, which had created a mindset shared by governments all over the world that showed an 'inability to recognise and work within the natural law of limits in any living system'. It was the beginning of a movement towards localism, of thinking more carefully about how what we buy, what we eat, what we wear impacts on people and the planet.

Twelve years on, climate change has already begun to devastate livelihoods and threaten whole nations. Low lying atoll nations like the Maldives will be hit hardest as the sea levels rise, while for Indian Himalayan hill farmers, Kamla Joshi and Bhuvan Chand Joshi, the apocalypse is already at their door. Where once there was a rainy season, the rains now last nine months of the year. 'The biggest problem is the wild animals', they write in Extinction Rebellion's 2019 handbook *This Is Not a Drill*. 'There never was much danger of wild animals. Their numbers have increased. They destroy the fields, cause so much damage to farming.' Their climate has changed largely through deforestation: 'Cutting the trees makes all the flowers and jungles fall', write the Joshis. They have no way of protecting their family, and as they watch their neighbours' houses float away and the glaciers melt in the mountains as the Earth warms, disease spreads through their community. 'All the germs and insects are born in the rain', they write. With poverty and disease comes migration and the inevitable social unrest that we can witness all over the world. 'We just get stressed', say the Joshis, who now have to buy in what they used to grow. 'There is a shortage of everything. But we can't migrate. Where would we go?'

The world faces an unprecedented polarity between the haves and the have-nots, with the UN.org recording 783 million people living below the international poverty line of US$1.90 a day. Combating global poverty by 2030 was the first of 17 Sustainable Development Goals (SDGs) for 2030 set by the United Nations General Assembly in 2015. The combined threat from climate change, food security, peak oil and obesity is setting the agenda for global economies; learning how to create new cultural and political values about food is one of the most important roles of the modern storyteller, and this book considers what the TV chef and food influencers can achieve.

Michelle Phillipov, in her 2016 article, 'The new politics of food: Television and the media/food industries', says that it is the 'complex dynamics of interaction between media, emergent cultural values surrounding food' and the way these coalesce that creates new and vitally important narratives, and this is urgent and timely work to do: with 60 per cent of greenhouse gases created by the production of food, the health of the nation is increasingly concerned about the health of the planet, and we're running out of time. To paraphrase Vivienne Westwood, fashion's favourite activist, there's too much to do to do nothing at all.

So how could storytelling save the planet? And which comes first: the chicken or the egg? Does television imitate life or do producers construct reality by spotting a trend and, through the 'magic' of TV, creating the Next Big Thing? This book is about the magic of television, who constructs it and why, and, in a postmodern society, whether or not we care. Stories about food tell us who we are and what we can be, and how television narrates our own stories has been told before by academics and TV producers. But in this, the first book to bring the voices behind Lifestyle TV to the debate about media narratives, both camps have been invited to the table to explore the construction of our modern world through food programmes. Through a series of interviews with some of the most influential gamechangers in British TV, the book examines the role of TV on food cultures around the world – from the British food makeover by Jamie Oliver and Nigella Lawson, for example, to the role of the copycat Jamies in reawakening food memories in Eastern Europe after the political ruptures of the twentieth century. This feat of storytelling on global economic, social and cultural frameworks is told by the people who made it happen, and those who analyse its impact.

This is a book filled with optimism. Rather than the dystopian, apocalyptic visions of the future that proliferate and dominate, this book explores ideas for a tangible utopia where the lessons we have learned from Lifestyle TV can help us to create more hopeful narratives. It aims to enable and empower media students and food activists to harness the potential of televisual storytelling across the many platforms now available for influencing. It is for chefs and food writers to add a little academic seasoning to their storytelling and enjoy a little deconstruction with their dessert. It is for media academics to hear from those behind the camera. Neither the academics nor the producers I talked to had been interviewed in this way before; as each was offered the thoughts and theories from the 'other camp', philosophies were passed across the table like salt and pepper, inspiring us all to think about issues of representation and narratology in new ways: 'You're making me think of lots of things while we're having this conversation' (Jane Root, 2013); 'It was interesting, because when I was looking at your email, I was sort of thinking about how it feels to me' (Pat Llewellyn, 2013); 'You've got some profound themes going on there' (Peter Bazalgette, 2016); 'I think that's a compelling answer to that question' (Signe Rousseau, 2016). Rather than relying purely on citing academics, I called some of them, emailed others and met some for coffee to put the producers' thoughts directly to them. I did the same with the producers.

The book is written in four parts, the first two focussing specifically on British TV and food culture. Part One paints a picture of the cultural, historical and industrial landscape of Britain in the 1980s and 1990s, and the role of the BBC in creating a food phenomenon on television. It examines how BBC Two chiefs, Mark Thompson and Jane Root, brought their fascination with food to the screen to encourage a new generation of TV producers to fetishize taste and romanticise ingredients, which led to an explosion in supermarket sales. The book asks why and how producers create a hierarchy of narratives in TV Food, and how conscious they are of creating stories that audiences then take up in narratives that they tell of themselves and their nation.

Part Two explores the relationship between storytelling and myth-making, and the narratives that TV food programmes use to create consumer tribes led by different chefs: Jamie for the lads, Gordon for the wannabes and Nigella for the dinner party crowd underpinned by the discourses of Bourdieu's economic, cultural and symbolic capital, and Gramsci's concept of hegemony. It asks if the impact of these narratives on the economics of the food industry has changed the face of high streets across the world, as restaurants, gourmet food chains and new café culture signify 'taste' and identify markets. It interrogates how new habits of consumption are constructed and how these practices might be used to contribute to a discourse about sustainable food culture.

One of the central ideas to emerge from the book is one of stable and unstable food cultures, the canvases upon which food can paint a new identity. Part Three focuses on how TV Food created a national identity for the temporarily unstable food cultures of Hungary and Australia, and the power and limitations this introduced to Italy's famously stable food culture. It looks at the Jamie Oliver narrative that was consciously copied from the British originals by TV creators/producers to put Hungary back in touch with its food heritage, reminding its people of who they are. Considering Hungary's most successful food bloggers and TV producers, the book examines the construction of a new Budapest 'cool' as a particularly successful form of storytelling. It also explores how storytelling has limited the story of Italy by romanticising its food, and how, like the storytelling of Australia which has created one of the best culinary cultures in the world, it has obscured part of these countries' histories – and their present – and redefined their identities.

Part Four draws together the arguments of producers and academics, and concludes how TV food must tell us new stories to influence change. With climate change, food security, peak oil and obesity setting the agenda in global economies, it asks how TV and the Internet deal with austerity narratives, and explores how stories about food can be used to influence the impact of human activity on the planet.

The cast

THE PRODUCERS

Mark Thompson: BBC Head of Factual Programmes, 1994–96; BBC Two Controller, 1996–99; Director of BBC National and Regional Broadcasting, 1999–2000; BBC Director General, 2004–12; Chief Executive Officer of the New York Times Company *leading* its digital innovation in cross-platform storytelling, 2012–present.

Jane Root: Head of the BBC Independent Commissioning Group, 1997–99; BBC Two Controller, 1999–2004; CEO Nutopia (*How We Get to Next*, PBS, 2014; BBC Two, 2015). Nutopia is based in London and Washington DC, featuring cross-platform huge-scale documentary series, such as *How We Got to Now* (PBS, 2014; BBC Two, 2015) and *The Story of Us* (History Channel, 2010).

Pat Llewellyn: Producer at Wall to Wall, (*Grow Your Greens, Eat Your Greens*, Channel 4, 1993); CEO of Optomen Productions (*Two Fat Ladies*, BBC Two, 1996–99; *The Naked Chef*, BBC Two, 1999–2001; *The F Word*, Channel 4, 2005–10; *Kitchen Nightmares*, Channel 4, 2004–14; *Heston's Feasts*, Channel 4, 2009–10). Optomen is an international distributor of format shows such as Gordon Ramsay's *Kitchen Nightmares*, *Great British Menu* (BBC, 2006–present) *The F Word, Mary: Queen of Shops* (BBC Two, 2007–08), *Police, Camera Action!* (ITV, 1994–2010) and *Two Fat Ladies*, with offices in London and New York.

Nicola Moody: Head of BBC Factual, 1999–2000; BBC Controller of Factual Commissioning, 2000–03.

Zoe Collins: Creative Director of Jamie Oliver Media Group.

Jo Ralling: Director of Sugar Smart Campaign and UK Partnerships at Jamie Oliver Food Foundation; Food Revolution Day Political Campaign Manager, 2014–15; Chief Operations Officer at Jamie Oliver Media Group, 2006–14; Head of Communications at the Food Foundation.

Peter Bazalgette: Bazal Productions (*Food and Drink*, BBC Two, 1982–2002; *Ready Steady Cook*, BBC Two, 1994–2010).

Nick Thorogood: Creator and Head of UK Food, 2000–04. Launched Scripps channels in Europe, Middle East, and Africa (EMEA), including Food Network, 2010–15.

Amanda Murphy: Executive Producer of *Supernanny* (Channel 4, 2004–08); Senior Reader in Media Arts at Royal Holloway University 2015–present.

Susan Elkington: Former executive vice president in Content Development, Acquisitions and Programming, Film and General Entertainment at Chello-media, the content division of Liberty Global, 2005–13

Niki Page: Former distribution executive at Freemantle, 2011–13; Head of Acquisitions in Factual & Factual Entertainment at Sky Vision, 2014–present.

Jamie Munro: Former managing director of Shine International, 2012–present (*MasterChef*, BBC, 1990–present).

Paula Trafford: Executive Producer at KEO Films, 2011–present, (*Victoria Wood's Nice Cup of Tea*, BBC Two, 2013; *Ottolenghi's Mediterranean Feast*, Channel 4, 2012; *Eat, Drink, Cook China*, Channel 4, 2016).

Philip Lymbery: CEO of Compassion in World Farming, 2005–present.

Tim Mead: Owner of Yeo Valley Farms, 1990–present.

Ben Williamson: Former senior international media director at People for the Ethical Treatment of Animals (PETA), 2015–18.

THE ACADEMICS

Dr Louise Fitzgerald: Lecturer in Film and Screen Studies at the University of Brighton.

Dr Signe Rousseau: Part-time Lecturer at the University of Cape Town, 2000–present.

Dr Sonia Massari: Director of Gustolab International Institute for Food Studies, Rome, 2008–present.

Anita Biressi: Professor of Media and Society in the Department of Media, Culture and Language at the University of Roehampton, London.

Heather Nunn: Professor of Culture and Politics at Roehampton University, London.

THE CHEFS

Ken Hom: TV Chef.

Peter Gordon: Chef Proprietor, the Sugar Club (1995–2001), The Providores (2001–19).

Jamie Oliver: TV Chef.

Nigella Lawson: TV Cook.

Nadiya Hussain: TV Cook.

Marco Pierre White: Chef.

Bosh! Ian Theasby and Henry Firth: YouTube Cooks.

Rick Stein: TV Chef.

Matt Tebbutt: TV Chef.

Hairy Bikers, Si King and Dave Myers: TV Chefs.

Part One

Birth of the cool

It's September 2019, and for the first time in three years, I'm not preparing to head to the Abergavenny Food Festival. I wade through the press release which lists the foodie heavyweights who will be packing another 30,000 visitors into my old home town and consider the many I've interviewed for the *delicious.* podcast for *delicious.* magazine: Elly Pear, Emiko Davies, Pete Brown, Trine Hahnemann, Tom Hunt, Cyrus Todiwala, Chetna Makan, Romy Gill, Georgina Hayden, Tim Lang, Angela Clutton, Sarah Dickins, Nick Miller, Aine Morris… every one of them with something BIG to say about the story of food. Jose Pizarro and Franco Taruschio are hosting the Young Chef Award competition, and I'm thrown back not just into Jose's kitchen to make strawberry gazpacho, but to Franco's impossibly glamorous Italian dining room at the Walnut Tree circa 1974. Nobody other than Franco cooked Italian food then in Abergavenny, but word had it among my older friends who had bagged the tip-heavy waitressing jobs, that there was a six-month waiting list packed with *Japanese* surnames! The Walnut Tree: just the name made me dream of what Japanese visitors would come all this way to eat.

My teen-hood in Abergavenny was an era of café-less streets and brownie-less bakeries, where iced buns were an occasional treat and bread came sliced. Saturdays were for rugby rather than for shopping, and the few locals popping out for essentials would have a transistor radio glued to their ear or peer through the Rediffusion shop window for the latest score. Market Days were the highlight of the week in Abergavenny, the livestock market on a Tuesday at the back of the food and clothes stalls a hive of activity as farmers from the Black Mountains and Brecon Beacons surrounding this gateway to Wales bid on their beasts before spending the rest of the day in the pub. Everyone came to town on Market Day, to buy, to sell, to parade – as we teens did – then only on Tuesday and Friday, now on Saturday too – a tradition practised for centuries which may give a clue to its unusual place in Welsh food history.

These days the market's Brewery Yard, which was a car park back then, has been redeveloped into 'a vibrant events space', with terraces, seating areas and a piazza. At the Abergavenny Food Festival, it is packed with stalls selling hedge-row cordials, heritage cheeses and sustainably packaged and locally sourced burrito-style sushi rolls. I'm not surprised: Abergavenny in the 1970s was a pretty dull place, for a teenager at least. But it had at its heart a relationship with food that was unusual in the Britain of the time. The excellence of local produce – although we didn't call it that then – was taken for granted. But the storytelling had not yet begun: the rump steaks at Edwards the Butcher would only later be branded 'Welsh Black beef', yet back in 1975, they still flew off the shelf. Down the road towards the War Memorial, Vin Sullivan had been importing everything from Polish cooked meats to Parisian vegetables since the 1960s. My parents used to tell me with hushed reverence, how Vin Sullivan, Harrods and Fortnum & Mason were the only three food emporia in the 1970s to import Iceberg Lettuces in the winter from Florida. Ignoring the food miles, Vin Sullivan has learned to tell its own stories, and boasts about its early bold buying practice in a section called 'Product Innovation' on its website. It claims a UK first in airfreighting fresh Dublin Bay prawns from Ireland, ostrich from South Africa, crocodile from Australia and bison from Canada. And all the while, we had to go to Shackleton the Chemist to buy our olive oil.

How Abergavenny became the food festival capital of the UK is a metaphor for this book, a tale of how tradition, relationship with the land and a shot in the arm of innovation and celebrity would cast a spell over my home town and the rest of the country. Visiting TV chefs such as Jamie Oliver would heighten the reality of Abergavenny's easy relationship with good food until its very name would confer a new status on those who exhibited at its food festival. Their stories would be told on BBC Radio 4's legendary *The Food Programme*, and some would even become finalists in its Food and Farming Awards, which were launched a year later in 2000. The powerful storytellers of the British media would pull further focus on what was already there, wrapping tales of Black beef and Abergavenny British soft goat's cheese into digestible stories to be retold, earning stripes of culinary capital for foodies at the cutting edge of Britain's emerging food culture.

What happened to Abergavenny had already begun in 1980s Notting Hill, where a tiny band of chefs was quietly stirring a food revolution. Just down the road in White City, BBC Worldwide began to sprawl out from BBC TV Centre, where fans would queue for hours for a glimpse of their heroes driving through the famous gates to record *Top of the Pops*. BBC Worldwide was a product of the Thatcher era, created to sell the BBC across the world and driven by a new breed of television salespeople proving that there was an international market hungry for British stories.

Notting Hill was a cab ride away from BBC Worldwide and a place already tried and tested in the art of renaissance. It had already housed the first wave of

Caribbean immigrants as HMT *Empire Windrush* ferried its cargo of would-be bus drivers and nurses to British shores, and with them the smells and tastes of home. Pricking the nostrils of the curious and inciting the fury of those less so, Notting Hill would become synonymous with class, clash and culinary experimentation over the next 30 years.

Just streets away, Ladbroke Grove was the fulcrum of rebellion-squatter and hippy-outsider culture, a place already defined by breaking the rules. Portobello with its bric-à-brac stalls and second-hand street markets joined the sweeping crescents of Notting Hill and old-fashioned upper-class Britain. A maelstrom of different influences, with British working culture sitting side by side with middle-class hippies and immigrants from Ireland to Jamaica, this tiny area of West London was increasingly becoming a ripped-up and patched-together multi-coloured canvas on which to etch a new Britain.

The intersecting influences of the music, art and food of Notting Hill between 1950 and 1990 is a story for another book, but it was this extraordinary perfect storm, prodded by Thatcher's conspicuous consumerism, which led to a revolution in eating out, with a tiny number of restaurants, mostly in W1 and W11, beginning to play with big ideas around food and eating, and attracting some of the most entrepreneurial chefs in the UK.

Of course, many other factors were involved: TV chef Antony Worrall Thompson told me for my 2008 Jamie Oliver biography, *The Jamie Oliver Effect: The Man, the Food, the Revolution*, that it was the recession of 1980 that was responsible for the creation of London's café society. He said that it mimicked Madrid, Paris, New York: 'We'd never had that. We ate out for special occasions but we didn't eat out as a matter of course. When prices came down in Britain, a lot of executives traded down because they didn't want their employees seeing them pay lots of money for food, and afterwards they'd say, "actually, I quite enjoyed that. It wasn't all stiff and starchy."'

Some of them would go on to change London's eating habits forever. Rose Gray of the River Café has been making crepes at the Rainbow Theatre since the 1970s; some of her best ideas came from her travels across Europe, which she brought back with her to what might be known today as a pop-up business.

'I saw people making crepes on the streets in Paris and thought "what a great idea"', she told me for the Oliver biography. 'I bought six crepe machines and, with various girlfriends helping me, I used to make crepes at pop concerts like Pink Floyd and Rod Stewart. I remember the Alice Cooper gig particularly because everyone was so stoned that they came rushing to my crepe stand. I used to do bitter chocolate with crème fraiche and marrons glacés with sour cherries and honey and nuts.'

Gray would later take her turn in the kitchen at 192 Kensington Park Road, one of London's landmark moments in its food history as chef Alistair Little led the way towards a simpler culinary culture in the capital with a focus of Mediterranean recipes and the freshest of ingredients. Little had come from l'Escargot, where he set up the kitchen for Nick Lander and his wife, Jancis Robinson, who would go on to become the wine presenter of BBC Two's *Food and Drink* (1982–2002). Gray was at 192 for just six weeks prior to setting up River Café with Ruth Rogers in 1987, but she joined Little and Rowley Leigh (Kensington Place), Dan Evans (Odette's) and Adam Robinson (the Brackenbury) in helping to make 192 the kind of place that was name-checked by Martin Amis in *Money* and Helen Fielding in *Bridget Jones' Diary*, as noted by Leo Hickman in 2002. Owned by the founders of the Groucho Club, Soho's celebrity private drinking haven, 192 opened in 1983. It had the feeling of a cross between Central Perk and the Queen Vic, according to journalist Nick Foulkes for *The Evening Standard*, who spoke to a key member of the 192 team as it closed in 2002: 'I think it started because Ben (Wordsworth), Tony (Mackintosh), Tchaik (Chassay) and John Armit (a wine salesman) lived round the corner and wanted somewhere to eat, and there really was nothing in Notting Hill', said front-of-house manager Mary-Lou Sturridge, who started working at 192 in 1986. 'It sounds silly now, but in the early 1980s, 192 was about as far north in Notting Hill as some people dared go.'

192 gave birth to what became known as 'modern British' food, the cool, innovative style that mixed French with Italian – as much from New York as Tuscany – with the confidence, creativity and expression of an artist. The menu changed twice a day and would include ground-breaking dishes such as buffalo mozzarella and panettone bread-and-butter pudding, ideas that came from their creators' travel diaries rather than just an Elizabeth David cookbook. The menu would roll off a Millennial's tongue these days, but, as Leo Hickman wrote in *The Guardian* in 2002, 1980s–90s London 'had never seen dishes like vegetable tempura, carpaccio of beef, chicken liver mousse with red onion marmalade, rocket and pousse side salad, gravadlax and potato rosti'.

Peter Gordon came to London as a young chef from New Zealand in 1989, spearheading a new movement in Antipodean food at his Sugar Club in Notting Hill. His recipe ideas came in the form of scribbles on the back of his traveller's guides to South East Asia, gathered like so many young Australians and New Zealanders on his great OE, or Overseas Experience. He was one of the first Antipodean chefs to stop and stay in London.

Cooking in the British capital was becoming exciting; and before the words 'celebrity chef' were even part of the national vocabulary, Marco Pierre White was breaking new ground in a kitchen in Wandsworth. He had attracted the attention of Fay Maschler, the food critic of the *London Evening Standard* who is credited with charting the rise of the capital's gastro-scene since the 1970s. As she reflected on her 40 years of eating at the best restaurants in London for her 70th birthday in 2015, she said that her favourite was Marco Pierre White's Harveys in Wandsworth (1987–93): 'I've never eaten better food than when he cooked at Harveys. He had almost become the food. He would identify with a piece of salmon so closely that he'd understand exactly what to do with it.' Alistair Little told me for *The Jamie Oliver Effect* (2008) 'Marco did something that was different. He reworked food in a really intelligent manner. He had a good look at it and broke it down, and modernised it into Nouvelle cuisine. He kind of dumbed it down but in a really good way'.

By the age of 33, White had become the youngest chef ever to be awarded three Michelin stars, but it was more than his ability to cook that influenced a new generation of chefs in the late 1980s: his rock-star swagger, tousled hair and smouldering gastro-punk attitude, combined with a modern European style of cooking, captured in his book, *White Heat* (1990), with moody black-and-white photographs of his fiery kitchen by advertising photographer, Bob Carlos Clarke, summed up a new spirit of perfectionism and drive. His punk attitude was part of the package: 'If I came to your house for dinner an hour late, then criticised all your furniture and your wife's haircut, and said all your opinions were stupid, how would you feel?' he wrote in *White Heat*. 'People still come here and expect a three-course meal in an hour. What do they think I do – pull rabbits out of a fucking hat? I'm not a magician.'

The swearing and the swagger were almost as exciting as the food itself for young chefs like Jean-Christophe Novelli: 'Marco was the transition between the past and the future', he told me when I was researching the Jamie Oliver book in 2008. 'What France had brought to the market was a traditional style, but it meant that you just do the same thing all the time. Marco went to the edges of that. He thought, "fuck that recipe, let's do a dauphinoise with shellfish reduction!" He pushed the boundaries of cooking and had an attitude that wasn't traditional. He was very rock and roll – he gave these young chefs freedom of expression.' White knows his place in this very British revolution, marked as it is by story and style, but as someone who has been accused of encouraging the bullying culture of the late-twentieth-century British kitchen, he says it was hard. Reflecting in *The Caterer* in 2007, he wrote: 'I saw the tail end of the Escoffier world, and stepped into the modern world. Very few chefs had heard of Michelin and there were no celebrity chefs. Like the foreign legion, the industry accepted everybody. Young boys knocked on back doors to learn their trade, you didn't need qualifications. Lots of people were from working-class backgrounds. When you went for an interview you never asked how much you were going to earn, how many hours you were going to work, or in what section. If you ended up washing up, who cared? You were in a great house. When I went to the Box Tree, I got £26 a week, live-out. If I had to go in two hours early to do what I had to do well and properly, to be ready for service, I did it, I didn't question it.'

But Marco Pierre White told me for the *delicious.* podcast (January 2020) that he was a creation of one of the most successful PR campaigns in food history. 'The truth is that I never tried to be rock and roll. Was I really those things or were they a product of exaggeration? The people I hold responsible for the modern-day chef, who made it cool and sexy was not me: it was Bob Carlos Clarke and Alan Crompton-Batt. Alan Crompton-Batt was the man who invented restaurant PR, and Bob Carlos Clarke took those images of me as a young man. I wasn't trying to be rock and roll. Maybe I was working so hard that I didn't have time to have my hair cut. Maybe I was sufficiently privileged to date and court pretty girls. I lived in Chelsea, not because I thought Chelsea was cool, but because La Tante Claire and Le Gavroche [the London restaurants where he trained from 16 years old] were in Chelsea, so by default I ended up there.'

He put his punky image down to the music that he listened to: 'When I started (in food), I was a teenager. It was the Pistols with Lydon, with Matlock, with Jones, and the world was changing. You had Che Guevara, you had the Pistols, you had Marc Bolan, individuals who contributed to that change. And maybe I contributed too. But there were lots of very, very good cooks and I just happened to be in the right place at the right time.'

He also told me how he met Alan Crompton-Batt. 'When I finished work at Gavroche, I used to go up the New Kings Road, and Alan was the manager of a brasserie called Kennedy's. I used to tell him stories of the Box Tree [in Ilkley, where White first trained as a chef]. Alan used to be an Egon Ronay inspector.' After training at La Tante Claire and Le Gavroche in London, White moved on to work with Raymond Blanc at Le Manoir aux Quat'Saisons, before coming back to London, aged 24, to take over his first restaurant, Harveys in Wandsworth, where as co-owner and head chef, he won his first Michelin star almost immediately. 'When I came back [to London]', he told me, 'Alan and his wife Elizabeth had set up this PR company for chefs. He looked after Nico [Ladenis] and people like that.' It was Crompton-Batt who would catapult him to stardom by commissioning photographer Bob Carlos Clarke to capture the fiery and gastro-punk energy of White's kitchen at Harveys in the iconic black-and-white photography of *White Heat*, and he fanned White's fiery outbursts in the press until a legend was born.

It was an image which would launch a new generation of chefs. Eight-year-old Jamie Oliver liked to hang out in the kitchen of his parents' pub in Clavering, Essex, where the 16-year-old chefs aped this new culinary king. *Saturday Kitchen* (BBC, 2002–present) and *Food Unwrapped* (Channel 4, 2012–present) presenter, Matt Tebbutt told me for the *delicious.* podcast (December 2019) that his first cookbook was *White Heat*: 'You flick through the pages, and you got this kind of chain-smoking rock star, who did make food sexy. Because, before that time, the chefs were big-hat-wearing, sort of hotel, a bit fat… you know, that typical stereotype. But this guy was totally different, and we all looked at him and thought, "oh god, I want to do that." '

White preferred to gather Michelin stars than appear on television. This was before Jamie Oliver and the rise of the celebrity chef, when TV chefs were on Daytime TV and good food was still a status symbol rather than just something to eat at home. Supermarkets were yet to stock the kinds of ingredients White would use in his kitchen, including the wines that would encourage the middle classes to try fine dining at home. This was the Thatcher era of conspicuous consumption in which being seen to eat out was the cultural capital of the day, a mark of sophistication and worldliness which the then Prime Minister had insisted would contribute to the 'sell' of her British brand on the world market. This currency of social mobility would blindside those who had considered British food culture to be little more than under-seasoned, over-industrialised and unloved fuel; Nouvelle Cuisine, with its works of art on a plate, would barely provide enough sustenance to get back to work after a business lunch, but it looked good, and that was enough for a nation more interested in style than content – for a short while at least.

London was changing fast. After the post-war period of rationing and the previous 100 years of industrial revolution formalising, scheduling and taming the country's workforce, Britain was searching for identity. Teenage boys had thrown off the suits of their fathers while hems had moved up and down to the changing beats of the generations. During this intense period of reform, it was only food that was left out to dry.

In his fascinating book, *British Food: An Extraordinary Thousand Years of History* (2002), food historian Colin Spencer says that it is when a country is at peace with itself that food can become the focus of the party. He notices a pattern for elegant dining during periods of social stasis, and describes the reign of Henry II, which oversaw 35 years of political stability, as a period of aesthetic exploration: 'A culture of a period is all of a piece, and a rich elite fascinated by hem lines, shades of dye, types of fur lining and curling tongs also want the food they eat to have the same skill, time and delicacy spent upon it.' The household of Henry II may well have loved the art on the plates of 1980s London, but going home hungry would have been unthinkable.

A. A. Gill, the late British food writer and restaurant critic, credited Worrall Thompson with the invention of Nouvelle Cuisine, the culinary trend which attempted to make food an art form, with its dainty, decorative dishes adding a new dimension to eating out. In retrospect, Worrall Thompson is not proud of the overpriced stylised food craze that swept through London in the mid-1980s and which revealed the city's superficial interest in style over content: 'It was a French invention', he told me for my 2008 biography of Jamie Oliver, 'but they went back into their escargot shells when they realised what a horrendous nightmare they created, and the English just went on from there.' But it changed the appetite for eating out in Britain, something that Antony Worrall Thompson attributes to women, previously an untapped market who were now paying the bills too. Popping into a stylish restaurant for a starter and a dessert, both beautiful and tiny, accompanied by a glass of wine was an acceptable business lunch for many people who had previously associated eating out with gluttony.

Permission to shift the image of eating out away from the 'fat cats' and onto the 'beautiful people' exploded the market, creating demand for ever more exciting ideas in the kitchen, if still only in this tiny corner of Britain. Robin Godwin wrote in the *London Evening Standard* in 2015 that the most exciting period for London restaurants was the mid-1980s 'when figures such as Rose Gray (River Café), Rowley Leigh (Kensington Place) and Simon Hopkinson (Bibendum) burst on to the scene. Before then, you really struggled to find anyone actually using their intelligence in a kitchen'.

Young chef Sally Clarke had become obsessed with the legendary Alice Waters at Chez Panisse in Berkeley, California, whose radical idea to create a daily-changing menu was inspired by what she had observed in Paris and the South of France as a student in 1965. Waters had gone home to Berkeley and, in 1971, created a neighbourhood bistro with a choice of just three dishes per course, dependent only on the best available organic produce of the day. Waters' influence has been ascribed to the markets of France, the touch, feel and smell, the sensuality of fresh ingredients which inspired a love and respect for provenance. She describes it as 'her awakening' to Andrew Friedman, in his 2018 biography of the birth of American modern food culture, *Chefs, Drugs and Rock & Roll*. But she says that it was in the soil of American counter-culture that her philosophy had initially seeded at the University of Berkeley, a couple of blocks from where Chez Panisse now attracts food fans from all over the world. 'We arrived [...] front and centre of the Free Speech Movement', she tells Friedman, recalling a 'lot of drugs, a lot of parties [...] I was a little bit into Ferlinghetti and that sort of beatnik side'. Filmmaker and restaurateur, Tony Bill, agrees that creative ideas were ripened by the heat of the anti-Vietnam War and civil rights movements, that he and Waters were part of a generation motivated by revolution. He tells Friedman, 'There's no creative effort [...] that wasn't questioned by my generation.' After art, music, movies and literature, food was the last to the table: 'All of these things were thought to be the bailiwick of the privileged few who laid down the rules and said how things were to taste, look, sound and read', Bill tells him. 'And food was just maybe the caboose of that train.'

Waters would inspire a new trend for making simple but elegant and exciting new food from the best ingredients, and Clarke would bring her influence home to West London, and to the chefs and foodies who were ravenous for cool new ideas. 'It wasn't a new philosophy', she told me for my 2008 biography of Jamie Oliver. 'It had been around since the beginning of time but we'd moved so far away from it.' She said that what was happening in Berkeley was a reworking of the classic French: 'We were just further down the wrong path and there were people here who understood European philosophy. We learned from (food writers like) Elizabeth David and Richard Olney who had a lot less imprisonment around fancy cookery. We were free in America to do what we wanted to do – for good or bad. There was a big free speech movement in Berkeley and everyone was setting up businesses in what they believed in, run the way you want it. There was an entrepreneurial culture as well as this beautiful climate that allowed us to grow great produce.' She told me that New York City hadn't advanced in the same way. 'They're still catching up. It's more difficult there. There's a sense of not knowing what regional cuisine can be.'

Colin Spencer suggests, in *British Food* (2002), that although the immediate success of Elizabeth David was due to the 'strength of her prose', its impact was because 'our national atavism had been pricked alert and awoke to a world that had once been ours and that we now needed to regain. The shallots, garlic and saffron, the almonds and pistachios, the mixture of sweet and savoury, of dried fruits and lemon zest, of lentils and chick peas were all somehow vaguely familiar.' Our intangible food memory of the ancient spice trade with the East, was, Spencer suggests, almost part of British DNA. It's one possible reason for the explosion of interest in Notting Hill. Waters' protégée, Sally Clarke, came to London from California and quickly spotted a cluster of interesting cooks on either side of Notting Hill Gate who had also read Elizabeth David. She remembered how it spoke to a London hungry for change: 'Alistair Little had just opened down the road at Kensington Park Road', she told me for *The Jamie Oliver Effect*, referring to 192, 'and Simon Hopkinson was cooking at Hilaire in South Kensington. Rowley Leigh hadn't quite opened at Kensington Place, but [...] Alistair and Simon were the two most exciting new chefs [in London]. They were cooking seasonally and they were cooking food that was from named farms and producers. They were definitely cooking in the Elizabeth David web.'

Clarke's opened on the Kensington side of Notting Hill in 1984 and immediately attracted a mix of Kensington locals and Californians. By the end of the decade, she had also attracted the attention of a young cookery student called

Jamie Oliver who, like the Notting Hill chefs, was fascinated by this new emphasis on freshness and seasonality.

In an interview for the *delicious.* podcast (April 2017), Peter Gordon remembered the food vibe on the streets of Notting Hill: 'There was The First Floor restaurant on the corner of Portobello Road, we had Books for Cooks, which was a fantastic shop where Clarissa Dickson Wright used to sit and sell you books. Notting Hill at the time was the foodie sort of destination in London. I remember Kensington Place was open just around the corner. Sally Clarke was just down there. And it seemed to be the centre of attention for food. But I think it was just a place, a centre of attention. It wasn't in the West End: people were doing food that wasn't just British or French.' The success of the Sugar Club, his Notting Hill restaurant which brought culinary ideas from the New World into this mix of new Mediterranean, was accompanied by a youthful Kiwi surfie style which ramped up the cool in West London's scene. Gordon was one of Nigel Slater's guests on his first Channel 4 series in 1998, *Nigel Slater's Real Food Show*, along with a young food writer called Nigella Lawson.

Gordon believes that Britain has always been creative in its fashion, its music and its art, and that food was the last bastion. 'You've got an environment where you can encourage creativity and invention', he told me. 'Whether that's the creativity of Heston Blumenthal or the simplicity of Fergus Henderson, or, you know, someone like the chap at Lyle's (James Lowe) who's doing little funky things. I think creativity is important. For a long time, you couldn't bend the rules, and actually what happened during that period in the late 1980s was that everyone was breaking the rules. You had an American and an English woman running one of the best Italian restaurants in England (River Café). You've got Alistair Little doing his lovely Italian European stuff that lightened everything up. I remember having some beautiful figs and Parma ham at Alistair Little's and just thinking, "oh, this is heaven." I hadn't had it that good before.'

The food was on the table, but that has never been enough for Britain, which loves its storytelling as much as its style. By the mid-1980s, the London food scene was a media-fed revolution in an aspirant society in which good-looking young role models showed off how to live. New style magazines *i-D* and *The Face*, which both launched in 1980 and targeted men – gay and straight – as well as women for the first time, featured 'hot' young chefs such as Alistair Little and his good friend from Cambridge University, Rowley Leigh. The pair would bring together the neighbourhood cool of 192, mix it with the aspirational elegance of Neal Street and the borrowed culture of l'Escargot, and create Kensington Place, a temple of conspicuous consumerism. With over 300 covers and showy window display of the Beautiful People at lunch, Kensington Place was all about looking good, and would set the scene for designer Terence Conran's gastrodomes: Bibendum in South Kensington, which reworked the French brasserie into a tableau of style and cool; and Quaglino's, the enormous theatre of food in Mayfair where walking to your table became as much an art form as what was on the table. It was about mimicking the best of New York, Sydney and LA, rather than Milan or Paris: 'To be fashionable a restaurant needs a buzz', Alan Yau told Kathryn Flett in 2005 for *The Guardian*. 'I remember the first time I went to Balthazar Brasserie in New York a few years ago. I got a late flight and arrived around midnight on a Monday. I went there and I just thought "wow": the energy level was incredible. The Mercer, also in Manhattan, has a similar vibe. You can't create a so-called fashionable restaurant artificially – if you do, it feels superficial. You can control certain things, like the size of tables (they should never be too big) and the space between them (not too vast), and the lighting and music to enhance the dining experience but you can do all of that and still not create the right environment.'

Style was a way of enticing the British palate to try something new. The Thatcher government had downgraded cookery classes on the school curriculum in 1988, while at the same time, the introduction of microwave meals had encouraged millions to become what Carolyn Steele in her 2008 book, *Hungry City: How Food Shapes Our Lives*, calls 'fuellies, happy to let food take a back seat as we get on with our busy lives, unconscious of what it takes to keep us fuelled.' As the Thatcher era became synonymous with industry closure and hardship in some parts of the country and enormous city bonuses in the capital, food became symbolically conflicted, with mixed messages from 'experts' and the food industry on how to eat inexpensive healthy food, and with microwaving fast becoming the preferred way to safeguard nutritional value while preparing quick TV dinners for the family. As food became shrink-wrapped, so consumers lost connection with ingredients and the sense of what to do with them.

While the rest of the country was limited to rare chef finds, where to eat was part of the aspirational storyline for some Londoners. In 1983, the first *Time Out Guide to Eating Out in London*, costing £1.75, was published, listing 1,000 'dining, drinking and lunching places in town'. It was an immediate success and became an annual publication. Nouvelle Cuisine, the craze for small but beautifully designed dishes on vast plates, came and went, but the mash-up of elegant, cool restaurants with the demand for fresh seasonal produce in the kitchens was here to stay. As chefs from all over the world – notably Australia and New Zealand – caught the word on the wind, including a stint in a London restaurant was a must on the Overseas Experience.

The opening of Terence Conran's Quaglino's in 1993 with Australian chef, Martin Webb, at the helm, was a metaphor for post-Thatcherism/pre-Britpop Britishness. Webb brought the Mod Oz tradition to London, introducing

Eurasian fusion of classics like saddle of hare, roasted and served with morels and celeriac from his Freemantle restaurant, Café Polperro. But as diners sashayed down Quaglino's art deco staircase and through the 450 tables of this cavernous Parisian brasserie style restaurant, it wasn't always Mod Oz that they were thinking of. Channelling the spirit of the 1920s when, run by its original owner, Giovanni Quaglino, it had attracted the future Edward VIII and the Mountbattens, Charlie Chaplin and Evelyn Waugh who came to dine and tango, stylish young Londoners went to Quaglino's to be seen to eat. On its revival in 2014, Zoe Williams wrote in *The Telegraph* in 2014, 'Quaglino's, when I were a lass, was the height of Mayfair wonder, slick but never crazily pricey, the perfect destination for urban know-it-alls who wanted to be considered discerning but never cared overmuch what they ate.'

Conran played the crowd: hindsight shows us that he made a clever move in democratising eating out which led to an unprecedented interest in dining at home and a demand for chic living/eating space. As he opened his 12 restaurants in London, including the Blue Print Café in 1989, which was situated on the first floor of the Design Museum, the juxtaposition between style and substance became obvious; even today, Terence Conran's influence over the preparation of food as well as dining, both at home and out, is profound.

His designs around the home and in the kitchen in particular introduced more affordable but good-looking utensils into the modern kitchen as early as the 1960s, when the first Habitat home store opened on London's Fulham Road. His pasta makers and yakitori skillets brought new ideas from around the world to the British high street about what to do in the kitchen, and, according to Conran's 1995 biographer, Nicholas Ind, won Habitat the accolade of being 'the most exciting new store since Biba'. With many of the influential chefs of the modern British era, Conran shared a love of French cooking, but while he borrowed design ideas from the cavernous golden-era brasseries like La Couple, it was, according to Ind, French city's 'authenticity, robustness, simplicity and substance' that he admired, rather than the 'unnecessary decoration and preciousness' of the perception of French food in Britain.

Conran was a pioneer in democratising design and diversity, bringing home ideas from across the world. His travels were our gain. At Pont de la Tour at Shad Thames, Ind suggests he created a food experience, 'a collection of food-related activities which appeal to those who are particularly interested in the variety of quality of food and drink'. This would draw people other than just diners to his gastrodome and thrill them with smells, tastes and inspiration. It opened in 1991 with not only a bar, grill and *salon privé*, but also a bakery and a wine merchant, steadily luring a new crowd and expanding the desire for the new food scene beyond the 'Beautiful People'.

Conran's Bibendum, an enormous art deco building in South Kensington which had been the headquarters of the French tyre company, and Mezzo, with 700 tables in the heart of Soho, played up the food storytelling. Conran was creating an experience in eating which was, as Popham writes in *Consuming Geographies: We Are Where We Eat* (1997), an 'escape from mundane English reality. In other cultures, to eat in a good restaurant is to commune with the soul of one's nation or region or city, to enter into a sort of dialogue about identity. In London, it is to flee – whether to Thailand, to Provence or, at Mezzo, to a fantasy of the Jazz Age.'

John Torode was head chef at Soho restaurant, Mezzo and co-author of the 1997 *Mezzo Cookbook*, which celebrated his Australian pedigree of what was known then as 'Mod Oz': the culinary fusion of Australia's migrant communities. Mod Oz had already transformed the Melbourne and Sydney food scene, but Torode's book spoke to a hip London crowd who wanted to be seen in the vast new Conran-designed food emporia, Mezzo, Bluebird, Quaglino and Bibendum. Conspicuous consumption may have started off as being seen to eat out, but food, style and architectural design together was now beginning to push new buying habits in the capital's supermarkets: lemongrass, galangal, fish sauce and star anise, once found only in Chinese supermarkets, were beginning to find their way onto the shelves of metropolitan Sainsbury's and Tesco. It's hard to remember how parochial food was in the early/mid-1990s: 'There was no soy sauce in the cupboard, no mirin, no sake, ginger, coriander, galangal or lemongrass', Torode told me, remembering the early days of the Conran empire when he was head chef at Pont de la Tour.

In 1980s London, eating tiny portions at Kensington Place would amass your cultural capital without altering the line of your Alaia skin tight dress. Kathryn Flett, editor of *i-D* magazine, lived and breathed the paradox: 'Fashionability and fine food make for an edgy, insecure, bitchy sort of a friendship, slippery and hard to define', she wrote in *The Guardian* in 2005. 'If you're on a big night out wearing, for example, a brand-new and fabulous pair of Georgina Goodman heels accessorised by a suitably expensive dress, you'll want to be seen, not seen to be stuffing your face.'

By the 1990s, food was lifestyle, in the more affluent cities of the world at least. It was the cultural capital de jour, the evidence of travel and the mark of sophistication. For the executives at BBC and Channel 4, it was edgy, cool and compulsive, and the stuff of great storytelling.

The manufacture of delight

The birth of Channel 4 in November 1982, a largely commercially funded public service television channel, provided more than just a fourth channel to British broadcasting. Like the tiny clutch of London restaurants changing British food culture, it blasted an energy through television audiences and developed a new set of narratives for British society, telling stories of an increasingly diverse world in ways we had never seen before. Series like Channel 4's *Network 7*(1987–88) and *The Media Show* (1988–94) would showcase new ideas in storytelling and break new talent both on-screen and behind the camera. Janet Street Porter and her revolutionary ideas behind *Network 7*, an entertainment youth strand designed to look and feel like the mother of all hangovers for an as yet untargeted youth audience, would be quickly poached by Alan Yentob at BBC Two, while Jane Root, who founded Wall to Wall with Alex Graham, would go on to head up the BBC Independent Commissioning Group in 1997 and become its first woman controller in 1999.

Channel 4 was a pioneer in capturing the spirit of Britain at a time when it was searching for a new post-austerity identity by doing what Britain has always done best – storytelling through fashion, art and music, self-deprecating comedy, and social realism. At Channel 4, it could often happen in the same programme, as in its most memorable successes, *The Tube* and *Brookside*. An unruly, amphetamined version of the BBC's *Top of the Pops*, *The Tube* broke brand-new ground by bringing bands from underground music scenes live to living rooms around the country, often regardless of sound quality and slick production values. The 'talent' was found among witty young journalists, Paula Yates and Muriel Gray, and musician Jools Holland, whose use of the 'f word' in a trailer for the show would eventually bring about its demise. If *The Tube* captured the narrative of British music, fashion and style, *Brookside* did the same for British TV's well-established narrative of social realism, with its stories of life on a suburban Liverpool housing estate, complete with family struggles, domestic violence, class wars and sex scandals.

Wild and fresh as Channel 4 was in the 1980s, as it put a Doc Marten up the backside of British TV, it was BBC Two where mouthy journalist Janet Street Porter was able to bring her tabloid punk to a new concept of programming. As the new Head of Youth and Entertainment Features at the BBC in 1987, under the direction of BBC Two Controller Alan Yentob, she introduced her hip new narratives in *Def II* (1988–94), which pioneered *Rough Guides*, a stylish travelogue presented by former *Network 7* stars, the late Magenta Devine and Sankha Guha.

The impact was profound: while it may be hard to find the legacy of *The Tube*, *The Media Show* and *Network 7* on the current Channel 4 (and, arguably, in its viewers), Street Porter's approach to factual entertainment would set off a mind-bomb across the BBC. How it would change TV News is the story for another book, but Mark Thompson, who had just left *Newsnight* to become the editor of the *Nine O'Clock News* at the astonishingly tender age of 30 in 1988, may well have had his notepad out. Street Porter's *Reportage* (BBC Two, 1988–94), which was part of the *Def II* strand and aired weekly at 6 pm on Mondays and Wednesdays targeting teenagers, took news seriously but loosened its tie. Its presenters were cooler, cleverer versions of their audience and told stories just slightly out of their reach. They brought new worlds to young people who had until now been patronised or neglected by television, educating, inspiring and modelling new ways of being cool.

A cab ride away from the BBC in Wood Lane, W12 was the new frontier in British food culture. Here, BBC executives, including BBC Two boss Mark Thompson and Head of Independent Commissioning Jane Root, would lunch with independent producers and plot a new era in Factual TV. With Root heading up the BBC's brand-new Independent Commissioning Group, the gates were open for the first time to 'indies': independent, often small companies pitching for up to 25 per cent of the channel's programming. Thompson remembers those 'power' lunches at 192, Notting Hill's first celebrity magnet 'neighbourhood' restaurant, though having started as a researcher at the BBC in 1979, he had been soaking up the food scene in Notting Hill for a while. 'London was beginning to happen around the BBC in the 1980s', he told me in 2013.

Thompson and Root sniffed the winds of change and spotted a way of bringing an early form of Britpop onto the plates of Britain. Jane Root had produced *The Media Show* for Channel 4 from 1987 to 1991 for her own production company, Wall to Wall, and had already been approached by the channel to consider the ways in which food could be made 'younger and fresher'. But in her new role at BBC Two, a meeting of minds with Mark Thompson, now controller at BBC Two, would create a new feel for the channel based on something much more authentic than the usual drive for the Next Big Thing. Thompson and Root shared unusually foodie childhoods in the 1960s and 1970s, which set them apart from their peers. Thompson's best friend at a British boarding school had lived in the Philippines during their early school days and would stay with him during half-term breaks. At the age of 13, his friend moved to Rome and returned the favour by inviting Thompson to stay with him. 'Until I was 18 or 19, I was totally immersed in Italian food every half-term', he recalled. 'I watched his mother cook what was just ordinary Roman food, but this was when spaghetti was still in tins in the UK. I became incredibly interested in food.' Back home in London, he noticed that his male friends did not share his passion. 'It was a male/female thing', he said. 'It was more unusual to be into food. London (food scene) was beginning to happen around the BBC in the 1980s. There wasn't so much money around before then. It felt exceptional to cook. There were little niches around, like Books for Cooks, and a few delis in Portobello. It was a counter culture. It was a bit like liking classical music or being gay at that time. It was edgy and cool.'

Jane Root had grown up in Essex, but it was her mother who influenced Root's unusual interest in food. She had grown up in East London during the Second World War, spending much of her childhood in bomb shelters during the Blitz, surviving, like the rest of Britain, on rations. Root described how her mother's choice of taking evening classes in cookery was 'crazy' for a young working-class woman in East London at that time. Yet, this influence on Root would have enormous impact on British television. 'She endlessly experimented in our family with new ingredients. I remember her cutting up a whole bulb of raw garlic and putting it into a salad and everyone's head exploding. And she said, "ah, maybe that didn't work." And the first time I had an avocado and a red pepper [...] She was always experimenting.'

It's important to emphasise just how unusual it would have been for senior television management of a certain age in London at that time to share this experience, and both Root and Thompson mentioned this in my interviews with them. Pat Llewellyn, an independent producer who had developed new ideas around food programmes with Root at Wall to Wall, also had a childhood immersed in food. Llewellyn's parents ran a small hotel and restaurant in South Wales, an area not known for its cooking in those days and, miles away from the nearest big city, it was an unlikely spot to find customers interested in being seen to eat in the 'right place'. 'My parents were very into feeding people generously and sending people away happy', Llewellyn told me for my 2008 biography of Jamie Oliver. 'They knew about food from the ground up: "my dad's side of the family were all farmers or grew their own food, but my mother had an understanding of what was going on in the 1970s and brought a tiny bit of sophistication to the place. She read everything – Elizabeth David and all those Robert Carrier part-works.

According to Root, speaking in 2013, her mother wasn't on the 'same social level' as Llewellyn's. She was a home cook, but from her earliest memories, there were many family stories about food. 'I remember the first time she bought asparagus. She was newly married. She cooked it for about 20 minutes in the way you used to cook spinach, and it was inedible. 'She remembered it was [about] being very brave. My parents were working-class kids who were making their way. They were really passionate about possibilities of the new world and food was part of that. As a family, we used to eat Vesta curries, you know, horrible things but at the time you thought, "hey, we're going to eat foreign food." ' Her father, like mine, had been in the Army, hers in India, mine across Africa and the Far East, and both were unusual among their peers in loving the local dishes.

This passion for food was about more than chopping and cooking: Root explained that growing up thinking about how things looked and tasted felt like 'possibility in a new world', and would inspire many of the series she commissioned or produced at the BBC and Channel 4, and as president at Discovery Networks. 'A lot of programmes I made as an exec or a commissioning editor were things that my family were obsessed with', she said. 'That's where all those programmes on industrial archaeology I made came from. It was about being brave and trying out new things.'

As the first female controller of BBC Two (1999–2004), she would bring with her the spirit of freelance journalism, from her work on women's magazines like *Honey* and *Cosmopolitan*, as well as the lifestyle pages of *The Guardian*. She would introduce some of the most successful exports, such as *What Not to Wear* (2001–07), *Top Gear* (2002–present) and *Who Do You Think You Are* (2004–present) to the BBC, creating trends from the audience's increasing interest in hobbying – or, the new buzz word in television – 'leisure'. She would also commission Pat Llewellyn to produce *The Naked Chef* (1999–2001), which not only gave her the moniker 'high priestess of Lifestyle TV' but also heralded Llewellyn as one of the most influential producers in television.

Thompson and Root worked closely together from 1997 as they navigated the new territory being carved out by the independent production companies. 'The indies were fascinated by food', Thompson told me in 2013. The BBC had already created Delia's Smith educative series *Family Fayre* (1973–75), *Delia Smith's Cookery Course* (1978–81), *One Is Fun* (1985) as well as her seasonal collections in the 1990s. 'I had to pivot that', he told me. How to develop Delia to stand up against an influx of fresh food ideas was Thompson's biggest challenge. Delia Smith was the BBC's signature dish, attracting vast audiences with her quiet, school-marm charm and detailed instructions on how to cook. 'She was our biggest star', he said. 'She had an ability to empty supermarket shelves.'

But with the new kid on the block, Channel 4, putting up a good fight in the ratings war, it was time to rethink what other ingredients might create a new flavour in BBC Food.

By the end of the 1980s, the BBC had launched its own food magazine, *BBC Good Food*, filled with chat and ideas about food from TV chefs such as Antony Worrall Thompson, Keith Floyd, Ken Hom and Madhur Jaffrey. BBC Two featured some of the new stars of the London scene such as Gary Rhodes, who was reinventing 'British' food, including faggots and oxtail, at The Greenhouse in Mayfair, gently changing TV food from a 'how to' documentary style into a more aspirational 'lifestyle' genre.

Early cookery shows were about teaching a busier Britain to cook; TV's first celebrity chef, Moira Meighn's snappily titled *Suggestions for Dishes to be Prepared and Cooked in 15 Minutes* demonstrated single-ring cookery in 1936 while Philip Harben's *Cookery* (1946–51), *Cookery Lesson* with co-presenter Marguerite Patten and *What's Cooking* (1956) did what they said on the tin. From 1949, Fanny Cradock was hired to bring a sense of theatre to what had been instructional but dull. Nick Thorogood bought ten episodes for a retrospective for Food Network and was struck by how artificial the content was. He told me, 'She was never really married to Johnnie of course. She was never really the daughter of an aristocrat.' Against the backdrop of aspirational cookery and a new era of mass consumerism, encouraged by the post-war boom and the rise of advertising across the western world, a media-constructed housewife was encouraged to believe that consumer goods; whiter, cleaner clothes; and impressive cookery skills would connect her to the fantasy of the 'good society' perpetuated by the mass media. The myth of the 1950s housewife in apron and stilettos symbolised a glamour that was designed to rework the traditions of cleaning and cooking into something that promised control over one's life. In the US, it was even called 'The American Dream'.

Fanny Cradock tapped into this market on British TV throughout the 1950s and 1960s with all the artifice that it stood for. She even wore a ball gown to present her early shows, an ironic nod to their performative nature, perhaps. Thorogood recalled the kind of tips she would offer the audience: 'In one show, she makes a brandy butter which she dyes bright fluorescent green, and she says, "and you can make it months in advance and keep it in the fridge."'

Thorogood put the viewing experience of the time into context. 'As a child of that era, we had the same meals every night of the week: roast on Sunday, leftovers on Monday, poached eggs on Friday, whatever. We never had anything fancy like a dressed chicken or a whipped brandy butter. So I think TV has always been good at broadening those horizons while creating a false culture'.

Media executive Peter Bazalgette believed that Cradock had the entertainment gene. 'She was a lousy cook but she was a good entertainer. And she used to
do live food shows for the *Daily Telegraph* in the 1950s. There was one wonderful occasion when they were rehearsing and the presenter, McDonald Hobley
arrived. She said, "I'm stuffing a turkey would you kindly f**k off!" and the
presenter got on a train and went back to London! But the point is she was very
strong-minded, very entertaining. She understood the idea of cabaret. She had
Johnnie doing the wine – so actually a lot of what happened later' (for example,
in Bazalgette's *Food and Drink* on BBC Two) was there.'

In 1968, *The Galloping Gourmet* romped into the BBC's Continuing Education
Department, whose remit was to teach the nation to cook. The department had
already started to commission a wider range of cookery programmes and would
quickly begin to reflect the richer food culture of Britain's changing demographic
and the increase in business travel in the 1980s introducing Britons to international cuisines. It inspired a small but significant interest in the different roles
that food could play in our lives, from health to fine dining and cultural fusion.
In 1982, *Ken Hom's Chinese Cookery* and *Madhur Jaffrey's Indian Cookery* brought
an exotic addition to the channel, which had also just commissioned *Food and
Drink*, the first British food show to discuss the subject seriously without the
'how to' format.

The popularity of Hom and Jaffrey is an early example of the British audience's interest in food stories, taking it out of the studio and on location, giving
the first hint that food could be about much more than chopping and cooking.
Paula Trafford, Hom's executive producer on the 2016 BBC Two show *Eat, Drink,
Cook China* explained how important early family experiences are in shaping a
relationship with food. 'Ken Hom's mother tried to keep his identity by doing
a Chinese lunchbox at school', she told me. 'He felt alienated from his Chinese
roots, and realised how important it was to hang on to his identity. Food was a
big part of that.'

While Glyn Christian was to bring the first cookery show shot on location
to BBC Two in *A Cook's Tour* in 1982, it was Keith Floyd who in 1985's *Floyd
on Fish* (BBC Two) brought a new attitude to food programmes, extending *The
Galloping Gourmet*'s portrait of a food loving lush to the travelogue of a bon
viveur. But it was his style that Tom Jaine, in his obituary of Keith Floyd in *The
Guardian*, described as 'inspired by chaos', which was to shake up the Food TV
of the 1980s. His informal attitude would loosen the stays around food, which
was still at this time an uncomfortable fit with the British way of life. 'Keith
Floyd gave birth to that whole style of TV programme in the 1980s', Antony
Worrall Thompson told me in 2008, 'and then we wanted more and more of
it. Dinner parties were all carrot and coriander soup, floating nasturtiums and

fish that had been cooked to death. We were desperate for knowledge but we didn't put it into practice very often. Suddenly, Floyd made everything very relaxed. It was radical – telling the camera to come in and have a look, while Floyd himself was having a glass of wine. Robert Carrier was in a studio; *The Galloping Gourmet* was entertainment, but then it disappeared completely; and when the Roux Brothers and Delia came along, it was about education. Floyd was about bringing it back to entertainment again.'

Rick Stein remembered the genius of Floyd's director, his friend, the late David Pritchard, who deliberately developed 'that blokey way of bossing the cameraman around'. In December 2019, I talked to him for the *delicious.* podcast about his BBC Two TV series and book, *Rick Stein's Secret France* (2019), which are dedicated to Pritchard who died while Stein was filming the series. He believes that Pritchard's was a conscious decision to be 'a bit contrary to the way that Delia Smith was doing it at the time. It had to be us boys being naughty and drinking too much and being rude about French cooks.'

Pritchard's thumbed nose attitude even extended to the way that he pitched his programmes to the BBC. I asked Stein about the legendary story of the lunch they shared in which their tablecloth became a proposal for their first series travelling through France, *Rick Stein's French Odyssey* (BBC Two, 2005). The apocryphal version has it that after a very good lunch in which he and Pritchard had drawn a map of France on a white tablecloth, zigzagged 'like a mark of Zorro' tracing the towns they wanted to film, they wrapped it up and took it directly to their BBC commissioning editor. 'Well, maybe it was a bit of A4', Stein told me in 2019, although he admitted to drawing the idea on the tablecloth first. 'But in a way we liked to use it [the story] as an example of how bureaucracy threatens the BBC. We like to think that they backed us on a whim.'

The informal feel of Floyd was replicated in the Stein series, with the duo's sheer delight in delicious food and drink at the core. Fifteen years later, in 2019, *Secret France* was more than an homage to their shared road trip through food: 'French cooking was where we started, really', Stein said. 'It was the first great revelation about how to cook really lovely food and how to drink really nice wine with it as well.' Pritchard's thumbprint is all over the series: 'It was about his nostalgia for motoring through France in the 1970s and 1980s. He knew that he was going to go, and he wanted to be in a place he remembered very fondly.'

While BBC Two became the home of food, taking its viewers to exotic locations and explaining what food meant to the rest of the world, *Food and Drink* was the channel's flagship food magazine programme from 1982 to 2002. It was produced by Peter Bazalgette, who brought to it the spirit of tabloid journalism of Esther Rantzen's *That's Life* (BBC One, 1973–94), where he had been a researcher. Rantzen's would-be husband and producer of the show, Desmond

Wilcox, had been 'inspired' by the format of the 1960s consumer affairs show, *On the Braden Beat*, which also featured comics Peter Cook and Tim Brooke-Taylor, and witty folk singer Jake Thackray. Bazalgette feasted on the ideas, learning on the job that factual information could be entertaining. His pitch for the food consumer magazine show would lead to the series, which ran from 1982 to 2002, and secured his place in television history. He remembered a seminal moment in 1985:'One of the *Food and Drink* presenters – a guy called Chris Kelly – made a film at the Dorchester about some dinner that Anton Mosimann was cooking for because he was the chef there at the time. When he came back afterwards having made the film he said, "he's a really interesting guy, Anton Mosimann; what would it be like if we sent him to cook for an ordinary family?" So I said, "yeah, let's do that." ' Mossiman was sent to a council house in Sheffield and, on a budget of what Bazalgette remembers as 'just under five quid', he cooked a three-course Sunday lunch. 'It was an overnight sensation. That's when the celebrity chef started. And it was Chris Kelly's idea.' Bazalgette smiled, 'I've probably got a bit of an entertainment gene in myself.'

Bazalgette would go on to create format entertainment cookery shows which would sell around the world, like BBC Two's *Ready Steady Cook* (1994–2000; *Ready… Set… Cook!* in the US [Food Network, 1995–2001]) and BBC One's *Can't Cook, Won't Cook* (1995–2000), and mastermind the birth of reality TV with the UK's version of *Big Brother* (Channel 4, 2000–10; Channel 5, 2011–18). Bazalgette explained how under the control of Michael Jackson at BBC Two (1993–96), *Ready Steady Cook* became the first formatted cookery/entertainment show: '[Jackson said,] "I think I'd like a sort of food show in the afternoons, I think it could be quite entertaining, I don't know what it is. Can you do something?" I don't suppose I did it on my own, but that's how I came up with the basic format for *Ready Steady Cook*! A producer did all the wonderful casting and everything else.' The competition between two celebrity chefs was about making the best recipe with a bag of ingredients bought on a budget of £5, and was an early example of Bazalgette's drive to democratise television by making what had been considered an elitist subject more accessible, but it was dismissed by food pundits. 'There were a lot of posh gits, stuck up food critics who derided it', Bazalgette remembered. 'But actually, it had a lot of extremely clever talented chefs working on it. They invented a sort of new cuisine – everything had to be cooked in 20 minutes.' Making a soufflé in a microwave, using traditional techniques but adapting them to the needs of the clock, was what Bazalgette called 'cuisine in miniature'. The show has been reprised in 2020 with a focus on less waste and more eco-conscious cookery.

Bazalgette would go on to become chair of the British Arts Council and, in 2016, non-executive chairman of ITV. He is widely credited with being one of the most influential men in independent television and in food culture. Like Thompson, Root and Llewellyn, he also had an unusually foodie childhood. He admits to having a charmed life: as the great-great-grandson of Sir Joseph Bazalgette, the Victorian civil engineer responsible for the design of London sewers, he had a privileged upbringing, with seasonal produce grown in the family's three-acre garden. 'We had a gardener who used to come and ask my mum what she wanted that day for lunch and dinner and he would go away and cut it, pick it', he told me. 'There was this constant supply of fresh fruit and vegetables from the gardens which we used to eat and which my mother used to cook in different ways. She loved cooking, and my father was particularly into wine, so I knew quite a lot about food and liked it.' Like Thompson, he was unusual among his male friends in learning to cook before he went to university. 'I remember being in demand with some friends to cook for dinner. I don't think I did it very well. It was a dog on its hind legs: it wasn't done well but you were surprised to see it done at all.'

I told him that Mark Thompson was also one of the very few men he knew who *liked* to cook at university, and Bazalgette laughed and asked if it had done anything for his sex life. It's a telling remark: for Thompson, being able to cook was 'about iconoclasm and identity, eccentricity'; for Bazalgette it was 'not just to make you salivate but something to make you laugh and something to make you smile, something to make you think there's some joy in this.' Bazalgette's model created a light touch in Factual Entertainment, and he would go on to make successful shows in other subjects such as the makeover formats of *Ground Force* and *Changing Rooms*, using this same entertaining, aspirational approach to revolutionise gardening and DIY. Compared with their competitors which he described as 'bloodless', these shows were about emotion. 'They created narrative and joy and surprise and reveals.'

Food and Drink was, according to Bazalgette, more about 'entertainment, human interest, narrative and information' than the high emotion of the makeover shows; humanity, warmth and charm rather than their jeopardy and big finishes. The show also played a vital part in the TV food revolution: by the end of the 1990s, *Food and Drink* would spearhead the changing relationship between the BBC and the supermarkets. As viewers responded to the suggestions of wine experts Jilly Goolden and Oz Clarke, supermarket buyers expanded their wine offer and explored new markets to feed the audience's insatiable desire for recommendations. It took the confidence of a TV maverick to negotiate one of the central principles of the BBC: 'We drove a coach and horses through that', said Bazalgette, referring to the BBC ban on product placement. 'You could say we were leading it, following it or going in lockstep with it; I don't know which of those three, but the supermarket revolution (went) from having about two thousand lines (in wine) to having seven or eight thousand lines. And that was when suddenly you could buy 30 different sorts of olive oil from six different countries. We popularised that. We would taste these things and recommend particular products. When Jilly and Oz used to recommend a wine, it might sell quarter of a million bottles.'

Delia Smith did the same for ingredients, most notably, cranberries, which she recommended in the 1995 book and BBC Two series, *Delia Smith's Winter Collection*. *How to Cook* (BBC Two, 1999–2002) and its accompanying BBC books caused a rush on eggs, lump-free flour and omelette pans. It seemed that audiences could not get enough: 'TV cooking sensation Delia Smith has thrown manufacturers of obscure ingredients into a production frenzy ahead of her new series *How to Cook – Part Two*', warned BBC News in 2000. The show advised on store cupboard ingredients, with Delia recommending a new set of basics, including Maldon Sea Salt and Worcestershire Sauce'.

BBC Two was now the third most watched channel in the UK and had won the prestigious 'Channel of the Year' two years running at the Edinburgh International Television Festival. Jane Root was controller from 1999 to 2004 and continued the relationship with the retailers 'We actually had to start telling the supermarkets in advance what ingredients […] were going to be her [Delia's] magic ingredients. The power of Delia was that she could say that dried cranberries are this most amazing thing. It was like six months in advance to source the ingredients otherwise people were so upset. People were outraged if freshly ground pepper was nowhere to be found', Root told me. People were learning to cook through entertainment shows, bringing a new joy to the educative aspect of food and translating it directly into both economic and cultural capital at the supermarket. 'It was a time when the public were voting with their feet', Bazalgette told me. 'They were taking these practical suggestions from Delia and Michael Barry (co-presenter with Chris Kelly of *Food and Drink*) and others, and going to the supermarket and buying it.'

Jane Root referred to BBC Two shows like *Food and Drink* and *Delia* as 'serious', but the former glossy magazine editor noticed that they lacked a certain something. 'What they didn't have was visual delight and visual joy', she told me. Peter Bazalgette agreed, at least with the criticism of Delia. 'It was like being told what to do by a primary school headmistress. Delia was authentic and people trusted her, but she wasn't there to entertain people. She wasn't even there to make them smile. She was there to tell them how to boil an egg, and woe betide you if you didn't do it the way she said you ought to', he said.

It was Thompson and Root who would change this in Delia's *How to Cook*. Thompson had already begun to rethink food at the BBC: 'Rick Stein had just arrived. He was a teacher too but we'd introduced a bit of character – like the dog. We were hanging around quaysides in Cornwall. We were beginning to open out of the TV studio into what you might call lifestyle.' Suddenly, Delia felt stuck and out of date. Research about food in the '1990s was driven by fear', Thompson told me. 'With food viewers aging, we were asking if there were different ways to do food.' Inspired by a cookbook his mother had given him when he had gone to university, he had a radical idea. 'I said, "why don't we start from scratch?" Let's teach Britain to cook.' The result, Delia's series *How to Cook*, would run over three series and 28 episodes.

Seamus Geoghegan was director of the lifestyle and multimedia division at BBC Worldwide at the time, overseeing magazines such as *BBC Good Food* and *Gardeners' World*, and believes that without Thompson, Root and Llewellyn, BBC TV food would have been a very different offer. He agreed with me that it was their unusually personal interest in food that was the driver. 'It was that passion that they had for the subject and belief in the talent to deliver it', he told me. I relayed the story Thompson had told me about his half terms in Rome. It didn't surprise Geoghegan. 'I didn't know what Mark's backstory was, but I knew he had to have one because Delia was extremely – and I mean extremely – support-ive of Mark. Others had tried to woo Delia back. Delia needs to absolutely feel and know that it's heartfelt.' Referring to *How to Cook*, Geoghegan said: 'I mean she's a very, very straightforward lady – and brilliant at it – but she didn't just want it to be another series. It had to have a reason for being.'

Thompson had created a revolution in food and successfully pinned it on Delia. While she had been appearing on the BBC from 1979 to 1999, the focus in Britain had shifted from cuisine to health. 'It was about the quality of ingre-dients, cooking for friends' Jane Root told me in 2013. 'We were encouraging documentary makers to think about food migrating from arts and other sectors.' By the time Root took charge of BBC Two in 1999, cooking had moved from the educative model to entertainment, bringing delight along with helpful tips. 'Delia was the bridge between these worlds', said Root. 'Delia was based on the idea that you would create this masterpiece in the kitchen and then take it through to the sitting room and everyone would ooh and aah over it.'

Root insisted that Food TV had to be about 'enjoyment rather than working hard at it'. It had to be about delight. 'It reminds me of many years later working with David Attenborough on *Planet Earth* [BBC One, 2006]. At the time when it started, there were these huge discussions at the BBC and Discovery, and David said, "you have to fall in love with the world before you can save it." That was the line that we all followed: fall in love first and that will motivate you to save it. I think there was that thing about love and pleasure. It was a kind of break-through.'

But the idea may not have arisen if the BBC hadn't commissioned a piece of research which Root remembered as one of the most influential moments on her watch in Food TV. The research was not about food itself, but about how people felt about food. 'We asked people what extra thing they'd like to have in their kitchen', she told me in 2013. 'And the answer was a sofa. For me, that was a really breakthrough moment. I remember talking to Peter Bazalgette about it and various production teams. For me, it was this idea that we had shifted as a culture from food being made in a kitchen completely separate to your family to food being the essence of a social thing. The home cook's obsession about cooking was making a risotto, drinking a glass of wine with your best friend in the kitchen while people are standing around talking. It was about that level of informality and friendship.'

The research would inspire a new way of looking at food at BBC Two, which would then spread to Channel 4 and open out new ways of telling stories about food across British TV, and it ultimately made its way to the high street. 'We wanted to make it into something to do with preparation that was more social', explained Thompson in 2013. 'I wasn't so keen on this idea of "Lifestyle TV". It never quite captured what I thought was going on', he told me. His own passion for cooking, inspired by his holidays as a schoolboy in Rome, underpinned a developing ideology at the BBC. He wanted to explore the meta-values of food, what it said about the individual cook, his/her world and the way they think: 'It's about an attitude to life. Unlocking it was a kind of expressionism. Collectively, we took that underlying metaphor to create something new.'

Delia was also one of the catalysts behind what would become the Jamie Oliver phenomenon. Jane Root explained: 'At that time, Delia was making all these noises about retiring which she continued to do on and off for years. So we were all like, "please don't go, Delia." But we were wondering if she ever did retire, who would we get to have that position. So we were actively looking.' Root and Mark Thompson watched with interest as the independent production companies brought a new flavour to the mix. 'We were beginning to change the mould with the introduction of indies', Thompson told me. 'We'd made *An Italian Christmas: Recipes from the River Café* (BBC Two, 1996). They were really hot in the 1990s. We needed to think who we were going to get next.' Channel 4 were in the lead in the ratings race with *Nigel Slater's Real Food Show* (1998) and *Nigella Bites* (1999), and the cult of the individual making food into lifestyle and the kitchen into the leisure zone of the home was finding purchase. Pat Llewellyn spotted her moment and approached Thompson. He remembered the moment: 'Pat came to me and said, "you've lost the battle but there's this boy…"'

The making of Britishness

Against the backdrop of a style-driven, food fetishizing capital, 1980s Britain appeared to have lost its sense of humour. Conspicuous consumerism was not funny: it was a display of aspiration and super-affluence among the young, up-and-coming professional known as the 'yuppy'. As Thatcher's dream of an individualistic society found its roots, the rise of the superchef seemed to be more about feeding the ego than competing with a rising trend in world-class cuisine that was coming out of Melbourne, Sydney, San Francisco and New York. Foreign travel – both for business and increasingly for pleasure as the cost of flights came down – was encouraging a more worldly British public to bring home new ideas, flavours and aspirational taste, and television was reflecting the conflicting stories that we were beginning to tell about ourselves.

The 1980s and 1990s were also an era of 'moral panic' around food and not just in Britain as the media seized on a series of scares. In the UK in 1986, 'mad cow disease' or bovine spongiform encephalopathy (BSE) was first identified in cattle, yet despite fears that eating beef could affect humans and an admission by the government that a new brain disease, a variant of Creutzfeld Jakobs disease (vCJD), was probably linked to BSE, in 1990, the then Agriculture Minister John Selwyn Gummer appeared before the media to eat a hamburger with his daughter. In 1995, 19-year-old Stephen Churchill became the first known victim of vCJD. In 1988, two million chickens were slaughtered after Junior Health Minister at the time, Edwina Currie, suggested that 'most egg production' in Britain was tainted with salmonella. And the incidence of reported listeria infections increased dramatically during the 1980s across the world: in 1985, a Mexican-style cheese was thought to be responsible for 142 cases, with 48 deaths in Los Angeles in 1985. In the late 1980s, an outbreak in the UK was associated with pâté causing more than 350 cases with over ninety deaths. Throughout the 1990s, listeria was linked to smoked mussels in New Zealand, raw milk soft cheese, pork tongue in jelly, 'rillettes' or potted pork in France, pasteurized chocolate milk in the US, frankfurters in the US and butter in Finland. It seemed safer to eat food out of a tin or from a shrink-wrapped supermarket packet than to buy meat from a butcher or eggs or cheese from a farm shop or deli. When John Major's government published its *Health of the Nation* report in 1992 evidencing the link between the great British diet of saturated fats and dairy with cancer and heart disease, we were told that we had got it all wrong. What we needed was a more Mediterranean diet of olive oil, fruit and vegetables, and red wine.

It would take another ten years before food scares and anxiety about the role of food in our lives led to the rebirth of artisan foods in the UK after centuries of industrialisation ruptured our relationship with the source of food production. The link between high-welfare meat and the importance of keeping grazing animals on British soil was yet to become clear, and it would be another decade before the new fashion for weekend trips with the kids to the farm shop would lead to articles in the broadsheets about rewilding and mob-grazing.

But it would not halt the rise of the restaurant experience or the reinvention of 'British' food, as the narrative of aspiration found its latest home. In 1995, Terence Conran opened his latest gastrodome, the 700-seater Mezzo in London's Soho, a theatre of food to be seen eating the latest trends. At the same time, Gary Rhodes, chef at The Greenhouse restaurant in Mayfair, was commissioned by BBC Education to tour the UK to rediscover the Britishness of our indigenous culinary culture. His braised oxtail, Lancashire hotpot and boiled bacon with pearl barley and lentils, in the 1994 BBC Two series *Rhodes Around Britain* and the accompanying BBC book, created a national conversation on what it meant to be British at a time when meat and farming seemed very scary indeed.

Pat Llewellyn was watching these elements come together to create the perfect storm. She told me in 2013 that she was thinking about her next food series after the success of the 1993 Channel 4 series *Grow Your Greens, Eat Your Greens*, and observing what Rick Stein and Gary Rhodes were doing on BBC Two. 'They were both very anti-supermarket. I'm not saying they started nose-to-tail but their values of proper food and buying British did feel very different to what was going on on the telly.'

Llewellyn wanted to do something different. 'I wanted to reflect what people were doing domestically.' Like me, Llewellyn had worked on Channel 4's magazine series, *Food File*, where storytelling and eccentric characters created a new narrative around British ingredients. Llewellyn remembered it well: 'We were always finding kipper-smokers in god knows where or going to see sausage makers.'

This style of televisual storytelling served to ground the heady fashionista food culture that characterised London in the mid-1990s, and brought it home to the hills and coasts of Britain. Homing in on the passion of the farmers, these 'foodies' were the people who grew it rather than those who just chose the dish to go with the dress.

Llewellyn pulled focus on the characters behind British food. 'I'd done *Eat Your Greens* with Jane Root and Sophie Grigson, and that was all about crazy people doing things with vegetables, and I'd met Clarissa (Dickson Wright) on that shoot. She was growing cardoons on a friend's garden in Skegness or something. I thought she was great and we kept in touch. I wanted to do something else with her and it took a while to work out what that was.'

The result was Llewellyn's ground-breaking BBC Two series *Two Fat Ladies* (1996–99), a triumph of British storytelling. As Clarissa Dickson Wright and Jennifer Paterson rode on motorbike and sidecar through the breath-taking British countryside, stopping in idyllic country villages to cook game, or preparing a feast for a lacrosse team at an exclusive school for girls, they caricatured a Britain recognisable from Ealing comedies and period dramas. Bossy and eccentric, Dickson Wright has been compared to the stout British matron, Margaret Rutherford, who starred in the Ealing comedy *Passport to Pimlico* (1949), a film that is all about British national identity and austerity politics, and as Miss Marple in the 1960s, calling upon a nostalgia often found since in British food programmes. *Two Fat Ladies* created an almost tactile quality to a screen experience with its utterly delightful gluttony and pastiche of the British upper classes. It was about friendship, adventure and fun, providing new opportunities to play with food while encouraging viewers to salivate over the dishes they made. Nicola Moody worked with Jane Root as Head of Factual while Llewellyn was making *Two Fat Ladies*, which Llwellyn described to me as 'hilarious and wonderful: the British eccentric at play'(2013). Its opening sequence set the scene for the parody of Britishness which would sell across the world: a fairy-tale storybook opens to reveal a cartoon of Jennifer and Clarissa aboard motorbike and sidecar accompanied by 1960s style children's storytime music. We hear a roar as the two fat ladies blast off the page to a jazz score, dodging bottles of olive oil and plates of seafood. 'Grab that crab, Clarissa', sing-speaks Jennifer as Clarissa joins her with, 'Eat that meat, Jennifer.' 'Fasten your taste buds for a gastronomic ride', they both growl as the trumpet screams and the cartoon bikers hurtle off-screen. The cartoon morphs as the real-life Two Fat Ladies ride through the wintery lanes of Winchester to meet choristers of the city's cathedral, whom they plan to feed stuffed goose and Christmas pudding bombe after their last service on Christmas Day.

The combination of high production values and quirky storytelling (*Two Fat Ladies*; *Nigella Bites*; *The Naked Chef* became a powerful and sophisticated branding for British Food. But unhampered by the kind of stable food culture which underpins most countries' sense of identity, producers like Llewellyn could create one. And drawing on Britain's imperial tradition to manipulate its storyline and punch above its weight, these caricatures of Britishness sold effortlessly across the globe.

Pat Llewellyn told me how *Two Fat Ladies* came about: 'I'd gone off in all sorts of different directions to start with. I started off thinking, "oh my gosh, I've got this posh middle-aged woman so maybe I need a young working-class wine writer or something." I was trying to find a pair for her. I started off looking for the opposite because she was quite a strong flavour. And then it was a friend of mine who met Jennifer at a party and he said, "oh my god I've just met another of your posh old girls." He said she's even posher than Clarissa. He was a friend of mine who I'd worked with on Wall to Wall. And I thought, "well, let's go for it. If we're going to do posh and fat and middle-aged, let's do it with knobs on." '

While Clarissa Dickson Wright and Jennifer Paterson as the *Two Fat Ladies* were an inspired antidote to the fashionable foodies eating out in London's growing food scene, they were also a deliberate poke in the eye at the government's advice on healthy eating. 'There was that whole Mediterranean diet thing going on', said Llewellyn (2013) about the response to the government's *Health of the Nation* report, which advised a diet rich in olive oil and fresh fruit and vegetables. 'There was lots of butter and they revelled in eating fat and things that weren't conventionally good for you', said Llewellyn. 'I think in a way that was part of the appeal. There was a lot of (she gestures a two-finger salute) going on.'

Two Fat Ladies was about the subversion of what society would expect of women of a certain age and class, a parody of the bawdy dame. 'I do think that its success was due to the fact that they were middle-aged and naughty and badly behaved', said Llewellyn. 'Jennifer smoked and drank on telly. It was outrageously bad behaviour.' It was perhaps a nod to the late-nineteenth-century Russian philosopher Bakhtin's notion of Carnivalesque, which derives from the medieval Feast of Fools when church officials would deliberately challenge authority through loutish behaviour. Interestingly, Paterson's uncle with whom she lived, was a Gentleman at Arms to the Cardinal Archbishops of Westminster.

In *Two Fat Ladies*, Clarissa Dickson Wright and Jennifer Paterson found licence to prod at the dominant representation of women on television: they not only drank too much, smoked and ate too much butter, but they also rode around the country on Paterson's Triumph Thunderbird motorbike with Dickson Wright stuffed into its sidecar. Their love of excess spilled over televisual boundaries, upsetting assumptions about class and femininity. Bakhtin suggested that humour and chaos have the power to challenge assumptions about the status quo, but academic Louise Fitzgerald believes that Bakhtin's carnival is only temporary: 'The rebellion is short-lived and works only to reinstate the social order because carnival is always sanctioned by those in authority as a way of mediating any form of rebellion. It's why slaves were given a day off for carnival by their owners, a seemingly benevolent act that actually worked to downplay acts of rebellion for the slaves (2016)'. She believes that these women would not have been seen as a signifier of femininity in the first place because their age and weight already take up 'too much space'. They are not feminine enough for the carnival to work', she told me. She added that their class status allows them to behave in this manner: 'We would expect them to be eccentric and to behave in ways that other women would not be allowed to behave. It might have been much more Carnivalesque to have had two middle-class yummy mummies behaving in such subversive ways.' Llewellyn told me that she finds class 'really interesting. It's a rich source for telly, isn't it? We categorise people all the time in telly. I think we were probably having a bit of fun and poking a bit of fun at their toffeeness' (2013).

In the US, *Two Fat Ladies* represented the antithesis of political correctness. David Richards wrote in the *Washington Post*: 'If excess poundage is considered an idiosyncrasy or, at most, an inconvenience in Great Britain, it takes on the dimensions of a moral flaw in the United States. Fat equals indulgence. Indulgence is weakness and weakness is deplorable. In that sense, the *Two Fat Ladies*, blissfully unconcerned with any such foolishness, are liberators, come to free the adipose from self-loathing.'

Thorogood says that the show is still doing tremendously well on the Cooking Channel in the US. 'Now I find that fascinating', he told me (2016). 'Two very British people from a very specific sort of background put together in a way that was interestingly constructed but appear to have this great jolly-hockey-sticks friendship, which they may well have done by the time they filmed the series. And they make this food that's very British: "let's put in seven pints of cream and make a fabulous big set custard." And yet it's appealing hugely to a US market. I find that very interesting.'

The gamechangers

Although Mark Thompson and Jane Root should be credited with being the creators of Food TV in Britain, they are, arguably, the midwives of a style created
by Pat Llewellyn.

Llewellyn had worked on Channel 4's *Food File*, the series responsible for
Hugh Fearnley-Whittingstall's first TV appearance. She had also responded to
one of the first calls for lifestyle entertainment ideas, by producing *Grow Your
Greens, Eat Your Greens* (1993), also for Channel 4, with Sophie Grigson at Wall
to Wall, before joining Optomen in 1994, where she would conceive and produce
Two Fat Ladies.

Jane Root had first seen the 'visual delight and visual joy' she wanted from
BBC Two's food programmes in Llewellyn's *Grow Your Greens*... 'I still remember that series with such warmth and affection because it really was about people
who just loved it. And Pat's pumpkin grower show was just this wonderful country guy who talked about his pumpkins. And Clarissa Dickson Wright was there
talking about cardoons. And it was really wonderful', she told me. Root had been
executive producer on the series at Wall to Wall. 'I remember we took a decision
really early on that we weren't going to talk about anything to do with pests.
People can figure that out somewhere else. The food was going to be delightful.'

She said that it felt revolutionary: 'I think it was that we moved from food
being really serious to being enjoyable. Sophie was in her later twenties, early
thirties, as we all were, and it felt like it was our generation that were grasping
that and being a bit more exuberant about it.'

A Channel 4 executive told me that Root was a gamechanger. 'Jane says it's
all about tips and tricks: she was the first person to structure shows in a documentary way so that if I were a viewer, I'd learn something.' Sophie Grigson's
pedigree – her mother was the influential food writer and journalist, Jane Grigson – added to her credibility to front shows about the best of British food, but
the idea of how to create a fresh style for a show about meat required a different
set of skills. 'Sophie would have had powerful philosophies', said the same Channel 4 executive. 'She may have brought the idea that what was needed was the

curve ball from vegetables (*Grow Your Greens…*) to meat (*Sophie's Meat Course*, Channel 4, 1995), but it would have been something that she and Jane Root would have devised together. 'It would have been about bringing a body of cooking knowledge to someone like me who didn't know that stuff', she said. It was the pursuit of 'delight' that introduced a haptic, sensually immersive experience to Food TV, engaging viewers with the visceral pleasures of *Two Fat Ladies*, which endowed the screen experience with an almost tactile quality, which Llewellyn knew how to recreate with Jamie Oliver.

Nicola Moody worked with Jane Root as Head of Factual while Llewellyn was making *Two Fat Ladies* and told me that Llewellyn knew more about food than anyone, 'perhaps even more than Clarissa', but that it was her ability to tell stories that sold British food programmes to the world. 'She came to us with a taster tape of Jamie', said Moody, remembering the moment when Llewellyn introduced Oliver to the Factual team at BBC Two. 'It was no more than five minutes in a pokey little kitchen with Jamie cutting up some green beans, as far as I remember. It wasn't beautifully shot but it had lots of energy.'

Jamie Oliver had first been seen on television in 1996 in a Christmas special on the River Café, the Hammersmith canteen run by Richard Rogers's wife, Ruth, and her partner, Rose Gray, one of the original chefs at the influential 192 in Notting Hill. Ruth Rogers told me how effortless Oliver was in front of the camera: 'Jamie was frying mushrooms. Rose says she thinks he was doing something else, but I think he was frying mushrooms. He could talk to the camera and be himself and that's a very difficult thing to do. You're doing two things: you're trying to inform and educate and you have to be at ease with yourself and the camera in order to do that. And he was there.'

Llewellyn had been looking for a new chef and went to see him at the River Café. As he made pasta, she spotted her star. 'My mother has this thing that you can tell someone who can really cook by the way they use their hands and I've inherited that from her', she told me for my 2008 Jamie Oliver biography, *The Jamie Oliver Effect: The Man, the Food, the Revolution*. 'I don't know what it is. He looked like he'd been doing it all his life – which he had.' She took a taster tape to Jane Root who remembered what it was that greenlit the astonishing story of Jamie Oliver: 'Pat Llewellyn came in and showed me three minutes of Jamie', said Root in 2013. 'It chimed with this thing about friendship and informality. He felt like he was all about that.'

Nicola Moody described the BBC Two of the time as a place ready to have a go. She remembered Mark Thomson saying, 'OK, why not? Let's have a go.' 'It really wasn't much more than that', she said in 2013. I suggested that it was a heady mix of politics and culture at a time when supermarkets had begun to sell good wines and dinner parties could be more like a restaurant experience.

I asked if BBC Two was trying to reflect this melting pot of aspiration and style, but she disagreed. 'I don't remember thinking that the world has changed and we need something to reflect that. I remember thinking that everything looked a bit boring and we needed something new. Maybe it's the same thing.' Moody said that BBC Two was feeling a bit old at the time. 'It [the audience] was very female and late thirties.' The average BBC Two viewer is now nearer 50, but at the time, Thompson, Root and Moody, who were also in their thirties, were keen to mirror some of the youthful dynamism that was evidenced by Britpop, the politically branded creativity that defined Britain in the mid/late-1990s. The then British Prime Minister, Tony Blair, had pulled focus on a handful of successful British artists such as Tracey Emin and the band Oasis to define a new 'cool'. 'Jamie felt like he was part of that young British art movement', said Moody. 'He was full of energy and fun and had an attitude. He was about freedom of expression. He wasn't "trendy" yet, and "cool" isn't the right word', she said. 'There had been a lot of youth programmes that had been too cool. No one wanted that anymore. This was about aspiration, the idea that you could live in a city and have a good life.'

Nicola Moody commissioned a pilot, but despite having found their man, it didn't work. The chaotic informality of the screen test had been replaced by Oliver trying to explain over-complicated recipes in catering French to camera. 'He gabbled so much', Llewellyn told me. 'He was completely raw and everything came out at once.' Nicola Moody remembered it well. 'It was shot too conventionally, with the camera on legs. Jamie was talking down the lens. It didn't have the energy that we'd seen in the taster which was handheld I'm pretty sure. It was dull. The mise-en-place was all done: everything was laid out in little bowls, ready to go. It didn't seem like him. It all seemed very old-fashioned. It was not what we wanted.'

Llewellyn had to tell Jane Root who, as Head of Independent Commissioning, was the executive lead. Root remembered the moment: 'I was driving somewhere and I was talking to Pat for an hour on the phone and we were just like, "oh my god, it's all going wrong. What are we going to do?"' Root gave her permission to dump £60,000 worth of pilot, lose the little bowls and start again. 'Pat got rid of the director and all this cutting up. He couldn't really talk to camera then – it seems like a weird thing to remember, but she had that thing about talking to him from behind the camera', she told me.

Moody suggested that what Llewellyn did next was revolutionary: by taking the camera off the legs (tripod) and asking the questions herself off-camera, taking away the bowls and simplifying the recipes, Llewellyn was able to 'produce' the 'mockney geezer' TV chef out of the young chef whom she had witnessed effortlessly making pasta while chatting to his team at the River Café. Moody was clear who created Jamie Oliver at that time: 'Jamie was just the talent', she said. 'He wouldn't have been involved with the creative decision.'

TV food changed forever with *The Naked Chef*. Nick Thorogood remembers it well: 'What was amazing about Jamie was he went, "oh, we're going to have a handful of flour," and he threw it, not into a bowl, but on a counter. "And a bit of this and a bit of that!" and if you remember, every piece of the language went from precision into abstract. "Oh, you bish bosh …." ' He agreed that what Pat Llewellyn did was unprecedented: 'If you remember in Season One and Season Two, it is Pat off-camera literally saying to him, "what are you doing? Why have you done this?" and that brought the story to life. What was fascinating for me with that was that it had thrown out every convention, every rule of television before it in the food area – and many other areas actually'.

Llewellyn's instinctive decisions, her skill in 'producing' talent is to heighten or accentuate what is already there. Interestingly, John Diamond and his wife Nigella Lawson had just also had spectacular success, this time on Channel 4, after Diamond encouraged the relaxed, playful side of his wife to come out on the screen, transforming a camera-shy journalist into a vampy domestic goddess. Far from duplicity, this talent for producing a heightened reality is described by Catherine Constable in Sue Thornham's 2007 *Women, Feminism and Media* as a 'pure play of appearances that is not deceptive, but rather possesses a particular authenticity'.

Authenticity in television is a contested term: in the discourse of mediated message-making, making telly is all about who holds the power and who sets the agenda. There can be no 'real' on the screen, media theorist Heather Nunn told me in 2017, 'You can't have any access to him [Jamie Oliver] other than through those highly mediated images.'

Nicola Moody illustrated this as she described in 2013 how the Youth TV movement, created by Janet Street Porter, prompted TV to 'move away from authenticity' through programmes like BBC Two's *Reportage*, which equated less physical movement with being what she called 'cool and authoritative'. Moody was editor of the programme and remembers being told by an executive to make sure that her presenters didn't move their hands too much. 'It was very controlled: it was cool to be calm, like [the black-bobbed, shades-clad, super-stylish presenter] Magenta Devine.'

As producer of Jamie Oliver in *The Naked Chef*, Pat Llewellyn brought an end to this era, and arguably to our relationship with food and style in Britain. After Gary Rhodes, Ainsley Harriott and Rick Stein, Llewellyn's Oliver offered something completely different. 'It was semi-real, semi-imagined', Mark Thompson explained in 2013. 'It was ambitious food that was practical and approachable. [Jamie] was a bit of an antidote, a different wave to the Gary Rhodes thing. The aspiration was to be a home chef, to have an incredibly delightful home experience. Sophie [Grigson] did a bit of it, Jamie hugely contributed, but it wasn't about locking yourself in the kitchen and being on *MasterChef* [BBC, 1990–present]. It was about it being part of your family life.'

Llewellyn would become one of the most influential producers in television. She had a 'vast effect on popular culture', according to journalist Howard Byrom. 'She's shaped the way we think about food, the way we treat the people who cook it, and, by proxy, the way it's marketed from the barrow boys to supermarkets.' He called her 'the scullery Spielberg, the culinary Cecil B de Mille', and said that 'thanks to her, mild-mannered housewives now smash garlic with their fists, toss salads with their bare hands, and taste the dressing by dipping in their fingers and slurping rather loudly'.

Part Two

Creating a national conversation

In 2016, the UK was reeling from the news that *The Great British Bake Off* (BBC, 2010– 16; Channel 4, 2017– present), that bastion of Britishness with its basketful of national treasures, its sweet smell of diversity and its wholesome values, in which Granny knows best and an older man with a twinkle in his eye can still make an audience salivate, had been sold. The highest bidder was Channel 4, that brash, trashy youth channel with its eye on the money and its heart in the headlines, which paid £25 million a year, four times the BBC fee. Love or money: it's a dualism that strikes at the heart of Britishness and its notions of taste.

The BBC One show (2014–16), made, rather ironically in retrospect, by Love Productions, first came to air on BBC Two in 2010 and struck gold with its classic sense of Britishness at a time when the UK was suffering an identity crisis. '[*The Great British Bake Off*] GBBO is a classic example of public service broadcasting – it aims to unite the nation around a common pastime and highlights the multicultural face of Britain – and deserves its place in peak-time schedules', wrote Professor Des Freedman in *The Conversation* in 2016, the morning after the news of the sale. Its presenters Sue Perkins and Mel Giedroyc were old school comics with their seaside postcard puns and genuinely warm hugs for the contributors, whose soggy bottoms reduced them to tears. When they threw in their tea towels within hours of the news of the move to Channel 4, social media was buzzing with national distress.

The pair issued a statement: 'The BBC nurtured the show from its infancy and helped give it its distinctive warmth and charm, growing it from an audience of two million to nearly 15 [million] at its peak.' Using their trademark puns, they said, 'We've had the most amazing time on *GBBO*, and have loved seeing it rise and rise like a pair of yeasted Latvian baps. We're not going with the dough. We wish all the future bakers every success.' Love over money; status quo over change: these are the choices of our national treasures and represent the duality of modern Britishness and how it is represented in broadcasting. While social media debated whether *GBBO* could be *GBBO* without Mel and Sue – or the BBC – suspicion fell over expert judges Paul Hollywood and Mary Berry as we waited to hear whether they would follow the money or stand by their fellow presenters. According to journalist, Claire Corkery, Mary Berry's husband, Paul Hunnings told *The Daily Mail* newspaper in that late summer of 2016 that they too might pull out of the show: 'Paul is currently in LA and hasn't had a chance to talk to Mary. But they have always said they are in it together.' By the end of the month, Mary Berry said she couldn't leave her fellow presenters. Only Hollywood stayed silent.

Suddenly, baking was big business and that left a nasty taste in the mouth. Love Productions, which took the series from a small show on BBC Two to ten million viewers on primetime BBC One, was seen as money-grabbing: *The Sun*'s headline represented the hypocrisy at the centre of British identity: 'Great British *GBBO* creators Richard McKerrow and wife Anna Beattie have raked in enough dough from the hit show to own two homes worth £6 million!', making much of McKerrow's background as a 'public schoolboy' and the champagne socialist's friendship with former Labour leader Ed Miliband. In fact, McKerrow's relationship with Channel 4 is long and deep: he was a commissioning editor there and launched Ramsay's *Boiling Point* (1999) and *Nigel Slater's Real Food Show*. But feelings were running high: when ITV's *This Morning* (1988–present) presenters Phil Schofield and Holly Willoughby joked that they might be replacing Mel and Sue, Twitter reminded them that it was not funny: 'How dare Holly and Phil mess with people's #gbbo emotions, I'm on the edge', tweeted @TooManyEmmas. @scottygb shouted, 'STOP PLAYING WITH US "THIS MORNING" WE'VE SUFFERED ENOUGH ALREADY THIS WEEK' (Vincent, 2016).

The critics were happy enough: 'The BBC needs to take risks and should be constantly renewing its offer and developing new ideas', wrote Freedman in 2016. 'In this context, throwing £25m a year at a single brand is not necessarily an imaginative use of public money [...] Channel 4's willingness to invest heavily in the programme reveals quite a lot about the way in which it now interprets its remit to provide "high quality and diverse" programming and to foster innovation and creativity.'

Hannah Ellis-Petersen in *The Guardian* reported that negotiations had broken down with the BBC over money and vision: 'The BBC was felt to be constrained by its licence fee settlement, whereas Channel 4 is said to have been happy to dip into its reserves to pay for the most watched show of 2015.' Within a day of the news, Channel 4 announced it was already planning a celebrity *GBBO* in aid of Stand Up to Cancer for its launch of the series. It noted that this is not the first time that the BBC has lost top talent to a better financial offer: after the BBC brought Jamie Oliver into the spotlight with *The Naked Chef*, he was signed by Channel 4. In 2010, his old friend Jimmy Doherty followed in his footsteps and transferred from the corporation to its commercial rival. As a publicly funded broadcaster, the BBC is limited in how commercial its programmes and present-ers can be. Indeed, it is not the first time the corporation has found itself in a sticky situation over the commercial fallout of a culinary hit.

The loss of Michel Roux Junior from *MasterChef* in 2014 is another exam-ple of the BBC's failure to keep the talent it grows. 'What's happened to GBBO epitomises the state of British television', wrote Freedman in 2016. 'For all the moments of inspiration and energy, our TV landscape remains obsessed with formulae and beholden to ratings.' He urged television to create more space for the 'dynamic independent sector that is fantastic at developing formats with huge export potential' and to vie with US corporations for the enormous spoils.

Yet *GBBO* draws from an idea of nostalgia, heritage, imperialism and the national story in ways that are comforting to us. *GBBO*'s focus on diversity reso-nates with a palpable national anxiety about the possible loss of part of Britain's national heritage through a programme that relies on a recall to imperialism: the marquee is a signifier of Britishness, and those with authority are white and priv-ileged. It is subverted slightly by presenter Noel Fielding's quirkiness, and his co-presenter Sandi Toksvig, as well as her predecessor Sue Perkins, are two of the most prominent lesbians on British TV. But *GBBO* is seen as valuable in its reflection or mirroring of a national storyline: as Stuart Hall wrote in his keynote speech, 'Whose Heritage? The Impact of Cultural Diversity on Britain's Living Heritage', at G-Mex in Manchester in November 1999: 'This gives the British idea of "Heritage" a peculiar inflection. The works and artefacts so conserved appear to be "of value" primarily in relation to the past. To be validated, they must take their place alongside what has been authorised as "valuable" on already estab-lished grounds in relation to the unfolding of a "national story" whose terms we already know. The Heritage thus becomes the material embodiment of the spirit of the nation, a collective representation of the British version of *tradition*, a concept pivotal to the lexicon of English virtue' (original emphasis).

Ask the average *Bake Off* viewer to name a previous winner, and Nadiya is likely to be top of the list. 'When John Waite and Edd Kimber won', said Nick Thorogood, 'the first thing that they did was to write a cookbook. It's about, "I'm a baker." But Nadiya wins the show and it's, "let's take Nadiya back to her heritage and do a travelogue." Thorogood was referring to BBC One's *The Chronicles of Nadiya* (2016), a two-part BBC documentary in which she travelled back to her family in Bangladesh to find the roots of her cooking/self. 'That is exactly what we've been saying about how the show has developed from being, "here's a show that tells you how to bake and how to cook into a show that is about representing our culture." That's really, really interesting', Thorogood said.

Media academic Louise Fitzgerald agreed, telling me: 'There has been a clear move towards the historical/nostalgic in austerity culture expressed within the media, within consumer culture and in the heightened embrace of the nation's past. British national identity or the national story continues to manifest itself in those signifiers that have been left over from the past: cricket, marquees on the lawn, gin, tea and cake, bunting and large English houses. Where once the use of these signifiers would have been seen as eccentric, they are now firmly established in the mainstream of middle-class white culture where the recession has largely factored as an opportunity to reboot established and enduring ideological precepts about class consumerism, gender and the state. Britain does not have a unified, coherent, identifiable self-image, either as a people or as a political entity – the focus is on virtues such as tolerance and decency'.

But *Bake Off* is perhaps the nearest that we can come to a contemporary story about British national identity, or at least what we might like it to be: diverse but assimilated, maintaining British traditions, overseen and judged by upholders of Britishness. The players are caricatures of Britishness: Mel and Sue were the prefects of an Ealing boarding school comedy, while Noel and Sandi continue in the rather eccentric, quick fire comedy vein, Noel's legacy of the groundbreaking *Mighty Boosh* echoing that earlier British comic pioneer, Monty Python. Mary Berry was the white-haired, well-dressed archetype of British manners, while Prue Leith, daringly colourful, is the headmistress of the most famous and well-respected cookery school in the UK. Paul Hollywood is still the self-made, Liverpudlian patriarch, the baker out of the card game Happy Families. *Bake Off*'s main narrative is that of a society divided by class, gender, race and ethnicity, but united by its common purpose – baking. It conjures up a time when Britain was the world's leader, a time of industrialisation, military greatness and empire, but it is produced at a time of heightened concerns about where we stand in the world, increased racism, fear of immigration and Brexit.

Creating capital

British food was given a makeover by television in the mid-1990s, with Delia Smith, Gary Rhodes and Rick Stein a more grounded response to the conspicuous consumerism that was happening in the elite fashionable restaurants in the capital. But it provided a more important role for audiences: television helped to spread food across a wider table, tapping into different audience groups, enabling them to define themselves as lads like Jamie, domestic goddesses like Nigella, he-men chefs like Gordon or alchemists like Heston. By the millennium, Channel 4 had ruptured the TV food model, taking food away from the conservative wine-tasting middle-class and giving it to the younger, flashier *Come Dine with Me* and *First Dates* twentieth-century foodies. But it also offered a new home to a new version of Jamie Oliver, one who would build a reputation as an interferer, a campaigner, a national hero. In the next chapters, we look at how media discourse and the television industry understand audiences in different ways to explore some of the discord between the two disciplines.

Between 1989 and 1993, *BBC Good Food* was the only food magazine on the bookstalls. It was the first in a line of enormously successful publications which capitalized on the growing interest in leisure (it was followed in 1991 by *Gardener's World* magazine). But according to Seamus Geoghegan, managing director at Eye to Eye Media, which publishes *Waitrose* and *delicious.* magazines, it was the launch of *Sainsbury's Magazine* in 1993, published by Delia Smith and her husband Michael Wynn-Jones, which shook the industry. Geoghegan was at BBC Worldwide from 1988 to 2002 and oversaw the launch of *Good Food* in 1989. He remembers how 'very, very powerful' *Sainsbury's Magazine* was, but that the launch was 'one which everyone forgets. *Good Food* was its own thing, but Sainsbury's and Delia brought in chefs/cooks that were authentic. Nigel Slater, Simon Hopkinson, et al., they were in *Sainsbury's Magazine* and nowhere else. And there became this real thing: these people can really cook, as opposed to these wannabe celebrities. *Sainsbury's Magazine* was immensely powerful and took a lot of copies off *Good Food*', he told me.

BBC Two was still the home of Food TV at this time, and was driven by entertainment and talent. BBC Worldwide had already begun to realise the pulling power of leisure among its audiences, and *BBC Good Food* was translating Food TV into theatrical events at enormous arenas like Birmingham's NEC. These live food events were a powerful way of connecting new audiences with food. Designed for mass appeal rather than as a niche middle-class foodie experience, they are still advertised today as an opportunity to gather some cultural capital. 'Experience the buzz of meeting your favourite chefs at a *BBC Good Food Show*!' proclaims the online invitation at BBCgoodfoodshow.com. 'Enjoy a day out with friends tasting exciting new flavours, stocking up on the latest kitchen kit and seeing the best-in-the-business cooking mouth-watering dishes in live demos and sharing their tricks of the trade in interviews.'

Geoghegan remembered the first time the TV chefs came off the screen and into the arena: 'They'd just set up what was to become the celebrity chef theatre for the first time and it was small, and of course it got overrun with people who wanted to sit down and see Ainsley and Antony Worrall Thompson at that stage. And that was the beginning of seeing the pulling power – the box-office appeal if you will – of the chefs.' The combination of the TV programmes, magazines and live appearances brought a rush on tickets and cleared the magazine shelves, creating a magic that would change the course of TV food. 'Alan Titchmarsh was the same', said Geoghegan of the Daytime TV host and presenter of BBC Two's *Gardener's World*. When *BBC Good Food* was released in print, you couldn't get a copy, according to Geoghegan. 'It's the age-old desire to make gods of humans', he told me. 'It's that "up close and personal" moment, that pointing, "oh look, that's so-and-so over there," or "I want to hear what they've got to say."'

The relationship between a TV audience and TV talent has changed immeasurably since BBC Worldwide created its relationship with print and live events. Geoghegan's role was to bring BBC Books closer to the channels, and to develop talent and programmes. 'It was about genre-facing rather than format-driven', he told me. 'So, all of a sudden, I had the books, the TV rights, as well as the magazines to manage.' He remembered first meeting Jane Root, then controller of BBC Two as she was addressing a colleague, tearing him off a strip for failing to sign up a hot young chef to BBC Books. 'She said something like, "I gifted you who I think is going to be the biggest thing since sliced bread and you f****d it up. You went off and lost out on what was a carte blanche to do a book."' He asked Root afterwards what the exchange had been about. 'She said, "I told them about this young guy that I've seen with Pat Llewellyn called Jamie Oliver who is going to be stratospheric, I guarantee you.' It was the first time Geoghegan had heard the name Jamie Oliver. 'BBC Books wouldn't have known a hit if it had knocked them on the nose', he said. 'I legged it down Fulham Palace Road into the River Café to meet Jamie and ask him what we'd done so badly to not get his book. He then introduced me to Pat's partner in Optomen, and who told me about how our pitch was so cruddy compared to Penguin Books who completely wowed Jamie. And that's why they got his book deal from that day to this.'

Seamus Geoghegan was at the helm of BBC Books during the reinvention of Delia in 1999 in *How to Cook*: 'Delia was our biggest author at the time so it was a massive moment', he told me. He puts the show's success entirely down to Mark Thompson. 'He held her hand and reassured her all of the way because she didn't want to come back and do just another "thing". He told her that there was a whole new generation out there that needed to know how to cook from her.'

Magazines and books have been instruction manuals for a better life since the beginning of the seventeenth century. Food historian, Colin Spencer, noted in his 2002 book the trend of titled ladies of this era to reveal the secrets of their boudoirs and their kitchens. The domestic goddesses of their day shared their beauty and culinary tips with a newly literate class, and Spencer suggests in his 2002 book that the cookery book became the first 'stimulus to fantasy'. The illiterate classes, however, which made up more than half the population, were in a perpetual cycle of debt and poverty, and as food manners and fashion and beauty became social indicators of those with and without property, so the classes divided. Echoing the stories of racism among second generation immigrants through the ages, so the newly landed looked down upon those they left behind, digging a social trench between them through the food on their table.

These female cookery writers did more for British food culture than provide bedtime reading: the period between the Civil War and the Industrial Revolution cemented the power of the middle classes to plan and grow their own produce, and women began to detail their pragmatic approach to keeping their families healthy. They wrote because they could, both in terms of skill and time, before the crushing scheduling of the day by the Industrial Revolution. Spencer notes that this was another dividing point between Britain and the continent, France in particular, where food was described by royal male cooks who were employed to perform with food in comparison with the more pragmatic British woman's desire to feed her family healthily and with some style. Hannah Wooley wrote several such books in the seventeenth century in which she details how to preserve as well as make syrups for colds and coughs, and shares a recipe for an aqua mirabilis made of sack, aqua vitae and many spices. She describes over 200 recipes from pickling cucumbers to stretching sheep gut, pies of lettuce and spinach and chickens and pigeons boiled in gooseberry and grape sauces. Matthew Hamlyn's 1988 book revisits some of her recipes in Hannah Woolley, *English Cookery of the Seventeenth Century*.

Cookery books were a means of documenting food history and instructing women in how to run a home as well as containing a compilation of ingredients and recipes. Mrs Beeton, whose bestselling *Book of Household Management* (1861) selling 60,000 copies in its first print run, was less about aspiration, as in the cookery books of the seventeenth century, and more about 'order and cleanliness' in the home as Spencer (2002) notes. It reflected the moral and pragmatic approach to running the home of Victorian Protestants. Mrs Beeton was the young wife of a publisher who advertised for recipes from housewives across Britain, and became a bestselling author when she tested and compiled them for her book on household management. Interestingly, she was seen as a leader, showing women how to run a well-managed home without smugness. But, as Spencer says, '[i]n reflecting a society, she also helped to propagate it'. Mrs Beeton was the very embodiment of the Victorian ideology of a woman's place being in the home. The Victorian housewife was not expected to cook, but she had to manage the household of staff looking after everything from babies to putting food on the table.

By the millennium, cookbooks had almost come full circle, with Nigella Lawson echoing the style of the seventeenth-century manuals with her 2000 book, *How to Be a Domestic Goddess.* Enhanced by design and photography, the modern cookbook is now a style guide to a 'better' life. But while the market is flooded with cookbooks covering every kind of cuisine, it seems that we still can't get enough. Distribution executive, Niki Page, told me that she believes the extraordinary book sales couldn't happen without television. 'I think people forget that TV is what makes these franchise/brands build. I keep going back to Jamie Oliver but he's just the best example of it. It's just incredible. So you've got TV and then the books spin-off which makes an incredible amount of money for them. But the book wouldn't do well without the series. Then there's all the sponsorship and all the pots and pans and spice and everything that goes with it, none of that would happen without the TV.'

The 2010s would change the story with the rise of social media usurping television's place as the most important influencer. *A Pinch of Nom*, which started as a slimmers' food blog by restaurateurs Kate Allinson and Kay Featherstone, who between them lost 76kg over three years, became the fastest-selling non-fiction book since records began, with more than 200,000 sales in three days in March 2019. Compare that to Jamie Oliver's 2005 bestseller, *Jamie's Italy*, which sold 154,769 copies in one week. *Deliciously Ella*, by Instagrammer Ella Mills, made her the fastest-selling debut cookbook author of all time, after selling 32,144 copies in one week. Fellow Instagrammer, Joe Wicks, sold 77,000 copies of his first book, *Lean in 15* in its first week of sales in December 2015. But by 2016, with an exponential rise in his Instagram following, it had sold 972,000 copies, making it the third bestselling book of the year. Diana Shipley in *The Guardian* says that it's no surprise that publishers are turning to Instagram to find their authors: 'We live in an image-focused society and a lot of a publisher's work has already been done if their new signing has already shaped their brand. Consider the authorial success of a YouTuber juggernaut such as gamer PewDiePie's book *This Book Loves You*, which reached top spot on the New York Times bestseller list in a week. Or Zoella, whose 2014 novel *Girl Online* sold more copies in one week (78,109) than any debut novel since records began, making the £100,000 advance she was paid to have it ghost-written seem like small potatoes.'

But whatever the platform, the story is still the same: the promise of a better life in exchange for following your hero. Influencers don't just change the way we cook and eat: they affect our decisions about how we cook and eat too, promoting everything from kitchen appliances to designer utensils. Food historians will note that this is nothing new and that, particularly in the UK, influence has always been motivated by keeping up with the Joneses. But while trends in kitchenware are cyclical, it was Sir Terence Conran again who reconceived the purpose of the kitchen in the 1970s. His designs at Habitat would change the way that we used the kitchen as a living space and would have an enormous influence on the way we eat. When BBC Research, commissioned by Jane Root, revealed that the sofa, the symbol of leisure time was the one extra thing that most people wanted in their kitchen, it would not be long before Ikea was building a bookshelf into their kitchen designs to allow for our cookbook fetish and to organise our living spaces around eating. Nick Thorogood was the head of UK Style (launched in 1997) on UKTV from 2001 to 2004, which was the biggest performing channel on weekends at the time. He said its success was driven by *Changing Rooms* and *Ground Force*, and, perhaps most importantly, by the arrival of Ikea. 'Suddenly there was a whole range of home improvement materials and (there was) this idea of really cheap, cheap, cheap, home design [which] said you can replace a whole room', said Thorogood. 'We saw an extraordinary uptake'.

Yet Carolyn Steele, in her 2013 book, *Hungry City*, says that we have never spent less on food than we do now: 'food shopping accounted for just 10 per cent of our income in 2007, down from 23 per cent in 1980. Eighty per cent of our groceries are bought in supermarkets, and when we shop for food, our choices are overwhelmingly influenced by cost, well ahead of taste, quality or healthiness. Yet while spend on real food decreases, programming increases: when listeners complained to Radio 4's media comment programme *Points of View* in 2014 that the BBC showed 21 hours of TV cookery in a week, food writer Rose Prince conducted her own audit for the *Daily Mail* of the past seven days. It reveals that if you also count the number of hours of telly cookery on other channels, including those on Sky and Food Network, the total comes to a staggering 434.5 hours – 18 days' worth of food TV in a week', Steele writes.

Food writer, Joe Warwick, in conversation with chef Henry Harris for *The Guardian* in 2012 (interview by Emine Saner), discussed the irony of the rise of Food TV alongside the demise of cooking skills: 'I think a lot of food TV is dumbed down because they're not aiming it at people who cook or have a knowledge of food, they're pushing it as entertainment.' As Harris told Warwick about how audiences had responded to his appearance on shows like *Saturday Kitchen* by ringing in for the recipe, Warwick reminded him that chefs like him only go on these shows for one reason: 'I was talking to a big-name US chef who said, "I hate doing television," and I asked him why he did it. He was opening a new restaurant and he said, "as soon as I do, there's a spike in custom." ' Warwick later added, 'There is so much interesting food. I would love a programme that goes to Japan and explains the food in detail. Will they put that on TV? No, it's too esoteric. I think they're being too obvious about it. We've had nothing to replace *Food and Drink*, which was cancelled more than 10 years ago. There's *The Food Programme* on Radio 4 – why haven't we got something like that on TV?'

Selling Britain to the world

By the early 2000s, with the voracious appetite of new channels devoted to food, a successful format was the Holy Grail. A single winning copyrighted idea that could be replicated across cultures, sold around the world and influence the way we live was highly lucrative for both producer and buyer, and commissioning editors were on the hunt. In 2016, Jamie Munro, former managing director of Shine International, explained why: 'The reason you're buying a TV format is because most commissioners are quite conservative and they realise that if a programme of theirs fails, they're out of a job. They've spent a lot of money on it and there's a real risk. So what most territories around the world tend to do is buy formats. They say, "ok, you've developed this, you've made this, you've learned from your mistakes and I can buy some of your success by buying a kit which will tell me how to do it and get some help from some flying producers who will tell me how to do it and give me that consultancy." ' Seamus Geoghegan said that there was a moment when the penny dropped at the BBC in the 1990s: 'I think that word – the format – raised its head, over and above everything: "oh, I get it, and it can travel," and "oh, and the rights involved at the back end" ' (2016). With budget constraints, there was suddenly a new way of thinking about production: if it is commercially attractive, as Geoghegan said, 'there's a way of greasing the wheels.'

One of the most powerful examples of how distribution affects narratives is the *MasterChef* format, which still reaches audiences of more than five million in the UK, as reported by Thinkbox in 2019, and sold to more than 50 territories around the world in 2017 a deal between BBC Worldwide and Shine International. Jamie Munro drove the deal to extend the original BBC Two show beyond the broadcast platform. The deal included plans to create live events, pioneered by the *BBC Good Food Show*, and rebrand *MasterChef* as *MasterChef Live*. 'Bookazines' and part-works, a branded *MasterChef* website would give it its own identity, with licence to create a cross-platform, on/off-screen experience.

MasterChef developed from an original idea by TV executives, Franc Roddam and John Silver as a Sunday afternoon watch on BBC Two in 1990 to primetime entertainment on BBC One in February 2005. It is now broadcast in 200 countries worldwide including in 47 locally produced versions. In 2016, Jamie Munro told me how it happened: 'It evolved as a brand, but as an entertainment brand rather than a food brand. What helped it as a show was that it started early evening so your kids started watching it quite young. They watched it after schoo – what else was there to watch? Then when it went to prime time, it took that audience with it.'

Munro was behind a multi-series three-year deal with the BBC in 2009, offering Shine a platform on the international arena. Initially, the format was sold to lifestyle channels rather than mainstream channels, but after its phenomenal success in Australia and America (where Gordon Ramsay was one of the judges), it became the brightest star in the Food TV firmament. 'Australia led the way', said Munro. 'It went massive there and then went full circle when some of the Australian influences came back in the UK show. The thing about *MasterChef* is that although it's about food, it's actually a competition. The UK series is still on not much more than a daytime budget, but in Australia they're on an *X Factor*-style budget.' The presidential debate in Australia was even rescheduled to avoid being up against the final of *MasterChef*. 'It got 50 per cent plus share', said Munro. 'That's down to the producers there who took it as it was and supersized it.' Seamus Geoghegan was at BBC Worldwide at the time. 'John (Torode) and Gregg (Wallace) were already doing what they're doing here, but it was quiet. It was a tame version. Australia – as only Australians can – turned up the heat, got the whole studio lights thing and whopped it, as they say.' Peter Bazalgette agreed: '*MasterChef* was a frankly rather staid little show, rather archly presented. It was Australia that reinvented it and it became a massive asset.' Shine continues to support the show in its various territories; in 2014, Shine CEO Nadine Nohr wrote in *TBI Vision*: 'It's a very crowded market for cooking, and *MasterChef* is the mother of cooking formats. It keeps selling into new territories, and the rate of re-order is amazing. That's because of the strength of the format and the nurturing it gets from the Shine Group in terms of remaking it and remaining true to its essence.'

MasterChef has launched its winners to astonishing success, with books and TV deals as well as restaurants: in Australia, Poh Ling Yeow, who was runner-up on the first series in 2009, has become a television superstar with three successful cookbooks, and she has featured in two headline television shows, four films and one TV series. Former electrician, Andy Allen, who won Season Four in 2012, is now owner and head chef at Sydney's The Blue Ducks, while also launching his own YouTube cookery channel. Julie Goodwin, who won the first season in Australia, has since conquered both the cooking and media industries with the publication of six cooking books as well as a bizarre CD of Christmas songs and recipes. She had a regular weekly cooking segment on Channel Nine's *Today* show before appearing as a contestant on *I'm A Celebrity… Get Me Out of Here!* She now hosts a breakfast radio segment on Star 104.5, which broadcasts across the New South Wales central coast.

As a format show, it has a different identity in each country, but in English-speaking territories such as Australia, South Africa and the US, its cast of experts is an international fusion: in the UK, New Zealander chef and British green-grocer, Gregg Wallace are matched with starry guest chefs while in the US and Australia, the judges are a mix of indigenous chefs, restaurateurs and British stars, with Gordon Ramsay in the US and Nigella Lawson, Jason Atherton and Marco Pierre White taking part over the years in Australia. Munro believes that the judges empower the audience to become food experts. 'For a competition show like *X Factor* or *Britain's Got Talent*, you sit at home and you're the judge. With *MasterChef*, how do you really understand how good it is? You're looking at something and you can see the expression on the judges' faces, but you're then saying that's good food.' Joe Bastianich, a judge on the US version on Fox, told *TBI Vision*: 'It's more than a food format; it's an aspirational show and shows how people can change their lives. For some people the food is irrelevant and it's just about the people, and for others it's all about the food and the process.'

The success of *MasterChef* across the world was a significant factor in the development of Food TV, with whole channels now dedicated to broadcasting food programmes, many of them formats which were bought from other territories. Nick Thorogood explained how the channel contributed to the explosion in cookery programmes worldwide in 2005, and tapped into a new C2D audience (2016). 'There was a gigantic step up', he told me. 'Food Network particularly did a massive reinvention of its schedule with some really well-invested shows that had a different ambition and went from the "in the kitchen" to much more entertaining TV with high production values.' Food TV had lived on the daytime schedule, the domain of the C2D audience: 'It was only when it moved out and started getting little hits in other bits of the schedule that people started saying, "hold on, what do we have to do to get into peak space?" *Hell's Kitchen* and, of course, *MasterChef* both went into mainstream entertainment slots and really did a huge job of shifting that perception.'

Food Network was already making some big shows like *Food Network Challenge* in the US. 'You'd get four fruit carvers', said Thorogood, 'and they'd have to carve a fruit representation of Hawaii in eight hours, filmed in front of an arena audience. It was huge-scale with loads of ambition and winnings of $10,000. It was the same with a show called *Chopped*. In many ways, it's like multiple rounds of *Ready Steady Cook* because they open a basket and there's ingredients you have to cook with but the scale of it, the production values, are so high. Look at

Iron Chef America, where you take what looks like a simple idea but add layers of production values that turned it into a big arena show.'

With wider audiences winkling Food TV out of its middle-class niche, the food channels went shopping for talent. The success of New York chef Anthony Bourdain's first book, *Kitchen Confidential* (2005), made Marco Pierre White look like an Andrex puppy, and brought a second wave of gastro-punk to the table. Food Network snapped him up. *A Cook's Tour* (2002–03) would blast cookery out of the kitchens and onto the streets of Bangkok to Ho Chi Minh to eat dog and cat, and to Iceland where he shared rotting shark innards with the locals. 'Bourdain stalked the screen, like a gaunt Joe Strummer, swearing like a longshoreman, occasionally actually drunk', wrote *The Guardian*'s Tim Hayward in Bourdain's obituary in June 2018, honouring the legendary contribution he made not just to Food TV but to food culture. Hayward argued that Bourdain pioneered a new form of early reality TV 'that freed him to immerse himself, scriptless, in the experiences he chose and communicate later with brilliant clarity'.

The Food Network also went shopping for programmes. 'America, UK, Australia or Australasia – they're the three countries that have driven TV food and that kind of lifestyle', said Thorogood. 'We were looking around the world to see who had the best programmes and the best looking. The best quality, although not (those with) the biggest budgets, were Australian.' By the early 2000s, British programmes such as *The Naked Chef* and *Nigella Bites* appeared on American and Australian TV and were gently mimicked, with Neil Perry protégée, Kylie Kwong, cooking food inspired by her mother on *Heart and Soul* for Australia's ABC from 2003, and Lifestyle's *Bill's Food* launching Bill Granger in 2004 as the Australian Jamie Oliver.

I asked Jamie Munro, who was responsible for the distribution of *MasterChef* whether a rather old-fashioned idea of Britain helped to sell food programmes. 'I think if it's BBC it definitely helps', he told me. The BBC, he explained, is associated with quality: 'I would say that the UK TV market is the best in terms of quality in the world.' Susan Elkington, formerly an executive at TV distributor Chellomedia, thinks that British food is perceived as 'less stuffy' than many stronger indigenous food cultures. 'It's more of a free market, a blend of post-war socialism, Thatcher meritocracy and New Labour funkiness', she told me. 'And it's come out in our food culture. We've put that on TV and turned it into really good entertainment, something more meaningful, and we're living and breathing it.' Elkington believes that British identity is formed from a conflation of moments. 'Post-war Britain has demonstrated an ability to be open to change and assimilation. It's shown in our food: you've got Mary Berry and Jamie Oliver and Raymond Blanc; you've got this range of society, age and personality – it's what makes us *us*. In some ways, we've demonstrated this massive transformation of our society more than other countries.' But to suggest that the British have an important influence on food culture worldwide is, Elkington told me, a big assumption. 'I don't think we make the best programmes', she said. 'We're obsessed that we've got the best news and sport. But *Al Jazeera* is much better. *'Allo 'Allo* and *Broadchurch* sell well but we've been exporting documentaries and natural history for much longer.' We may be great storytellers with high production values, but in terms of influence on the high street, Elkington suggested that audiences are not so fickle. 'Take Spain', she said. 'Everyone on the street would know Jamie Oliver, but when they go home, they won't buy anything other than Spanish food. You may know who Brad Pitt is, but you'll marry a Spanish man.' *MasterChef* may have appeared on Spanish TV since 2013, but Elkington believes that the audience is interested in the competition that pitches ordinary people who love food against each other, rather than the example of successful British food storytelling. 'Food TV is very good in Britain', she said, 'but it's not the best.'

Niki Page, formerly of Freemantle, which distributes Jamie Oliver programmes around the world, and now Head of Acquisitions in Factual and Factual Entertainment at Sky Vision, told me in 2016 that in terms of content, after America, British TV ties with Canada and Australia in joint second place. 'We thought that there was more value in some factual programming than there actually was', she said. 'But I think the genuine explosion was lifestyle. You can watch factual entertainment which is more niche but lifestyle programming is about something you want to become. You want to escape your everyday drudgery, family, kids and go into this stylish life.' I asked her why the world wanted to buy Jamie. 'Our food-programme making is so much better than in the US', she explained. 'It's very stylish. Lorraine Pascal is a super model. She's beautiful and she can cook. She's so stylised and stylish and you think, "right, I'm going to buy the book and cook like her and be like her." The US is more mumsy. Even though the demographic is probably the same, the chefs tends to be a bit older, like Martha Stewart and Anna Olson.'

Peter Bazalgette said the success of so many British food shows abroad, including his *Ready Steady Cook*, was more about a triumph in storytelling than the appeal of the food culture that they represented. 'We have a genius for taking factual information and essentially formatting it, giving it a narrative, giving it entertainment quality – a human quality', he said in 2016. I suggested that with an unstable food culture such as ours, it is easier to tell stories which appeal to those we tell it to, and Bazalgette agreed: 'We use food as a vehicle. That's the truth. I was using food as a vehicle to entertain people. *Come Dine with Me* uses food as a vehicle in entertainment wars. Can I entertain better than you? It's home vanity, which *Changing Rooms* was about as well. And *House Proud* and all that stuff.'

But, also in 2016, Susan Elkington put the impact of British TV's influence in perspective: 'McDonald's has a bigger impact on indigenous food culture. You don't need to overstate it. It's just TV entertainment.' She suggested that the Internet is more important than linear TV channels, as audiences search, discover and share food online. Food bloggers, YouTubers and ordinary people sharing pictures and recipes raise the interest in everyday food more than TV can ever do. 'People want to participate', she said. She argued that in such a multi-platform viewing culture, successful imported lifestyle formats, such as the Jamie Oliver shows, are about something more powerful than reminding audiences how to cook: she believes that they are enabling. 'There's the programme and then there's psyche. It allows the flowering of the personality, the self. It allows you to self-actualise through food. TV unlocks that which is most interesting. It's not an end in itself. It's not that there's more British food being made in Spain or France. There simply isn't.'

Dude food and fairy cakes

On British TV, food authority is divided by gender: the men are chefs – Tom Kerridge, Jamie Oliver, James Martin, Rick Stein, Michel Roux Junior – even if their shows are made in their own homes or around the world with their expert culinary commentary. Meanwhile, the women are home cooks – Nigella, Nadiya, Lorraine, Ching, Mary Berry. Women tend to be casually and often sexually costumed, wearing an apron rather than the white coat of the chef. Despite some impressive credentials, female hosts rarely mention cooking professionally and often acknowledge the difficulties of keeping up with the different food needs of the family, managing the budget or throwing a dinner party in half an hour. When men refer to cooking for the family, it is often presented as a leisurely or fun experience.

With the introduction of the barbeque, the amateur male cook was encouraged to prepare a meal for the family in a completely different way. Largely influenced by the traditional Sunday lunch of spit-roast lamb brought to the backyards of Australia and America by their Greek immigrants, the intention was to bring the smells and tastes of home to root themselves in this new, unstable Anglo-Celtic food culture. It quickly became associated with 'man food', a meaty connection with food from the land which was soon reflected on television. Men are still seen cooking in the wilderness or in open spaces, foraging, fishing and shooting on television while women shop at the markets of the world and swap recipes with other home cooks. Only Jamie Oliver seems to cross the gender line, making pasta with the Nonnas and, albeit in tears, cutting the throat of a lamb with farmers in the fields of Tuscany. The narratives of food campaigner and multi-millionaire businessman underpin his authority in the industry even while his empire fails.

Jane Root told me in 2013 that there has always been a divide between the home cook and the chef, and in the UK in the 1990s it was very much the era of the chef. She said that it was Jamie Oliver and his relationship with Pat Llewellyn who changed this, breaking the gendered binaries of male/female spaces. 'He actually was a chef but he did his programmes as a home cook', she said. 'It was

Jamie's whole thing – he trained at the River Café and he knew how to make something absolutely amazing out of spun sugar. He knew everything. But that was the magic of the Pat Llewellyn and Jamie combination: they were flirty and they did that thing that was just "bish bash bosh, what I like to eat with the lads".' She said it was a 'different wave to the Gary Rhodes thing' in *Rhodes Around Britain* on BBC Two in 1994. 'The aspiration was to be a home chef', she said, 'to have an incredibly delightful home experience. Sophie [Grigson] did a bit of it, but Jamie hugely contributed. It wasn't about locking yourself in the kitchen and being on *MasterChef*. It was about it being part of your family life.'

Nigella Lawson also broke the rules by creating her own image, a pastiche of a domestic goddess through the (many) television series produced by her own company, Pabulum Productions, from 2001. Even the word 'Pabulum' is an ironic swipe at the performance of television: it is described in the dictionary as '[a] substance that gives nourishment: food. Insipid intellectual nourishment'. She is Oxford University educated, financially astute and able to articulate her own ironic intention with what she calls 'gastro-porn', surely a feminist triumph if we are to measure her success by who is in the driving seat. It was she and her first husband, John Diamond, who had the idea for a cookery series based on her book, *How to Eat* (1998). It would offer a postmodern approach to cookery, bringing a knowing irony to the construction of taste by deliberately creating a glamorous, over-sexualized performance from its presenter.

Kudos, one of the most influential production companies in the UK, worked with the couple to create a cookery phenomenon which sold all over the world. Initially, the sell was simply a gap in the market: a senior producer at Kudos witnessed its genesis. 'We'd had Delia and Ainsley and Gary Rhodes, Keith Floyd and Rick Stein', one of the producers told me for my 2005 biography of Nigella, *Nigella Lawson: A Biography*. 'It was the time when Jamie had been on with *Naked Chef* and food had gone through the roof. Everyone wanted to know who was going to be the next Jamie. He'd done the lifestyle show, and Nigella offered something for the slightly older, aspirational family-oriented viewer. Everyone thought she would be a success. There was no doubt. It was partly her pedigree, partly the *Vogue* column, partly because the book had been very successful and was very easy to turn into TV: it was a beautifully written book and evoked a lifestyle. She seemed to be so full of stories.'

To acknowledge the roles of her agent, Ed Victor, one of the most powerful men in publishing; her father Nigel Lawson, Margaret Thatcher's chancellor; and her brother, the influential journalist Dominic Lawson, does not diminish her role in maximising her own potential as family breadwinner while her husband battled with terminal cancer. On the contrary, it shows what the personal story can add to Lifestyle TV. 'She'd had a lot of tragedy in her life and that gave her something that people could relate to', Bruce Goodison, told me for my biography. He explained how he used this idea of subjectivity: 'I wanted it to be about eating rather than cooking, with people dropping in for anything from leftovers to a fancy dinner. I wanted to open it up and make it about sociability, about life around the kitchen as the nucleus of the family. Everything moves around that. It's a lovely way of bringing the whole family in. It was about a woman who cooks while a bloke is dying of cancer, where everyone who came into the house is a character. It was more like an Almodóvar film than a cookery programme.'

Where once a privileged beauty teaching us how to cook might have been patronising and irrelevant, feminism has taught us to listen to each other's stories, and that subjectivity is about individual experiences that we can all learn from and which empower us. Nigella's domain is the home, but it is not the place of drudgery and housewifely duties that second-wave feminism (Betty Friedan, Kate Millet and Germaine Greer, for example) saw as an enslavement of women, but a place where a woman can pretend that she is a 'goddess' feeding her friends and family, revelling in her curves and reclaiming the right to feast. Her recipes are remembered from her grandmother and her mother, and are full of the legacy and lifestyle of the women in her life. 'She said that she wouldn't have done the book or the TV if it hadn't been for her mother', Goodison told me in 2005. 'Her whole philosophy came from her.'

But the performative element of Nigella, queen of gastro-porn, which made her such a global superstar was a conflation of whim and the ability of Lawson and her husband John Diamond to spot an opportunity. Diamond's friend Christopher Silvester told me for the biography in 2005: 'I really think that it was a natural process. John had tremendous chutzpah and Nigella was lacking in that kind of confidence. I'm sure that John would have actively encouraged her to do TV, and if she had any doubts, he would have dispelled them.' Goodison observed on set how the couple worked on drawing out a performance from her more playful, flirtatious side: 'You didn't get the sense of any cynicism about making her into a star, but there was a lot of preparation for what would happen after he died. She would always defer to him. She asked his opinion about everything, but she asked a lot of people too. It's a complex psychological area for her. She is a reluctant public face, but ambitious at the same time – although I'm not sure that she is anymore. She really believed in her book [*How to Eat*] and she wanted to make the most of it, and John really supported her in that.'

Lawson turned the glance into the gaze in 1999 with *Nigella Bites* on Channel 4. She deliberately roused our desire, cracking her eggs, 'allowing the whites to dribble slowly through her fingers', throwing her head back and dangling pasta over her outstretched tongue. 'You've got to feel more relaxed at the end of the day after a bit of squelching and squeezing like this', she says, before tipping a squid into her open mouth. Philosopher, Susan Bordo, in her 2003 book, *Unbearable Weight: Feminism, Western Culture, and the Body*, says that Nigella's 'gastroporn', a term Nigella admitted to inventing as a pre-emptive strike, 'would violate deeply sedimented expectations, (and) would be experienced by many as disgusting and transgressive. When women are positively depicted as sensuously voracious about food [...] their hunger for food is employed solely as a metaphor for their sexual appetite'. Nigella appeared to be in the driving seat, fully aware of the taboos she was trampling, rewriting the rules as her success spread across the world.

In *Television and Sexuality* (2004), Jane Arthurs argues that women who succumb to their desires (especially in terms of food) are seen as taking up too much space through their excess: Nigella grabs the space and fills it up. Lawson's triumph was in the mainstreaming of popular feminism through the re-imagining of domestic life. Louise Fitzgerald suggested to me Nigella became 'the pin-up girl for post-feminism, whereby femininity is once again a bodily property and women are encouraged to use their bodies in exchange for financial and cultural reward'.

R.M. Magee disagrees, in his article 'Food puritanism and food pornography: The gourmet semiotics of Martha and Nigella' (2007): 'Lawson's reconfiguration of the domestic goddess demonstrates just how far from food pornography her approach really is. She rejects the patriarchal oppression of the kitchen while embracing domestic comforts in the same way that one may embrace the pleasures of sex while turning away from the essential falsity and potential oppression of pornography. By combining and conflating sexual pleasure and gustatory pleasure, Lawson's "gastroporn" challenges the simplistic binary oppositions of Puritanism and pornography and suggests that the real experiences of food and sex are much more complex.'

Lawson subverts the male gaze to show us how we watch and are watched: 'The pornography of food pornography is not literal', says Magee, 'but Nigella deconstructs the notion by taking it literally. She conflates the sensual enjoyment of food with the sensual enjoyment of sex and plays with the results. What becomes obvious to her and her readers is that the food itself is important only so far as it provides enjoyment and nourishment. It does not work as an image that is to be carefully constructed and admired.' By contrast, Magee calls Martha Stewart's Domestic Goddess persona 'a hyper-real projection, while Lawson's Domestic Goddess playful image is not to be taken literally. In the mythological narrative that Stewart has so carefully and obsessively constructed, the image overtakes the person creating the image and becomes more real than the reality. Nigella self-consciously prods the image, manipulating it ironically to deconstruct both food Puritanism and food pornography'.

Lawson wrote in her 2001 book *Nigella Bites*, 'So what I'm talking about is not being a domestic goddess exactly, but feeling like one.' She writes of her 'fond, if ironic, dream: the unexpressed "I," ' perhaps suggesting that her Domestic Goddess persona is her alter-ego and one that she herself doesn't take too seriously. As Joanne Hollows says in her 2003 article, 'Feeling like a domestic goddess: Postfeminism and cooking', Nigella herself performs the Domestic Goddess, and knows that it is 'available only in fantasy'. She uses femininity as a tool of empowerment, yet feminist scholars would argue that this harks back to pre-feminism where femininity was a performance of a certain notion of what being a woman means.

I examined this with fellow academics, Lorna Stevens and Benedetta Capellini, in our 2015 article, '*Nigellissima*: An exploratory study of glamour, performativity and embodiment'. Through the theoretical lens of glamour, we looked at the complex process of how glamour is created, performed and ultimately embodied. We were interested in how it exemplifies the 'postmodern feminist position that recognises the sexed body, empowerment through the body and the body's subversive potential to take on symbolic identities'. Nigella Lawson, the food writer and journalist, we argued, 'has used a glamour aesthetic to mark out a particular masquerade of retro-femininity in order to develop a distinct and unique personal brand to create *Nigella*, and later *Nigellissima*. We looked at the etymology of the word 'glamour' in the *Oxford English Dictionary* definition and found a variety of meanings, each crucial to the storytelling of Nigella: '1. magic, enchantment, spell: 2. a. A magical or fictitious beauty attaching to any person or object: a delusive or alluring charm: b. Charm, attractiveness: physical allure, esp. feminine beauty: c. To affect with glamour, to charm, enchant'. She literally charms us with her performance, casting a spell, a wonderland where reality and image are blurred in a simulacrum of middle-class foodie lifestyle. Nigella is parodying constructed femininity and recuperating feminist politics.

I asked Lawson, when I interviewed her in 2019 for the *delicious.* podcast celebrating the vintage edition of *How to Eat*, if she set out to enchant us. She laughed, but told me that the real measure of glamour is that it doesn't exist. 'It's how you look at something', she said. 'The enchantment of cooking lies in its ordinariness. It's a bit like a spell: you are making a potion.' I asked her about the gastroporn, the licking of the fingers, the separating of the eggs through her fingers. 'It's rather disgusting', she said. 'It's such an odd reading to think it's alluring in anyway.' She denied that it was intentional. 'I'm just not a coquettish person', she said. 'I have got quite an element of camp about me, but, look, it's futile of me to dispute any of this because clearly I am in the minority.' She suggested that it is the intimate way she has of talking to her viewer that has been misinterpreted as suggestive. 'I feel this urgent need to convey what I need to convey. But it's not meant to be seductive.' I asked her what it was like to be listed as one of world's most beautiful women. 'It felt very embarrassing', she said, and dismissed it, reminding me that journalists 'sit around making lists all the time'. Rather than performing Nigellissima herself, she put its creation at the media's door. 'I don't recognise myself in those descriptions. TV creates glamour.' Jeanette Winterson wrote in the foreword to the vintage edition of *How to Eat*: 'Pleasure always starts in the mind', and I suggested to Nigella that she enchants people by taking her readers and viewers into her inner world. She agreed and told me how she does it: 'The senses are on the plain that food occupies. We have only language at our disposal to conjure up a physical world.' She told me that for her, story is everything. 'People have a very real need to connect, and when you're writing a book about food, you're connecting on a very deep level. You're bringing your family's food into [the reader's] family, into their life, and I think it's a tremendously powerful and moving thing to do.'

The glory of Nigella as the parodic figure in TV food is that the audience can take or leave the intention of Nigella Lawson, the journalist and food writer; Nigella herself is the first to say so: 'I can't be responsible for what people project onto me', she told me. Nick Thorogood told me that 'she has a very mixed audience'. I asked him if it included working-class men. 'Yes, actually', he said. '[Food Network] runs her nearly every day. The nature of its audience is that it is across all of the socio-economic groups because of the fact that it's on Freeview and the platform tends to bring in more C2DEs and slightly older.' He thinks that she works on a number of levels according to who is watching: 'I think there's something really interesting because from a male perspective, obviously there's a very attractive woman cooking very attractive food. From a female perspective, there's a successful woman who is not stick thin, not unachievably, unattainably perfect.' Despite the original intention of the myth-making, it is the 'authenticity' that, according to Thorogood, 'means that whoever you are, you share in her joy, even though actually a lot of the food that she cooks requires, I don't know, organic cocoa that they don't have in Morrisons. It may not be that accessible, but her enthusiasm makes it more accessible'.

Critics may suggest that audiences who can't afford organic cocoa may feel alienated by the tease of inaccessible food ideas and what they signify, but Thorogood says it works: 'I think part of the brilliance of what [Nigella] does is, you know, a bit like the end shot where she goes to the fridge, and puts her finger in and takes a bit of the cream from the trifle. We all get that: we all do it. And that's not about being of a class, having the money, it's understanding, "oh, I do love that, that's delicious, and I do that, and I get that." And I think that's where it becomes accessible.'

That leap of faith, the haptic or immersive vicariousness of Food TV, would become one of the biggest drivers behind the launch of food channels. Thorogood explained that it's all about the psychology of the viewing experience: 'Take *Saturday Kitchen*, what we always used to term the "Hangover Slot"', he told me. 'Back at Food Network, we very much led the way with male viewing figures on Saturday mornings, where you're feeling so rough from the night before that you can't get off the sofa to go and cook your own breakfast. So watching someone else eat really good food is almost good enough to make you feel better.'

Man vs food

The appetite for Food TV was stoked by the launch of Food Network in the USA in 1993 and, while it did not reach the UK until 2009, many of Britain's most successful shows were already in American sitting rooms by the millennium, including BBC Two's *Two Fat Ladies* and *The Naked Chef*, and Channel 4's *Nigella Bites*. The impact on American perception of the British was profound; Pat Llewellyn was the producer of the first two: 'I guess *Two Fat Ladies* was the first British food show that sort of took off abroad and was a kind of worldwide hit. And then Jamie came after that, and suddenly I think it kind of changed the way that people thought about British food really', she told me. But by the mid-2000s, American Food Network was developing a new programming strategy, pushing male chefs into prime time, with big macho cook-offs ramping up the competitive element of cooking. Tasha Oren argues in her 2013 article, 'On the line: Format, cooking and competition as television values', that the plan was to 'de-emphasise cooking how-to altogether by moving actual cooking shows – programmes in which largely female on-air talent prepared meals in a domestic kitchen setting – to a morning segment known as "in the kitchen" '. Oren says that it was a 'radical shift in tone, genre and narrative arc' that transformed Food TV in America, with programmes like Food Network's *The Next Iron Chef* (2007, 2009–12) and *Chopped* (2009–present); Fox's *Hell's Kitchen* (2005–present) and *MasterChef*; and Bravo's *Top Chef* (2006–present). Oren uses Food Network as an example of Food TV, which she says employed 'global-televisual-exchange, industry strategy and algorithmic logic […] which broadened viewership from home cooks to food lovers, and from older women to younger men' by the mid-2000s. As *foodies* became an identifiable group of consumers, what she calls the 'format-centric logic' which informs and then reinforces changing cultural values told the stories that audiences began to tell themselves. As the foodies amassed their cultural capital, Oren notes how television's higher production values used 'soft focus close-ups of sumptuous ingredients', and the introduction of salivatory TV or food porn. As female presenters were deliberately given the morning slots, they made way for a new wave of male hosts: 'professional chefs, decidedly not home cooks, were out in the social world, primarily restaurants, diners, food carts, cook-offs or BBQs (not domestic settings) and a sudden all-consuming, full-throttle pre-occupation with such "masculine" fare as pork belly, burgers, beer and BBQ.' The schism divided the audience – in America at least – into domestic daytime and professional night-time viewers.

The message was clear: women cook for love (family) while men cook for money. Oren cites *Iron Chef* – originally a Japanese show which premiered in Japan in 1993 and was bought by Food Network in 1999 – as the show that took TV food from the kitchen to the stadium. The show reached record ratings 'when the "New York Battle" pitted the stern Japanese Iron Chef Masaharu Morimoto against the cocky American Bobby Flay – who was vanquished and then scolded by Morimoto after the American chef jumped feet-first onto his cutting board at the battle's end'. This macho warrior-chef style programme would become *Iron Man America* by 2004, joined by the fire-breathing Gordon Ramsay in *Hell's Kitchen* and *Cooking Under Fire* (PBS, 2005–present).

Louise Fitzgerald noticed that the alpha male TV cook lends macho themes to TV cookery: 'Culinary culture is about science and butchery', she told me. 'Reputations are on the line as chefs strive to affirm their culinary prowess by beating challengers in programmes like *MasterChef* and (albeit more sedately) *Great British Bake Off.*' Political food campaigns are headed by male chefs: Hugh Fearnley-Whittingstall, Jamie Oliver, Heston Blumenthal and Gordon Ramsay. In Channel 4's *Big Fish Fight* season championing sustainable fishing in 2011, Ramsay is even threatened with a gun when he challenges a fish factory in China: a culinary Bond, perhaps. Hugh Fearnley-Whittingstall campaigned for free-range chickens to be sold in supermarkets, and Jamie Oliver's campaigns for better school dinners and a sugar tax changed government policy. 'While it is largely women who created the most influential Food TV', suggested Fitzger-ald, 'it is masculine skills of strength, expertise, vigour and authority that we see on-screen'.

But while Fitzgerald, Oren and others criticise the deliberate gendering of Food TV, former UK Food Network managing director, Nick Thorogood, told me that it was hard to find a woman in restaurant kitchens. 'We were constantly looking for the female chef and in my mind in order to refer to someone as a chef, as opposed to a cook, I would look to someone who was running a dynamic restaurant-kitchen.' But he said that 'the laddish culture' and the hours invested in running a restaurant means that women don't tend to choose the profession and are therefore rarely in the talent pool. He explained that after 14-hour days buzzing with adrenaline, the post-work drink is an essential part of the expe-rience. 'You might add a couple of hours in for people to come down at a party or over a drink', he told me. 'So if you had any ambition perhaps to take a career break and have children, it would be very hard to picture yourself surviving in those scenarios. I can see there might be moments where you would try to use your skill in a different way.' This is, of course the same for fathers who want to take an active part in the home. I asked him what had happened to the women we had seen on television when they were younger and prettier: 'Television is also a very cruel mistress', he said. 'It's very judgemental. And it's hard work. It eats up content: you've got to produce a lot of recipes. You've got to do a lot of stuff'.

But he said that the representation of maleness is similarly limiting for men. 'Until the 1990s, people felt women were at home cooking. They would never say a man was at home cooking. In restaurants there was definitely a culture of male chefs – it was a profession. Jamie did a great deal to change that. You then got men cooking. You didn't necessarily get women cheffing, but it liberated men to be allowed to cook. And it wasn't just Jamie. It was a lot of Pat's (Llewellyn) work', he said.

Thorogood was referring to Gordon Ramsay and Heston Blumenthal, whom Pat Llewellyn took from their restaurant kitchens to the small screen with astonishing success, as well as Hugh Fernley-Whittingstall, whose talent she had first spotted in the early 1990s as an assistant producer for Channel 4's *Food File*. Her skill in drawing an authentic performance from basic talent was often down to observation; she told me that Jamie Oliver seemed 'almost balletic' in the first studio kitchen she used for the *Naked Chef* pilot, which she knew would not work on-screen. 'We needed him to be familiar with the kitchen he was working in', she told me. 'He lived in a tiny flat in Hammersmith at the time, and the kitchen was long and skinny, which was impossible for us, so we found somewhere that was better for us to film'. In order for it to feel like home, Oliver and his then fiancée, Jools, had to move in. They would put the money they had paid to rent the Hammersmith flat into the pot which would go towards the new loft apartment, and Optomen Productions, who produced *The Naked Chef*, would pay the rest. 'The rent was four times as much, but our location fee topped that up', she told me.

Thorogood suggested that Jamie Oliver liberated the male cook: 'The Jamie Show (*The Naked Chef*) was about making cooking and his perceived lifestyle – the warehouse flat, the sliding down the banisters, the campervan and the friends and the scooter – it made it cool, not just for young women but for young men as well. And that whole sudden twist that you saw that actually good-looking male chefs are not just about appealing to women, they're saying to men, you can be cool and attract women in a way that, really, you hadn't seen. You had all sorts of flopsy, camp chefs coming through and you'd had a number of women cooks coming through, but you hadn't had that same sort of really dude-ish chef'. He told me how it broke down barriers among audiences and allowed him to think differently about who was viewing Food TV and why. 'I think that's really fascinating because of course one of the biggest things for us at Food Network was the "Dads and Lads" slot. We had a very interesting amount of shared viewing for *Man v. Food* [Travel Channel, 2008–present] and *Diners, Drive-Ins and Dives* [Food Network, 2006–present].' He told me that despite working in 'a 500-channel universe' with viewing on tablets and phones in various spaces, the figures showed a 'very high level of shared viewing, disproportionally you would imagine, to those food dude slots. The dads will watch with the children, with the mum. Everyone will watch together.'

The expansion of the food audience was now more male, more working class, and commissioning editors across the networks were on the hunt for new talent that was about more than food. It was about exploring *the world* through food. In the UK, the addition of the Hairy Bikers to BBC2's quirky canon of British storytelling in 2006 took Newcastle's best-mates-on-bikes on the road to find friendship and food on behalf of a wider audience back home. Si King and Dave Myers quickly became national treasures; they were living the dream – both theirs and their viewers' – exploring a world of food and reporting back with genuine warmth and enthusiasm. It was an instant hit. But not everyone believed that it would work. I asked the Bikers about the story I'd heard that a 'very senior person' at the BBC had decided that they weren't aspirational enough. 'It's true', Si told me for the *delicious.* podcast in December 2019. 'We're genuinely enthusiastic human beings. We came from the arse end of nothing, and to have the opportunity to live life the way we do is a privilege. There's not a day that goes by when we don't give thanks for that.' Dave sighed at the memory of the BBC's negativity: 'I think what we do to 95 per cent of the British public is *so* aspirational. We never patronise the viewers. We can be cheeky with each other but people come on our programmes and they're guests in our house and we're guests in theirs' (original emphasis). Si agreed: 'We're conduits for people's stories. We want to hear them and so do the viewers. That's what the Bikers shows are for. And they watch it for our friendship 'cos we have a crack on with each other'.

Behind the camera lies a more nuanced explanation of how gender works on TV, based on the rare ability to spot a storyteller. Pat Llewellyn told me in 2013 how she first saw the televisual potential of Gordon Ramsay, and it wasn't the hell raiser that we would see later. She hadn't been impressed by the machismo of his first appearance in Channel 4's *Boiling Point*: 'I thought, "no way on god's earth do I want to see and meet Gordon Ramsay. I know I'm going to hate him. He's awful." He felt very one-dimensional.' When she did, however, she said that his charisma filled the room. But it wasn't that which changed her mind. 'We had this lunch together in Baltic in Waterloo and it was empty. There were about three tables in there. And he said something like, "I can't believe there are so many empty tables. What they should do, and what I do at lunchtime if the dining room isn't full, is take the tables and chairs out and just put more space and then people don't realise the restaurant's empty." ' It was the moment that inspired *Kitchen Nightmares* (Channel 4, 2004–14). 'I still think it's the best thing he's done really', she said. 'It was trying to do something different. You know, a lot of people are cooking on television, but how do you get into the world of restaurants? Can you come at it from a different way? I suppose it was a sort of food programme by stealth really, because at the time (with) the sort of food that Gordon was cooking, I couldn't see how that could particularly translate to domestic telly and really turn people on.'

Llewelyn rang Nicola Moody, the then BBC Two Controller of Factual Commissioning. She remembered the conversation: 'I said, "why has no one put Gordon Ramsey on the telly? I mean what is going on? Why hasn't it happened? He's unbelievable!" And they were like, "oh no, we keep getting proposals for any old thing and he'll stick his name on anything" '. Although she acknowledged that much had happened to dent Ramsay's image since, Llewellyn believed that it was his authenticity at that time that made *Kitchen Nightmares* work so well across gender and class – and, crucially, across territories. 'I remember the first series of *Kitchen Nightmares*', she told me in 2013. 'We were filming up in a restaurant in the Lake District and the director rang me after the first day's shooting. And she said, "I don't know what to do. Gordon says this restaurant is in such a lot of trouble, and there's such a lot of work to do before we can really properly open for evening service that he doesn't want to film today." And I said, "what?" She said, "he won't film because he says he's got to fix the restaurant." And it was just one of those really extraordinary moments when I just thought, "oh my god, you know, Gordon that is why…" It was absolutely real for him. That first series, what he was trying to do for real was help people turn their businesses around.'

It was Llewellyn's producing skills that spotted the something in Oliver and Ramsay that would make them superstars and change the face of British food on- and off-screen. Most of the interviewees in this book who I argue were the architetects of TV food culture are women: Jane Root was the first female controller of BBC Two and was dubbed by the tabloids the high priestess of Life-style TV. Zoe Collins, Oliver's executive producer and right-hand woman, helped to shape his ideas into programmes as successful as Channel 4's *Jamie's Kitchen* (2002), *Jamie's School Dinners* (2005) and *Jamie's Ministry of Food*. Paula Trafford brought Ottolenghi to our screens, creating a new anthropological approach to storytelling about food, while Nicola Moody kite-marked British food in BBC Two's *Great British Menu* (2006–present), which she executive produced at Llewellyn's Optomen Productions until she joined Jane Root's Nutopia in 2016. Yet Llewellyn was not impressed by the roles for women in TV food 20 years on. She said, 'Maybe this is me being a bit bitter, but I was thinking about class and women and it feels to me that on BBC Two in particular there's this rash of beautiful young women who are models or who used to be models and have been promoted as cooking stars on the BBC. It feels so old-fashioned. It feels like we've gone back 20 years. The men have to have tons of authority and they can look like whatever they like. When I started, there was suddenly a market for food that hadn't been there before, both here and abroad. And there are books, people can launch very successful restaurants; look how much money Jamie has made. And I think that's what people expect'.

Food writer Rose Prince was asked to make a taster tape for a series after the publication of her first book in 2005, *The New English Kitchen: Changing the Way You Shop, Cook and Eat*, a practical guide to buying and cooking with quality ingredients and using up leftovers. She wrote in the *Daily Mail* in 2014 that although the broadcaster loved the idea, she 'was found wanting. My presenting skills were in part to blame but when, much later, I asked a senior commissioning editor what the problem really was, his answer was revealing. "Your problem is that you are too ordinary. A middle-aged, middle-class housewife trying to solve her cooking problems and keep to a budget is not what we look for any more." "Would Delia Smith get a show now if no one had ever heard of her?" I asked him. "No way. To be honest, women chefs need to be young or have model looks. Otherwise, we love the 'novelty' appearance of older women, like the *Two Fat Ladies* – and now Mary Berry," he explained. I guess I'd better wait until the wrinkles deepen, then try again.'

Storytelling and race

Access to Television's corridors of power is itself mediated by background and education, and the confidence and 'instinct' or 'intuition' that is attributed to the most successful executives and producers is still the result of access to an elite. All British television channels now have a diversity strategy aimed at including black and minority ethnic groups as well as women returners, although unpaid or low paid internships among many of the independent production companies still ensure a filtering system that excludes many of those the channels hope to attract. The result is evident on-screen. In this chapter, I look at how and why producers cast new talent, and at some of the ideas behind the representation of race and class on TV.

Lorraine Pascale, Nadiya Hussein, Andi Oliver and Romy Gill are among the very few women of ethnic minority backgrounds currently associated with cooking on British television. *The Great British Bake Off* has an exemplary cast drawn from Britain's ethnic minorities, while Food Network fishes from a rich pool of international talent. But in Britain, at least until the mid-1990s, there were very few people of colour in the kitchen. Madhur Jaffrey and Ken Hom instructed British audiences in how to make the nation's favourite foods with their 1980s shows on Indian and Chinese food, respectively, with Ching He Huang the only home-grown Chinese talent to carry on the mantle. But ethnic minority chefs who are major names in the British food industry, such as Cyrus Todiwala, Vivek Singh, Ching, Meera Sodha, Selina Periampillai, Atul Kochhar and Gordon Ramsay protégée, Ravinder Bhogal, are still bit-players, passing through on *Saturday Kitchen* or *Sunday Brunch* (Channel 4, 2012–present), or consultants in TV food, when compared to the white giants who don't even need a surname: Nigella, Jamie and Gordon. Only Nadiya can begin to make the same claim.

Nick Thorogood has run major food channels in the UK, as well as the Food Network in Europe, Middle East and Africa (EMEA). I asked why, if diversity has played such an enormous role in catapulting London onto the international culinary stage, there are still so few people of colour on British TV. He reminded me that television is supposed to represent its audience, and the 2011 Census for England and Wales showed that although 46 per cent of the foreign-born population identified with a White ethnic group, 33 per cent identified as Asian/Asian British and 13 per cent identified with Black/African/Caribbean/Black British (ONS). 'If you look at the level of the skills that you need in order to get an entry level job in TV, which is already a highly competitive well-paid industry', Thorogood told me, 'then it makes sense that smart, well-qualified people from diverse backgrounds might look for more available and better paid industries – and that sometimes means getting the mix of diversity in the talent pool is difficult.' Louise Fitzgerald argued that television must reflect the lives and opportunities of minorities: 'If people from these backgrounds don't see themselves represented on the screen then they won't see this as a viable option. I think Thorogood's argument is really flawed here', she told me. 'It's too easy and it maintains the absence of non-whites on the screen by saying they don't exist outside of the screen, and that's just not true.'

Thorogood produced some of Ainsley Harriott's first television appearances on *Good Morning with Anne and Nick* (BBC One, 1992–96). He said that it was Harriott's experience as a comedian that set him apart, and his ability to banter with hosts Anne Diamond and Nick Robinson was key: 'He had an amazing sharpness as a performer, a genuine passion for the food, and really fast-witted intelligence that you need if you're going to stand up there', he said. 'He has got a tremendous energy. He represents something really interesting which is the diversity of the UK, but in a very accessible way. He comes across as quite middle class in his own way, you know, but he comes from a family of entertainers and he knows how to entertain.' Thorogood is still good friends with Harriott, and told me that he also knew how to play the game: 'Even though there are tons of positive and wonderful and amazing things about him, all TV people need to find out how you fit in if you want enduring success. You can be the extraordinary freak out, the slightly different one, but you need something quite mainstream [to stay on the screen].' He said that what is really important is authenticity. 'There are chefs I could tell you about whom I've met whose agents have begged me to put them on TV, and I won't because I just don't believe they're authentic. If I can see it, the viewers will see it'.

South African TV presenter Siba Mtongana was first spotted by Nick Thorogood and Sue Walton for Food Network. Her series, *Siba's Table* (2013–present), aims to give a twist to traditional dishes of her youth and add to the fusion of indigenous and imported tastes that has done so well for Australian food culture. I asked about the process of casting her: 'We sat in a hotel lobby over a period of days, with maybe a hundred chefs coming in and out to meet us', he told me. 'The platform that we were operating on really loved what we were doing, but very much wanted us to try and find a black South African face because that was where they saw a big opportunity in their Satellite TV market – that's how they saw they were going to grow. The channels could [then] appeal to a sector of the [emerging black middle-classes] market referred to locally in South Africa as "Black Diamonds"'.

Mtongana was the food editor of the magazine *Drum*, which Thorogood knew was 'very much part of the black movement in South Africa'. His researchers had already spotted that she had a passion for and understanding of food, but her philosophy was what she could bring to the screen at a particularly interesting time for South Africa. 'She published her recipes and what was interesting about them in the magazine', said Thorogood. 'It was very clear it was about updating and saying, "this is the modern South African food," yet its roots were very much in the traditional. When we then met her, I have to say the second she walked in, we knew that we had found the person we were looking for'.

Her rise has been exceptional. *Siba's Table* is now broadcast in over 128 countries, including the US where the franchise is broadcast to 60 million homes on the Cooking Channel. *Oprah Magazine* listed Siba as one of the most influential African women in its 2014 Power List and, at the time of writing, she has another show in production for Food Network. Nick Thorogood is not surprised, as he told me: 'She has become a very important person because she represents something really, really fantastic about how South Africa looks forward, and is looking forward – not just through the development of its population – but through its food and its culture'.

Food Network, with its endless thirst for new presenters and ideas, targets talent like Siba who can fast-track cultural messages. Oklahoma award-winning blogger Ree Drummond is Food Network's *Pioneer Woman*: 'Take one sassy former city girl, her hunky rancher husband and a band of adorable kids and you have *Pioneer Woman*', drawls the Food Network show page. '*Pioneer Woman*' is the name of her blog that, with its elaborate photography, family stories and easy-to-follow recipes, won her the attention of the blogging community and then Food Network in 2010. Her books are similarly messaged – featuring recipes from an *Accidental Country Girl* to a *Pioneer Woman Cooks: Food from My Frontier* – making her TV career a shoe-in. Her subsequent autobiography, *From Black Heels to Tractor Wheels*, has been optioned as a major feature film, and Reese Witherspoon is said to be in talks with the producers to play the lead.

The last programme Thorogood made for Food Network was *Fabulous Food Academy*, with British Asian TV chef, Reza Mahammad, and white South African TV chef, Jenny Morris. 'They were two people who are experts at cooking and teaching. It's a very simple format going through a range of basics, categorised into different groups, with groups of contestants being taught how to cook a dish and then having to cook it', Thorogood told me. 'But it was very much about the interplay between the two of them. I wanted to get those two faces on screen together, because they had a fabulous chemistry. We had seen them together a lot because we had done a lot of live events where they were cooking, but the viewers hadn't seen it, because we never actually put chefs together in that way.' He described how he 'produced' the concept of black-and-white co-presenters specifically to maximise audiences: 'Jenny has a huge appeal to traditional white South Afrikaans and black African viewers', he explained. 'Reza has a massive appeal – I mean he was like a rock star – for what they called the coloured community, so the Indian community in Africa. So, to put the two together, we were reaching a very wide audience appeal, but also playing off a bit of personality but with genuine experts.'

Charlie Clare runs Casting House, which scouts for talent for production companies in the UK. He agreed that there is an issue around ethnicity on British Food TV. 'It's very hard to get anyone on television', he told me in 2017. 'When we do talent searches, we're talking to scores of people who are all great, and getting any one of them actually to have a series is really difficult.' He said it was particularly hard to find ethnic diversity. The British Asian community is culturally shy about going on television. And we regularly find people who are young British Asians that don't have that cultural thing. They agree to do things, then they tell their family, and then they decide not to do it.' He said that it is changing: 'In my career, the British Asian has noticeably become louder. This third generation is becoming much freer of its kind of shyness, and I think that is just beginning to come through in telly.' But with broadcasters stipulating the need to promote diversity on and off the screen, Clare told me that it means that casting people simply have to work harder to redress the balance. 'London doesn't reflect the rest of the country', he said. 'And so, where in London we have ethnic diversity, I don't know, at 30 per cent or more, you know, nationally, it's at most 15 per cent – as well as ethnic diversity, what people also want is regional diversity. So we find that we cast fewer people from London than anywhere else. It tends to be people that are outside London who want to do media stuff, and it's an interesting conundrum for us. I actually tell people that ethnic diversity is going to be very, relatively, expensive to put in their shows. They can't just expect it to come through naturally or organically.'

Working harder to get the reach is about time and money, and this is passed on to the production companies, a choice that executive producers have to make. 'They're not always happy to spend money, but everyone wants that ethnic diversity. Every brief has it, whatever they want, followed by, "oh yes, with ethnic diversity, and with regional diversity." They're the two things that everybody wants, and frankly needs. If I'd set up my business two or three years later, I think it would have been a smarter thing to have set it up with its focus on ethnic diversity.'

A good producer/director makes all the difference, and we have seen how Pat Llewellyn's intervention with Jamie Oliver was an essential part of his success as *The Naked Chef*. 'Rachel Khoo is a good example', said Clare of the Croydon-born TV cook who lived in Paris before moving to Sweden in 2016. 'So there's someone who is actually half Malaysian, and the reason she was successful was because she ended up in this slightly comical place where she was cooking from a small flat in Paris. But she already had book deals in the background. You know, there was talent there, and it was the quirk of that flat that made it all work.' Clare had already spotted Khoo's taster tape when he was working as a producer at Jamie Oliver's production company, Fresh One. 'She had a naturalness in front of the camera. The vast majority of people can't talk – even on Skype – like this', he said, referring to our conversation via screen. 'The talent and ability as a chef helps get the commissions and all that kind of stuff. But all I'm looking for is a total freeness in front of the camera that ultimately doesn't come across as self-conscious.' It means that the viewer on the other side of the screen feels like they're in their room. And that's the magic. You're looking for someone who takes the screen out of the interaction.'

I asked him in 2017 whether Nadiya Hussein had what it would take to go beyond *Bake Off* and the anthropological spin-off, BBC One's *The Chronicles of Nadiya*: 'I think Nadiya is great, and I think she is good talent', he said. 'But I think there's a little bit of the industry patting themselves on the back, and promoting her because they're so pleased to have finally nailed the ethnic diversity conundrum. And they are really searching – everyone is searching for great ethnic diversity talent. Lorraine Pascale has been there and she keeps coming back because there's no one else to fill that space. And Nadiya is there now. Nadiya will move into that space.' By 2019, Nadiya had indeed filled that space by bringing more than her heritage to the small screen. Her 2019 BBC One documentary, *Anxiety and Me*, which allowed viewers to follow her as she sought a diagnosis and treatment for her crippling panic attacks, was praised by viewers and critics.

In the complex area of ethnic diversity on the television, it is rarely about the colour of skin. Clare told me about a show he had made recently starring someone who is half Mauritian. 'And he was great', he told me. 'But he was so middle class that he didn't quite tick the box for anyone. Because he wasn't ethnically diverse: he just had some skin colour. And so we worked very hard to find something that was more representative of the communities we're trying to support.'

I asked why Levi Roots and other black chefs are not on television more often. Clare answered by telling me why Jamie Oliver gets away with cooking food from any ethnic community instead: 'He's got a really good understanding of what the British mother is prepared to go and buy and can translate it for them. You know, one confusing ingredient and then that's your whole audience switching off. Ultimately, that's a very restricting factor. As producers, we want ethnic diversity [but], the product of that show has got to ultimately appeal to a very British, and essentially a pretty white palette, because that is the biggest market.'

This does not address Madhur Jaffrey's or Ken Hom's popularity, of course. Clare told me that when he was working at Fresh One, there was plenty of ethnic diversity and some great talent that stood out. 'But ultimately, none of that talent was good enough to break through this kind of stranglehold, you know, the fact that we've got all these great people.' He said that the only one from that time that really came through was the white West Country chef, Tom Kerridge. I asked him why. 'Do you know what?' he said. 'He's just better than the others.' I suggested that *better at what?* was the real question, that according to the position of the viewer and the cultural context of the viewing, 'better' can mean different things. 'I totally back that there is a link between what people see and what people relate to, and who's leading who', he said. 'There will be more ethnic diversity on TV, but I think part of it is, as British Asians become more confident in being British, they can speak to that wider market in a more confident way.' At the end of 2019 *Great British Menu* (BBC Two) judge Andi Oliver was the first woman of colour to join the team of presenters on *Food Unwrapped* (Channel 4) and Indian chef and food writer Romy Gill is part of the 2020 revamp of *Ready Steady Cook* (BBC One).

London's food scene is largely to do with this new confidence in ethnic food, buoyed by a rich, diverse population with its myriad stable food cultures. It's a long time since Italian restaurants added ketchup to their tomato sauces to please their new neighbours in the 1970s, although the cream added to curries in the same era has led to chicken tikka masala becoming Britain's favourite dish. Nadiya Hussein told me for the *delicious.* podcast in 2019 that her father used to run Indian restaurants in the 1980s and 1990s, and never served the food that she and her family ate at home. 'Mum cooked traditional Bangladeshi food', she told me, 'but Dad cooked Indian food slightly tailored to the British palate with nuts and cream. It was like two different worlds – Mum's food and Dad's food.' She remembered admitting to her mother that she liked his food too. 'It felt like I was cheating on her', she laughed. 'There was this massive row, and she said, "well, I'm never going to eat that!" I love the way she cooks, but that lamb dhansak was really nice.'

Ken Hom sees a confidence growing in the food of British Chinatowns. This follows years of food which had been created by Chinese and Hong Kong immigrants eager to please their new neighbours: 'When I first came here in 1971, I said, "what is this?" ' he told me for the *delicious.* podcast in 2016. 'I can see now there's less and less of that. And it's not only in London. You have to go outside of London to places like Manchester, Leeds, Liverpool. And that's where you really feel how Chinese food has progressed. It's food that I can eat with my friends from Hong Kong and we say, "this is a Chinese meal. This is authentic." ' He said not only is it authentic, but it's better than ever, because so many different ingredients come in now from China. 'And, you have to remember', he added, 'that we're going to have an influx of Chinese living here, from China, and they demand the top-quality food. And that's a great benefit for all the British people.'

Storytelling and class

How television producers tell stories with impact is the theme of this book, and while cultural theorists argue over the how and why of the construction of messaging, most successful producers say that they feel it in their gut. A Channel 4 producer gave me an example of how 'instinct' works: 'The people who do well in Telly are temperature testers. In one way, their skills are finely tuned, but their ideas could also come from somewhere on the street. You might be Simon Cowell and do *X Factor* but there might be a pirate radio station somewhere where we'll find the next Plan B. It works in two ways. For us, what we revel in is the combination of experience and risk. Our strategy is to engage with fresh ideas. It's about whatever fresh is. Pat [Llewellyn] had a nose for fresh.'

A media executive identified the skill of a factual entertainment commissioning editor at Channel 4 as 'cross pollinating entertainment talent into factual to get a new brand. If I get a new product, I'll feel it out, think what kind of talent does this need on this show. We'll slip people on with a totally different bag of skills and we'll watch them cross pollinate. We understand what the ambitions of the show should be. It's instinct. We work in TV. That's what being a commissioning editor is.' She explained the production of a zeitgeist: 'If you get a successful show, it changes everyone's minds about the direction in which the fish needs to swim. That's a psyche that you develop from a combination of engaging with talent, engaging with the indies and engaging internally, and you get this balanced instinctive judgement about what the channel needs to keep on pushing itself forward.' She described people like Pat Llewellyn and Jane Root as 'creative thinkers [...] who can survive within the system. They're gamechangers. They're communicators and they're confident enough to do things. They're strategic enough to work the system and they're people who are instantly recognisable but who come in different shapes and forms.'

Crucially, it's also the ability to communicate those ideas to the people in charge of the channel. In a post-Marxist analysis, understanding the means of production of television texts is about more than the influence of the few over the many. Another Channel 4 executive explained how leaders are created at the channel: 'I think that what happens in TV is that some people are attracted to it, some fall into it, some people come through schemes. But the most powerful tool that drives people up the system is about self-preserving, about having an innate intelligence about how organisations work and how to fit in and how not to rock the boat. It's about how to add value and how not to piss people off. And when you've got that completely handled, you start developing the confidence of your own voice. But you never ever just go around expressing that voice. You modify: you're like a leopard waiting to pounce. You learn to manage conversations and strategies and skills. It's all about judging the moment.'

Thorogood added that TV storytelling is very often driven by socio-economics, and he explained how new ideas emerge: 'The thing that you got in the post-banker era was the celebration of blue-collar', he told me, referring to the crash in 2008 which was blamed on the international banking community. 'It's really fascinating that the [Food Network] shows that are doing really well are all about good honest food in the street, or food in the café, or food in the diner.' I asked him if he had deliberately commissioned or bought in shows that fed the man in the street. 'The ones that do well are bought in, like *Diners, Drive-Ins and Dives*, *Man v. Food*. From stuff that we've originated here, Andy Bates's *Street Feasts* [Food Network, 2013] does well – that whole street food revolution. You know, this is real workers' lunchtime food.' I suggested that the average blue-collar worker might be more likely to take a Tupperware of white bread sandwiches to work rather than an order of pulled pork and creamed beans from a local food truck. 'Yes and no', said Thorogood. 'I think the interesting thing is if we'd shown Richard E. Grant going to have lunch at The Ivy, our white-van-man would not feel there was any relationship there at all. But he has stopped off and had a cheeky burger from a roadside lay-by van. He has been to his local café and had his fry-up breakfast, or – I'm speaking in clichés which is perhaps a little unfair – but these are real experiences. [As an audience,] you understand accessible food. And those shows celebrate that accessible food. The whole point is that there are queues around the blocks to get into these diners or to get into local cafés or restaurants because they're affordable and they're accessible and it's very popular food. It's not some fabulously elite sweetbreads in sherry. It's burgers or it's fillet steak sandwiches or it's mac 'n' cheese.'

Understanding a channel's audience is crucial to the success of its shows. Pat Llewellyn, whose success with BBC One and Two as well as Channel 4 is unsurpassed, admitted to me just before her first episode of ITV's *Food Glorious Food* was broadcast in 2013 that she didn't 'know' the ITV viewer very well at all. The show, presented by Carol Vorderman and featuring judges including former *MasterChef* presenter, Lloyd Grossman, was a co-production between Optomen led by Llewellyn, the queen of Factual TV, and its king, Simon Cowell, and his own production company, Syco, which also makes *X Factor*. Llewellyn had never made a programme for ITV before, and ITV had not made primetime food shows. Despite the change in viewing habits, programmes are still made according to schedule, and with *Food Glorious Food* following *Coronation Street*, it was important to know that the audience was largely female, northern and over 55, not Llewellyn's usual foodie audience. 'None of us know how it's going to do', Llewellyn admitted.

The series was not successful: the first programme reached just 2.7 million viewers, a 12.7 per cent share of the audience between 8pm and 9pm, on its launch in February 2013, down 46 per cent on ITV's average for the Wednesday night slot over the previous three months. By contrast, BBC One's *Holiday Hit Squad*, presented by Angela Rippon, reached 3.8 million viewers at the same time, a 17.7 per cent share, as reported by Thinkbox in 2019. It was a spectacular fall from grace by Simon Cowell, which largely obscured that of Llewellyn. '*Food Glorious Food* managed to fumble an audience inheritance of more than eight million viewers from the preceding ITV show, *Coronation Street*', wrote John Plunkett in *The Guardian* in 2013.

Llewellyn told me how she and Simon Cowell came to work together. 'He had an idea for a food programme and couldn't sell it, which I was quite pleased to hear! Peter Bazalgette was on the board at Syco and he said, "why don't you phone Pat and see whether you could do it together?" Simon doesn't watch Food TV but he had an idea to search for the best family recipes in Britain. Simon loves his mother's roast potatoes and he was really amazed to find that her recipe was the same as his granny's and the recipe was passed down. It's a lovely idea. The Syco bit was that the winning dish gets onto the shelves of Marks & Spencer and you can buy it.'

I asked Peter Bazalgette in 2016, just after he had been appointed chairman of ITV, if food could ever work on primetime ITV. 'Well, apart from *Bake Off*, there isn't food on primetime on BBC One [either] I don't think', he said. 'It's mostly on BBC Two. *Bake Off* started on BBC Two, like *Changing Rooms* and *Ground Force* started on Two and went to One.' I also asked him about the difference between ITV and BBC Two primetime audiences when people are choosing to watch TV on Catch Up, and when there are so many new channels vying for sections of each of the traditional audiences at different times. 'In the old days when there were three channels', he said, 'you might have said, "oh, ITV is a very different audience to BBC," although actually the crossover was probably 50–60 per cent at least, if not 70–80 per cent. But today, there's no particular loyalty and there are hundreds of channels. There's no 'ITV viewer' in the way there used to be.'

The making of Jamie*

It would be pushing a point to suggest that television in the late 1980s and 1990s was largely produced by ideologically informed graduates of the Frankfurt and Birmingham Schools, but Jane Root, one of the TV executives credited with creating Lifestyle TV, graduated from London College of Communication in the early 1980s, where critical theory was part of the curriculum. She went on to study the philosophical and historical construction of society for an MA in International Relations at the famously Marxist Sussex University. She would later employ Jamie Oliver's producer, Pat Llewellyn, who studied film theory at the University of Westminster in the mid-1980s: 'I started off by doing quite "serious" telly', she told Susan Low for the *Daily Telegraph* in 2002. 'The first thing I ever commissioned was a philosophy series that included people such as Jacques Derrida.'

The Naked Chef was the first Lifestyle TV series to offer a wraparound culture of youth, good food, cool music, clothes, scooters and friends. From the kitchen shelves laden with unread cookery books to the barbecues of shrink-wrapped Tesco's Finest, Llewellyn and the commissioning team were constructing a show that was about aspiring to the Naked Chef's lifestyle and had very little to do with the real chef's personal passion for healthy eating; local, seasonal, sustainable sourcing; and compassionate animal husbandry.

As Oliver's media persona developed, he was seen on-screen as *The Naked Chef* and snapped by paparazzi off-screen popping around the corner from his flat to buy his vanilla pods and his fresh fish. London was represented in the series as an accessible, friendly village in which the corner shop was the centre of the community, where cheese shops and butchers lined nearby streets, waiting for cheeky chappies to stop by for a natter and a slice of something nice. It was a world of old-fashioned British values, even if the recipes were inspired by an Italian peasant diet. Off-screen, Jamie Oliver's world was quickly branded by the tabloids as stylish, youthful and healthy, with everything apparently within his reach; while his old school mates featured in his on-screen barbecues, off-screen he was Brad Pitt's new best friend, taking his protégé chefs from his Fifteen charity with him to Los Angeles to cook at Pitt's 40th birthday.

He was what Grant McCracken, in his 2005 book *Culture and Consumption II: Markets, Meaning, and Brand Management*, called a 'super-consumer', who is perceived to 'create the clear, coherent, and powerful selves that everyone seeks'.

It was the clarity of the message to his audience, the absolute promise that life would be 'pukka' if you cooked like Jamie, a message that Roland Barthes, in his seminal 1957 work, *Mythologies*, would describe as 'euphoric'. It was a perfect example of the Barthesian myth, as it distracted the Lifestyle TV audience from the mundane reality of their lives, and has become a staple of Factual Entertainment TV ever since.

Amanda Murphy is an award-winning executive producer and Senior Reader in Media Arts at Royal Holloway University, London. Like Root and Llewellyn, Murphy was a student of cultural theory, graduating in 1987 from Leeds with a degree in Communication and Cultural Studies. She thinks that although it may well have been only a small part of the self-help puzzle, the newly imagined Lifestyle TV was meeting the needs of its audience. 'Jamie is one of those larger than life [presenters] who've got a bit of character, a bit of skill and this transformational quality about them. That means that you can cast this super character who can transform whatever you want to transform and affect people's lives enormously.' She believes that it was the enormous potential of transformational television, which included Oliver's food programmes, that led to the apparent 'buy in' by the audience.

In their article 'Television as cultural forum' (1983), Newcomb and Hirsch call this 'buy in' a contract based on a mutual benefit for both TV producer and TV consumer. The matching of the creator (of the programme) with the audience in the making of meaning was later denounced by David Morley, in his 1992 book *Television, Audiences and Cultural Studies*, as facile, and Morley held up the imbalance of power as evidence. At the time, he may well have been right, in that the producers alone had 'power over a text and [...] power over the agenda within which the text is constructed and presented'. But Murphy believes that the development of technology has changed that contract, and that a relationship is emerging which is more about a mutual exploitation between audience and producer. 'In the past, TV audiences would just sit and watch – that was the culture', she told me in 2011. 'The whole dialogue was the broadcaster to the audience who passively absorbed. We're a more interactive society now – technology has changed us and we want to take part, we want to have our say, we want to vote. We've noticed that there's an opportunity now for us to do more than the curtain twitching that we used to do and for us to take part and change our lives and to do something that we wouldn't be mobilised to do ourselves. I think it's the same way therapy works.' She said there's lots of acceptance in this country that therapy can change your habits and attitudes for the better. 'That's come from America and TV has tapped into that. Rather than vote for people who are brave enough to go on TV and change their lives, it could be you. I think it's mobilised people to think that TV is the route for change, that it's a natural and known and accepted route for change.'

The offers of transformation ranged from being able to parent, clean, decorate and even sing better. But the big surprise was in the size of the audience that bought into Oliver's unique style of transformation through food. Seventy per cent of his five million viewers were young aspirant working-class men who were watching a TV chef for the first time, and they not only drank up his missionary zeal for good food, which promised so much more than mere nutritional value, but they also began to cook it themselves. Unlike Fanny Cradock, Graham Kerr, Keith Floyd and Delia Smith before him, Oliver was presented as the bloke next door, living the kind of life his audience dreamed of. This identification with him led to a new breed of 'lads' cooking around the barbecue, showing off to their girlfriends and buying the message that cooking is cool. The Naked Chef, both programme and presenter, was lifestyle. Oliver showed us what he and his friends liked to eat and drink: 'If I give them a nice roast lamb and a glass of wine, they're going to be well chuffed', he said in his first programme, blowing the cobwebs off the chef archetype and showing what food could do for social mobility. We met 'the lovely Jools', still at the time a glamorous but just-accessible girl-next-door whom he had met on the school playground. We were introduced to Uncle Alan, who 'used to look like Cliff Richard', and his children who podded peas for Jamie and effortlessly munched into roast chicken and coriander wraps on a picnic on Southend Pier.

Barthes critic Michael Moriarty, in his 1991 book *Roland Barthes*, might have equated this aspirant but ultimately farcical scene with Barthes's views on wrestling: 'This is "ludic and aesthetic in function [...] the duplicity of the event is part of the spectator's pleasure."' Barthes may have said that Jamie's picture of Essex children happily preparing healthy, slightly exotic food was the perfect myth, in that it was neither true nor false. Myth, just like Television, which manipulates real events featuring real people doing real things to create an edited programme representing the 'truth', is the compromise between the two. 'Myth hides nothing and flaunts nothing: it distorts', Barthes writes in *Mythologies*; 'myth is neither a lie nor a confession: it is an inflexion'. The fact that we can see the myth being created by this collection of television images is, for Barthes, the very essence of mythology. What Saussure called 'the sign' is to Barthes packed quite deliberately with meaning, and is hiding nothing as it constructs its message.

Amanda Murphy fully admits that producers consciously tap into the audience's aspiration for a better life: 'When we create these characters on TV, whether it's Gareth Malone, Ramsay, Jamie, Supernanny or the Dragons, the power of TV means that we can make people believe they can do things a bit better', she told me. I put Guy Redden's 2010 point to her, that Lifestyle TV divides us into those who are 'worth less' and those who are 'worth more'. 'But as a producer you can do more than that', Murphy told me: 'You can mobilise streets, villages, countries. You can take it to America. The power of actually getting an audience behind a message and making people feel better about themselves is to mobilise people en masse to do something more political. It's not that difficult. I think you consciously take it to bigger places. Someone like Jamie, he'll do huge community events that make people come together to believe that they can change something bigger. It's no longer about making a difference to you and your family, it's about something else. It happens on a larger scale.'

Murphy was responsible for devising Channel 4's parenting hit show, *Supernanny* (2004–08), and sold it to ABC America and 47 different territories for Ricochet TV. She explained how the original idea was developed in 2003 to fill a genre gap, that magic moment when a producer spots something that hasn't been done before: 'The original idea came from Nick Emmerson who was a father of two young girls at the time', explained Murphy. 'We'd had property, property, property. There wasn't quite so much food at that time, although Hugh [Fearnley-Whittingstall] was around. Nick was looking for interesting ideas and was clearly inspired by being a father.' She explains how consciously 'the message' was constructed: 'At first, all the chats were all very honest about audience figures and how to make a programme that, to use all those words that commissioning editors use, "makes a noise", "has attitude", "gets heard". From a selfish point of view, the producer just wants to make a programme that stands out.'

The team wanted to create a 'new Mary Poppins, but not necessarily a warm Mary Poppins', Murphy told me. 'She could be stern and she could be harsh because she would be more notable that way. It would have more edge.' Edgy, she explained, would mean the programme would be more talked about and would be a bigger series. Even the name 'Supernanny' was deliberate: 'She was unusual. She was larger than life. She wasn't your warm normal nanny or au pair. It was a superhero thing.'

Murphy and her team began to cast, and Jo Frost, with her unusual mix of stern authority and comparative youth, was the clear choice. 'She was quite ballsy, quite street', said Murphy. But however suitable the presenter is, the creation is not complete without the production process and its enhancements. 'We talked quite deliberately about the uniform', said Murphy. 'I commissioned the music that was slightly tense, like an edgy Mary Poppins coming to your street. We chose her shoes so they would click', she said, reminding me of the stomping, striding theme tune. 'We chose her uniform, put her hair up and found her some glasses that made her look more austere. We decided that she should be a little bit scary: we thought that if she had harsh edges, she'd have more impact and people would stand to attention when she walked in the room. Therefore the viewer would. Therefore the country would. Therefore, politically, she could do much more. It was a hugely conscious effort, from the styling of the uniform to the props to the music, the editing and the way I filmed her.' The success of the show was instant, attracting six million viewers and resulting in three bestselling books, a magazine and *Supernanny* spin-offs in 47 countries.

In 2015, *The Bookseller* reported that Jamie Oliver had broken through the £150 million unit mark for sales of his cookbooks, making him 'by far' the best-selling non-fiction author since accurate records began. Unlike Supernanny, his success also had an explosive impact on supermarket sales. His first-ever advertisement for a prawn curry pitched at the 'lads' night in' market rocketed the sale of prawns by 900 per cent in just six weeks at the beginning of his relationship with Sainsbury's in 2002. The sale of nutmegs had already shown what could happen after Oliver suggested in his series that it was 'just the job for a pukka Spaghetti Bolognese'. Weekly sales of jars of nutmeg rose from 1,400 to 6,000, prompting Sainsbury's to order two years' worth of stock. Buyers were even sent out into the field to source new supplies to meet demand. The vanilla pod also became a 'bestseller' after Oliver told us that he 'popped them in jars of sugar' and gave them away as presents. Barthes would not have been surprised; he wrote that the naturalisation of mythologies is a sign of their success. The fact that this apparent *embourgeoisement* of the audience could not really deliver them Oliver's lifestyle was obscured by what Barthes in *Mythologies* called the 'euphoric security of the myth' that owning these items could now provide.

The signified prawns, nutmegs and vanilla pods had very little to do with the myth of the super-ingredients that Jamie fans now had on their larder shelves. Like the brands that Arvidsson describes in his 2005 book, *Brands: Meaning and Value in Media Culture*, these innocuous ingredients also gave us what Arvidsson calls 'a source of shared beliefs, meanings and social connectedness within contemporary capitalism'. These products have not only merged 'aesthetics and economics, informational and commodity culture, they have come to play a more profound role in organizing or giving meaning to the everyday. In today's thoroughly branded existence, consumption can be seen to have taken on an enabling and productive quality, as a site or set of practices through which consumers construct the common social world that connects them to each other'.

Barthes would have been more sceptical about the motivation behind this normalising of myth, but the fact that it worked to form a stronger bond around certain tribes in society, a more cohesive branding of demographically differentiated audiences, would not have surprised him. *The Naked Chef* had clearly engaged a new audience and changed consumption patterns, and the man behind the myth quickly spotted the potential for revolution. Setting up his own production company after leaving Pat Llewellyn and the BBC for Sainsbury's and Channel 4, his new company, Fresh One, could now begin to use his unique style of energy and commitment to make much more than aspirational TV. He would be moving beyond the myth into TV that was what Barthes called in *Mythologies* 'initially and finally political'.

Jamie's Kitchen aimed to give under-achieving, often homeless young people a chance to transform their lives through cooking. It was the perfect extension of the Oliver brand's success to date: from aspiring to his lifestyle to buying the kind of food Oliver cooked, young working-class men bought the message that Jamie Oliver represented a better set of opportunities, whether it was about getting the girl or the job. But despite the inevitable cynical reactions, the intention behind this series and the next, *Jamie's School Dinners*, was about making real change. Amanda Murphy thinks it was always so with Jamie. 'I think that Jamie is a political animal: there's an intention in the programmes that he's involved in that they will have a big political impact', she told me.

Fresh One attempted to build a new approach to TV production based on the Oliver brand values of honesty and integrity. It worked, attracting the kind of people who would add to its kudos. Fiona Gately of Prince Charles's Duchy Originals was one of the consultants on *Jamie's School Dinners*. 'She is a very cool customer, a very clever woman', Tim Lang, Professor of Food Policy at City University and fellow consultant on the series, told me for my 2008 Jamie Oliver biography, *The Jamie Oliver Effect: The Man, The Food, The Revolution*. 'She's an astute woman with a strategic brain', he added. Lizzie Vann, Organix chief and food consultant, wrote the *Food for Life* document for the Soil Association on which *Jamie's School Dinners* was based, but delivered it to Jamie Oliver because she believed that his influence would be the most powerful. 'I put it on the counter' (at Fifteen, Oliver's new restaurant in London's Hoxton), Vann told me for the same book. 'He wasn't there but I said, "we've just finished watching *Jamie's Kitchen* and it's a great programme, but this is his next TV series."' The Soil Association supplied Fresh One with information about alternative ways of providing food to schools, and Tim Lang consulted on the politics. 'I'm a great fan of what they did and how [Oliver] grasped it immediately', he told me in 2008. 'He went into really dangerous territory. Fresh One was dealing with a political no-go area which stretched back 20 years, starting with the 1980 Education Act under the Tories', he said, referring to the outsourcing of school meals to the private sector.

Oliver's missionary zeal, which had informed his early desire to inspire young men to cook, had developed into campaigning for healthy school meals in *Jamie's School Dinners*, and more compassionate farming methods in Channel 4's *The Big Food Fight* (2009), *Jamie's Fowl Dinners* and *The Big Fish Fight* (2011). And in some cases, it worked: Oliver has now trained a new generation of socially excluded young people to become professional chefs through his Fifteen Foundation; his Ministries of Food, which set out to give simple recipes to families living on junk food, have spread to Australia; and his American Food Revolution, which battled against negative public opinion in a repeat performance of his post-*Naked Chef* era continues with Alice Waters, chef and champion of America's farmers' markets creating 'edible schoolyards', in which learning, growing and eating healthily were integrated into the curriculum through working on vegetable gardens. It even reached the office of Michelle Obama during her husband's presidency, and became key to her work with children and food. As we went to press (2020), news emerged that the Trump regime had reversed her reforms.

Largely as a result of *Jamie's School Dinners* in 2005, British schools, for a while at least, put emphasis on practical food experience, including cooking skills and food growing, helping to educate future food citizenship skills and increasing an understanding of how marketing affects food choices. According to the School Food Trust (SFT), the average school lunch in 2011 was lower in fat, sugar and salt than it was in 2005. Claire Rick from the SFT told me in 2012: 'Clearly, TV does have huge power. While concerns had been growing about the quality of school food in England for a long time, it was *Jamie's School Dinners* that really brought the issue into the living rooms of many parents. In that instance, TV certainly had power to raise awareness of the issue – but the really difficult and complex work comes afterwards, in engaging and continuing to work with the many different people involved [...] in many different ways, for the long-term.' In 2019, my interviews with the teenage food ambassadors of the Food Foundation revealed a very different story. Healthy foods in school are too expensive, if they are available at all, and where cookery lessons are offered, ingredients have to be brought in from home, a tough call for the 25 per cent of children living in food insecurity. The children's charter for the 2019 *Children's Future Food Inquiry* has demanded what they have tagged their #right2food.

Amanda Murphy told me that although it's not a driver for all producers, the potential for revolutionary TV is there. 'For some it is about audience figures, but lots of us do want to make an impact. I also made *Changing Sex*, which was about making people think differently about transsexuals. Daisy Asquith's film,

My New Home [2013] which I'm exec on, specifically wanted to contrast immigrant children's view of Britain in order to show British people how to look at themselves and how we treat immigrants. We consciously did it with that aim in five one-hour programmes.'

It is a small-scale revolution and a game of snakes and ladders for Oliver. Murphy, who took *Supernanny* to America, said that British producers need to think differently in the US. 'Americans don't like to see their people being humiliated. They're much more "everyone can do it": the postman can be the president. So sneering at someone because their cooking is not very good isn't acceptable in America. You take a superhero like Jamie to America and he's got to have a success rate that's growing and mushrooming before your eyes. It's got to have great warmth: that person couldn't cook and might have stuffed himself with loads of pizza, but rather than being told what to eat week in, week out, and having his fridge examined and being humiliated and embarrassed, he goes and learns how to cook. It's all framed in the positive. He then teaches someone else how to cook, who teaches someone else. That works in America. It's about working out where the sensibilities lie in the different countries and where you can grow the idea. When you can make it mushroom, then it becomes political.'

According to Moriarty in 1991, Barthes was a visionary 'in that he looked for Utopia and how desire could be realised, how happiness could best be achieved'. The key, Barthes believed, is in the motivation of the myth-makers, and so, for a genuine revolution in food, that motivation has to come from viewers as well as TV producers. The aspirant working class who bought into the values of the petite bourgeoisie in the early days of mass consumerism have been filled with half a century of social mobility, and many have more power now than when Barthes was first writing. Many are now in the driving seat of the food retail business and have clearly bought into the myth that the consumption of certain foods offers a fast track to a 'better' way of life. In an interview for my 2008 book about Jamie Oliver, Tim Lang said that '[change] is not about organic free-range cooking for the Jamie fans. It's when Morrisons commits to 15 per cent of British retailing. Now that would have an impact. Jamie or you or I or the Prime Minister make bugger all of an impact'. In 2019, Morrisons's TV advertisements and web presence make much of the supermarket's commitment to local producers, with all of its beef now British. With the use of 'real stories' in the making of its new myth, it presents itself as a supermarket that cares.

The mass media, with its sophisticated understanding of myth and its clever use of narratives to harness aspiration, is now exploiting its potential to generate ideas which can change the world. Television looks for new factual entertainment narratives which utilise the jeopardy of 'will they/won't they?' that was so engaging to *Jamie's Kitchen* and *Jamie's School Dinners* audiences. Can it now encourage the same audiences into more food growing, better local and seasonal sourcing, and a greater respect for what and how we eat? It seems that revolutionary ideas debated in University film societies and ideology seminars have, if not always consciously, filtered through to the production process of the mass media and become part of a new life-styling mission. With a clearer understanding of viewing patterns and desires through audience figures, television is now reinventing myths that have become the basis for change. Led by the feel-good factor of the myth, television illustrates how aspiration and consumption can successfully mask the dominant power relations in society, while introducing new discourses in food and lifestyle.

The material for change is already there: a sustainable food policy at the core of every council's vision of the future, reducing waste and carbon footprint and the cost of its related healthcare, would be packed with subplots and personalities. Edible schoolyards similar to the idea that Alice Waters has been promoting across America with Jamie Oliver since the late 1990s have cropped up all over Britain. As reported by the National Childhood Measurement Programme in 2011, the Brighton and Hove Food Partnership is quietly optimistic that working so closely with the council may have contributed to the drop in obesity rates among primary school children in the city for the first time in three years.

For Murphy, the political potential of Lifestyle TV is within reach: 'It's about the power of actually getting an audience behind a message, and on a small level making people feel better. [They think], "I'm not as bad as those people whose kids are so badly behaved", "I'm a better cook than that woman on *Can't Cook, Won't Cook.*" The next stage is to mobilise people en masse to do something more political. It's not that difficult.'

Jamie Oliver's television programmes work within an industry which creates myth emptied of history and filled with meaning, but Oliver himself is, as Barthes would have said 'initially and finally political', and he is able to exploit the potential of myth to make the change he wants to see in the world. The motivation of this unlikely member of the petite bourgeoisie who sells a lifestyle based on consumption and aspiration, and is one of the wealthiest men in the UK, seems to be genuinely revolutionary. Thurstan Crockett, freelance consultant, catalyst and campaigner, recognises a similar quality in some of the team leaders who inspire the city's working class to grow their own vegetables. 'People like authenticity', he told me. 'They understand that it's about intention.'

Alice Waters agrees: she has been a mentor to Oliver throughout his career, and as one of the first chefs to create her menus from local, seasonal ingredients of the day at San Francisco's Chez Panisse, has been making significant changes in the restaurant industry since the 1970s. Waters believes that Oliver has the quality of a revolutionary, as she told me for my 2008 book on Jamie. 'He has that rare quality: his compassion shows through however angry he is. It's never destructive. He's always someone who cares. And Americans really value that – everyone values that. It touches everyone.' I told her that she made him sound like Martin Luther King. 'Yes', she said. 'I'm I'm thinking of people like him who have that rare combination of radical politics and compassion.'

For Lifestyle TV to make fundamental and lasting changes to the way we consume, both at the supermarket and in our own homes, the ideologically informed producer cannot rely purely on an aspirant audience. Authenticity, the Holy Grail of TV production may be a complex concept in academic discourse, but it is, according to BBC Research, what audiences respond to. 'If you strip out the soaps and continuing dramas like *Casualty*', Gill Hudson, former editor of the *Radio Times* and graduate of Sussex University in the political late 1970s, told me, 'the programmes that people are really locked into are things like *Jamie's School Dinners, Spring Watch with Bill Oddie, Cold Blood, The Choir, Tribe* and *MasterChef*. I remember a reader said that what she really liked about these programmes is that you know that the presenters are the same off-screen as they are on. She used the word 'authentic'. People absolutely know the difference between pure entertainment and a bit of a show and something that is absolutely genuine that has a point and a purpose. It means that you really can tell when something comes from the heart.'

To producers and audiences, authenticity may be termed 'TV gold', but academics recognise its performative quality: we analyse it in terms of how meaning is constructed from it and often do not allow for the progressive changes that it can offer. The potential for transformation in television itself, through the motivation of its producers to create programmes that are what Barthes calls 'initially and finally political', and what Murphy describes as 'a starter for change'.

'You can't change people's lives forever in such a short period of time. The problem with some of these transformational TV programmes is that they walk in, put some Elastoplast over the problem, offer a quick fix solution and then walk away. And we all know the bigger picture. Therapy, self-help, real change takes much longer and is more complicated. You can't change people overnight but telly does. It almost creates false promises. But some people just need that kick up the bum. They are aspirational: they do want to make some change, but they can't be bothered to pick up the recipe book and try something new. Mostly it's to do with fear or lack of time and a whole array of other things, so telly gives them a bolster to do something else. In that sense, it does create a myth.'

Note

A version of this chapter was first published in the *Journal of Media Practice* (13:1, 2012).

The Odyssey narrative

Authenticity is a highly contested term in academia: media personalities are clearly *constructs*, a mix of talent, producers' visions and storylines, yet those who spot it call it 'TV gold'. Something about Jamie Oliver transgresses the rules. This chapter explores the making of Jamie Oliver as the authentic hero of modern television, and the production process of one of the most effective narratives in television at a time when we urgently need to change the story of how we eat.

In 2013, I had my first interview with Zoe Collins, Creative Director of the Jamie Oliver Media Group, who oversees all of Fresh One's food output. We would meet several more times over the course of writing this book, through the sugar tax and the dramatic failure of his restaurant business. She and Jamie Oliver had first met when she was a young production assistant at BBC Radio 1 in charge of the guests on the *Breakfast Show* with Zoe Ball. They got on well, and he asked her to join him when he left Pat Llewellyn's Optomen Productions to set up his own company, Fresh One Productions, in 2001. The story is told more comprehensively in my 2008 book about Jamie Oliver, but as Collins and I talked through his move from BBC Two to Channel 4, we reminisced about how the narratives had changed. From *The Naked Chef* of the Llewellyn era (1999–2001), Channel 4's handcuff deal demanded access to his 'real' life and introduced jeopardy to underscore new cliffhanger storylines.

When we first met, Britain was just emerging from the fallout of the 2008 global crash. Austerity was still foregrounding most people's daily choices, and the debate around climate change had moved beyond all reasonable doubt to become a major factor in influencing how we should buy our food. The cost of sustainable food was a very real tension between the slow and organic food movements and supermarkets like Tesco, which insisted on putting customer choice before the needs of the planet. Since 2005's *Jamie's School Dinners*, Fresh One produced *Jamie at Home*, also for Channel, 4 in 2007, which focussed on growing and cooking Oliver's own produce in his new family home in the Essex countryside. It fed into the allotment movement and was a gentle, instructional reminder of how simple life can be. But, in his walled medieval kitchen garden just outside London's commuter belt, it hardly spoke to the Tesco BOGOF (buy one get one free) customer. *Jamie's Ministry of Food, Jamie's Food Revolution* (ABC, 2010–11; titled *Jamie's American Food Revolution* on Channel 4) and *Jamie's Dream School* (Channel 4, 2011), which would bring together some of Britain's most inspiring artists, entrepreneurs, politicians and community leaders to persuade 20 young people to give education a second chance, would once again pitch Oliver in a new role as social guardian.

I asked Collins in 2013, how the socio-economics of the country affected new ideas for Jamie Oliver shows at Fresh One. 'One of the things that I think has changed over the years are our sympathies towards the audience', she said. 'Especially at the moment, when all of us are feeling the pinch. None of us are as flush as we used to be.' The blame for the crash had been placed at the door of the City, at the 'wanker-bankers', as Pat Llewellyn had called them in an earlier interview in 2013. Collins explained how it went to the heart of their creative planning: 'I think we have slightly less tolerance for people who we perceive to be not putting back into society and just sort of helping themselves. Our tolerance of that is low right now.' I asked what was next in terms of Jamie programmes. 'We don't know where we are', she said. 'We're sitting back at the moment. We don't want to go through the pain right now. We're looking at different subject areas.'

The pain she was referring to was the 'failure' of *Jamie's American Food Revolution* to transform American food habits and promote a healthier school lunch programme. The production company had worked with and consulted some of the most influential people in the country, including American food legend, Alice Waters, and the show was nominated for the VH1 Do Something TV Show Award for its efforts to promote healthy eating at public schools. It even won an Emmy for Outstanding Reality Program, but it was its low ratings that made the headlines. Much was made of it being replaced by the entertaining but lightweight *Dancing with the Stars*, a kick in the teeth for campaigning and a reminder of what America wanted from a night in front of the telly. Oliver himself was accused of putting his foreign nose in business that wasn't his; according to the *Daily Mail*, he was told by DJ Rod Willis on *Rocky n' Rod*, a country station morning show, 'We don't want to sit around eating lettuce all day! Who made you king?'

What made Jamie Oliver king was a Homeric journey through the gods and monsters of high ideals and human failure, of institutional and cultural brick walls, and a narrative that had audiences across the world rooting for a hero in a bleak world. From *Jamie's Kitchen*, the seven-part series which aired in 2002 following Oliver's new deal with Channel 4, to *Jamie's School Dinners*, the four-part series broadcast in 2005, Oliver played the vulnerable hero setting himself up against the system, including his own broadcaster, on behalf of the dispossessed – the homeless whom he would train to become chefs in his own restaurant, and the primary school children fed a diet which was more about food industry profits than nutritional balance. The first led to the opening, against all odds, of his first charity restaurant, Fifteen, and the training of 15 disadvantaged young people who would become his first brigade of chefs. The shows regularly reached audiences of five million in the UK, and the training programme ran for a further 14 years until it was transformed into the Fifteen Apprentice Programme, which aimed to have at least one chef in each of the now defunct Jamie's Italian restaurants in the UK.

In *Jamie's Ministry of Food*, the Odyssey narrative had Oliver, the warrior, arriving in Rotherham – where obesity levels are some of the highest in the UK – on a quest to teach the town to cook, and to tackle a series of personal challenges when he met eight people living on a diet of crisps and chocolate bars. As he taught them to cook simple recipes, they committed to sharing the recipes in a 'pass it on' campaign that would embed the learning, model the process and spread the skills. The idea was that it was not just the person who would be transformed, but the whole town – including Oliver himself, who had to confront his own expectations and sense of personal success and failure. I asked Collins in 2013 if there was a deliberate use of this narrative in the planning of the show. She told me that although Jamie would never call himself a 'hero', and she wouldn't 'have that conversation with him or talk about it in those terms', she would use that word with her team. 'And in the edit, we would probably think about it in that way', she added.

The series is one upon which academics have feasted, drawing as the show does on rich themes of patriarchy, neo-liberalism and the British brand of austerity rehashed so prolifically in the post-economic crash era. 'Our mission is to empower, educate and inspire as many people as possible to love and enjoy good food', proclaimed Jamie's Ministry of Food website. Borrowing from the ideology of Lord Woolton's Second World War Ministry of Food, the series used the language of austerity, with its themes of rationing and frugality juxtaposed with invention and resourcefulness as a metaphor for the British character. British food writer William Sitwell tells the forgotten story of Woolton as the architect of the British diet, which helped the fat rich lose weight and the malnourished poor achieve their calorie needs healthily. In his book, *Eggs or Anarchy* (2016), Sitwell describes how strict rationing was underpinned by an ethos based on simple pleasures and economical intelligence, and he encouraged rather than penalised the ingenuity of the great British cook who could make the most of the few ingredients on offer.

This rationing period following the Second World War is still recalled as a golden era when the state and the country worked together for the common good. Food writer Bee Wilson says that the certainty of just enough good food on the table during and just after the Second World War gave Britons a sense of being looked after: 'People still remember the blackcurrant puree they were given as children', she said on BBC Radio 4's *Start the Week* in 2016. It was also a rare acknowledgement by the British government of the role that healthy food plays in the spirit of a nation. For practical reasons, a nation must be healthy in times of hardship; the Japanese government, for example, broke a one-thousand-year taboo on eating meat by deliberately promoting a carnivorous diet in the late nineteenth century that would strengthen the nation in a period of major restoration. By the 1920s, it targeted the soldiers of the Imperial Army, urging Japanese housewives to cook recipes borrowed from China and India, such as katsu and stir fries, which were considered to be cheap and easy ways to build the health of men of fighting age. After the Second World War, in order to combat hunger in school, Japanese children were given white bread rolls flavoured with a strange curry powder mix and washed down with a glass of milk, which, Bee Wilson argues, would endow them with an eclectic palate that would give rise to a nation of adventurous food lovers, and one of the world's healthiest and most delicious national diets.

In *Jamie's Ministry of Food*, the theme of war summons that of the Great British Spirit, the make-do-and-mend principle of using what you've got to survive. As Oliver shows his class of eight how to cook with simple, inexpensive ingredients that could save the town from obesity, they become his foot soldiers. By learning a few recipes and taking responsibility for teaching the recipes to others, the 'Pass It On' campaign aimed to revive the spirit of the town, with the message being that people could save themselves. Oliver, the warrior, would then ride on to the next town to continue his quest.

In her 2011 article, 'Foucault's progeny: Jamie Oliver and the art of governing obesity', Megan Warin suggests that the narrative empowers the audience to demand change from the contributors to the shows. Turning the camera on a televisual activity, she suggests, could be described as a Foucauldian contract, an agreement between a community out of control that allows itself to be filmed while it attempts transformation. Warin writes, 'Through the lens of the camera, Oliver provides a window in which the audience observe and judge the everyday lives of the people of Rotherham. Like much documentary-based reality TV, the *Ministry of Food* operates as a panopticon, a model of surveillance in which Oliver becomes an omnipresent guard, policing' people's everyday lifestyles. But the disciplinary forces of surveillance have stepped outside Bentham's prison, and seep out into a social body, flowing through the networks of the socius.' She joins Ouellette and Hay, who argue in their 2008 book, *Better Living through Reality TV: Television and Post-Welfare Citizenship*, that this form of documentary-based reality TV has become a 'new form of cultural technology in which individuals and populations learn how to take care of themselves through self-monitoring, responsibility, choice and empowerment' in a 'televised form of governmentality'. *The Biggest Loser, You Are What You Eat, Honey, We're Killing the Kids, Fat Camp* and *Britain's Biggest Babies* (and the international versions of each of these shows) are cited by Warin as prime examples of this genre. Television becomes a social arbiter, willing those who can't cook, whose children are obese and threatening the national health of the country, to get into line. 'Reality TV is a milieu for education and intervention rather than a source of representation, and has thus become one of the most important resources for people to manage their "out of control" lives in world of risks and insecurities', wrote Warin in 2011.

Zoe Collins uses the same terminology to describe a TV producer's approach to television narratives. 'Producers don't like "out of control narrative lines"', she said, referring to journeys into the unknown and campaigns with uncertain outcomes, despite the fact that two of Fresh One's most successful series were *Jamie's School Dinners* and *Jamie's Kitchen* which were narratives predicated on uncertainty. But television is a useful tool: from a production perspective, the surveillance narrative encourages a response, an expectation of something about to happen. Casting is essential, as Amanda Murphy explained in relation to the transformational quality of Jamie: 'You can do this combined casting of this super character who can transform whatever you want to transform or affect people's lives enormously, and you cross-cast them with people who are needy or people with a passion for something that they need or want in life.' In their 2008 article, Ouellette and Hay could have been addressing Murphy: 'Everyday life has become a staple for reality TV, in which "needy" individuals and populations are targeted, and transformed into functioning citizens.'

Megan Warin argued in 2011 that *Jamie's Ministry of Food* broke new ground in that it spotted an opportunity for television to create a technological self-help community, with Oliver holding the puppet strings and audience expectation driving the need for narrative. She describes Oliver as 'Foucault's progeny': 'What distinguishes [*Jamie's*] *Ministry of Food* from other weight-loss reality shows, is the targeting of individuals and the whole community (and by implication, a whole region and nation of England). Rather than focussing on individual players in a competitive role play, the community approach presents a new form of reality TV that seemingly fits with social models of "new" public health.' This constitutes a new role for TV audiences, she argues, and demonstrates a 'new and intimate relationship between reality TV, health promotion and governmentality'. In 2008, Ouellette and Hay were on the same page as Warin: 'Reality TV is this rationalisation and comes to the fore as an "object of regulation" [and policy] designed to nurture citizenship and civil society, and an instrument for educating, improving, and shaping subjects.'

Jamie's Ministry of Food was not just about overcoming food demons: with the cameras in her home, Julie Critchlow, who led the 'Burger Wars' in response to Oliver's ban on fast food in *Jamie's School Dinners*, made her peace with her media-constructed enemy in the first of Oliver's *Ministry of Food* quests. In the opening episode, Critchlow and her mother meet Oliver for the first time after battling via the newspapers, and, after apologies on both sides, she agrees to sign up to be part of Oliver's 'Pass It On' campaign, in which eight food ambassadors learn to cook simple recipes and pass them on to two people who then do the same. In 15 steps, the whole of the town will be cooking and, by implication, will be made of better people. The message is clear: feuds can be laid to rest through the civilising effect of good food. I watched the episode with media academics, Professors Anita Biressi and Heather Nunn, who noticed that Oliver used the same device as he did in *Dream School*: 'He parachutes in and uses his experience to educate ambassadors that then go out and the message spreads', said Heather Nunn in 2017. This is the mushrooming that Murphy described to me in 2011. Nunn also suggested that a criticism of the show might be the absence of a broader context: 'It's a highly individualized approach to improving education about food, accessibility to food, stuff about the economics of food supplies. On the other hand, it's appealing and you can see how he's trying to address a certain level of ignorance. There's a very basic set of skills that people don't have now.'

Sally Munt, in her 2000 book *Cultural Studies and the Working Class*, writes that class is always constructed in ways that serve those in power: 'The primary interest has been in finding audiences who read against the grain. The approach has been to place the locus of responsibility onto readers, rather than producers. Isn't there a kind of shame existing here? Aspiration, in class terms, is largely concerned with escape, rather than the reconstruction of available icons.'

Jamie Oliver's willingness to 'cut through the crap' and 'get things done' resonated with the notion that Britain was a society in need of healing, and that local and national government were incapable of remedying the situation. But, in her 2012 book *Food Media*, Signe Rousseau argues that Oliver is practising what she terms 'everyday interference', and she questions why he should take on the task in place of an appointed advocate. She admits that the answer is complex, but suggests that Jamie Oliver has employed the special cachet of the TV chef, who is there to soothe the national brow with a clear authority at a time of food scares and diet-related health crises, all while waving the magic wand of celebrity. Rousseau goes on to say that the media has become a more democratic platform for social reform at a time when people have become more political but have also lost faith in politicians. It was an empowering moment for audiences who invested their belief in a man of the people who might change the world.

As the series rolled out across the UK and other territories, the campaign achieved some success. A study commissioned by the Food Foundation and led by the Department of Population Nutrition and Global Health at the University of Auckland, and the World Health Organisation Collaborating Centre for Obesity Prevention at Deakin University in Melbourne concluded that the campaign increased confidence in key skills areas including daily food preparation. Six months after the programme was completed, participants' daily vegetable consumption reportedly increased by more than one half serve. The series also evidenced an increase in the frequency of families eating together, as well as a reduction in the consumption of takeaway meals.

But the question remains: does it really work? If Jamie Oliver Television is, as Megan Warin suggests in her 2011 article, like a panopticon in which participants are surveyed 24/7, does it matter as long as they signed the consent form and the results are positive? If the criticism is of shaming the poor into eating more healthily, who is being more condescending: the TV producers who cast the participants, or those who presume (often without having watched the shows) that the participants' consent was not appropriately informed? In 2017, Nunn told me that to me how ultimately it is the audience ratings that determine a show's success, though academics may 'sneer' at what a good night in front of the telly is often all about: 'We (with Anita Biressi) wrote an article on sentimentality and *Secret Millionaire* and one of the things that we tried to grasp is that while there are so many things that we found troubling about *Secret Millionaire*. We sat there watching more and more, there were times when I thought the humanity of the shows – we'd be quite gripped. Sometimes I'd sit there and I'd feel like crying and I think it's because it's constructed but they are still people, just like us and you can feel an emotional connection even if they are produced for TV. One of the things that we said is that sentimentality is sneered at. It's seen as the lowest form of emotion.'

The making of dreams

When Jamie Oliver tried on a different archetype, this time as 'Expert' in education, the daggers were out. *Jamie's Dream School* was a response to Oliver's personal experience with young people and the education system following Channel 4's *Jamie's School Dinners* and *Jamie's Kitchen.* Oliver is one of Britain's great meritocrats: he left school with two GCSEs yet is one of the richest men in Britain and an internationally famous celebrity. It is his passion that drives him to choose the subjects of his programmes and leads him to explore the sociological and often psychological roots of the issues that he addresses. Despite his dyslexia (he read his first book, *The Hunger Games*, after watching his children enjoy the trilogy), he studied Food Nutrition through St Mary's University in Twickenham, Greater London in 2014, and in 2016 he started a Master's in the subject. He told *The Times* newspaper: 'It might take two or three years but I'm going to give it a good go. It's completely changed my life. It's proper geeky, I could go off on one.' Zoe Collins explained how the idea developed, telling me that he wanted to use the experience of 'having worked at Fifteen with all these young teenagers and seen how real practical skills can empower them and give them a sense of self-worth and self-respect and really propel them onwards'. He wanted to see if there was another way for education to be, she told me, that if what he had done for food with Fifteen could happen again: 'If we brought inspirational characters into the mix, can we together, each of us, do – and prove – something interesting?'

But as the series of seven episodes followed the experience of 20 young people who had 'failed' at school, Oliver's role of moral entrepreneur was given short shrift by the nation's teachers. 'Six Weeks summer holiday almost makes up for having the likes of #Jamieoliver make a mockery of your profession #jamiesdreamschool', tweeted one teacher. 'Completely irrelevant – teaching skills come 1st then excellent subject knowledge – didn't we see that proved by #jamiesdreamschool', wrote another. 'Why are #jamiesdreamschool students & staff giving evidence to the Ed Com in House of Commons! It's a TV show, a manufactured moment in time', tweeted another viewer. But 'I can't believe I am watching

BBC's Parliament channel at 7.30 am during the holidays but it's the committee on #jamiesdreamschool', said a fan for whom the initiative had worked.

'I am a huge fan of Jamie Oliver', wrote *The Telegraph's* TV critic, Allison Pearson in 2011. 'The young chef has a better gut instinct for what ails this country than any politician. Jamie knows that something is badly amiss when disruption is as endemic in our classrooms as kebabs are in our diet. When it comes to nourishing proudly ignorant young minds, however, the poor guy has bitten off more than he can chew.' Yet, with its narrative driven by the jeopardy of whether or not Britain's greatest actors, musicians, artists and business people could engage a class of truants and academic failures, *Dream School* did win. Rather than pitching the students against each other as in *The Apprentice* genre of reality competition TV, the Jamie Oliver narrative is about beating public expectation. As with his *Ministry of Food*, *Dream School* was about confounding the judgement of an unseen audience, both for the students who had been excluded from school (read society) and the 'teachers' who used their own entrepreneurial enthusiasm, authenticity and love for their subject to break through the barriers around learning and make dreams come true. Biressi and Nunn write in their 2013 book, *Class and Contemporary British Culture*, that Oliver 'legitimated an already developing public discourse that entrepreneurialism was a better solution to social problems than state intervention'. It seemed that under this narrative, *the People* really could take on the government. 'As the classmates headed to Downing Street for a meeting with then Prime Minister, David Cameron', write Biressi and Nunn, 'the 'arc of the series [...] travelled from individual struggles via a transformation narrative towards public engagement around social issues by non-state actors.'

Biressi and Nunn devote a whole chapter to critiquing *Jamie's Dream School* as an opportunity to explore the relationship between education and social mobility, and responsible citizenship. They focus on meritocracy and personal responsibility, considering 'ways in which educational choice is presented, taken up or passed by'. Their argument is set within the discourse of neo-liberalism which others have already explored (they note Becker's 2006; McCarthy's 2007; McMurria 2008; and Ouellette and Hay's 2008 *Better Living through Reality*). This neo-liberal framework is about 'choice, entrepreneurialism and self-reliance', and suggests that democracy is enabled by aspiration and choice. Effective citizens in the narratives of Reality and Lifestyle TV are those who can drive through social, educational and class barriers to where they need to be in order to climb the ladder and take their place in the world. Making the most of the wide range of economic and social determinants on offer, as Bourdieu points out in his 1984 book, *Distinction: A Social Critique of the Judgement of Taste*, citizens draw on their networks and milk their worlds for opportunities to gather cultural and social capital. Valerie Walkerdine adds, in her 2003 article 'Femininities: Reclassifying upward mobility and the neo-liberal subject': 'Within advanced neoliberalism the social state gives way to the enabling state, and is no longer responsible for providing all of society's needs for security, health, education and so on. Individuals, firms, organisations, schools, hospitals, parents and so on, must each and all take on a portion of the responsibility for their own well-being. The social and the economic are seen as antagonistic. Economic government is de-socialised in order to maximise the entrepreneurial conduct of the individual: politics must actively intervene in order to create the organisational and subjective conditions for entrepreneurship.'

Jamie's Dream School and *Jamie's Ministry of Food* were a fast-track way of introducing the underprivileged to the world of cultural capital through education and food, which would open the door to good health and better opportunities. Climbing the ladder in front of a judgemental audience was part of the deal. Academic, Signe Rousseau told me in 2016 that the concept of surveillance extends to Jamie Oliver himself: 'We're all watching the guy grow up, and that makes him vulnerable too. Obviously, there are bits of the narrative of Jamie's life that are constructed and we don't have access to everything, but I do get the sense that we have access to quite a lot.' She mentioned the scene in *Jamie's School Dinners* when Jamie read his wife a newspaper headline claiming that he had had an affair: 'they were having a bit of a thing on the street and he was in tears and she was in tears and it was great television', remembered Rousseau. 'It looked convincing enough to suggest that it wasn't scripted.'

Robert Thirkell was the series editor of *Jamie's School Dinners*, and in his 2010 book *CONFLICT: An Insider's Guide to Storytelling in Factual/Reality TV and Film*, he explains how he used the quest narrative with such success: 'Narrative drive, the arc of the film', he writes, 'is small questions and small answers which all contribute to the big question and big answer. We have to embark on a scene with the expectation that it will take us somewhere different at the end than where it began.' He articulated the big question for *Jamie's School Dinners* in 'fairy-tale terms: "an evil giant – big bad food – was rampaging round the land, leading to illness in children and even eventually to their early death. The government didn't seem to know what to do about it." As the audience boo and hiss, enter Jamie Oliver, stage left: "could plucky Jamie slay the monster of big bad food and show the wicked king – i.e. the government – that it could be done better?" '

But the fairy tale didn't work with the big guys. *Jamie's Food Revolution Jamie's American Food Revolution* on Channel 4) was the moment when Lifestyle TV came face to face with the realities of life's stories: after his initial success in the US as the archetypal British cheeky chappie in *The Naked Chef*, the failure of Jamie Oliver to change the American diet was about the inability of Entertainment TV to tackle the systemic issues underscoring the big questions, which Thirkell refers to in his book. In this case, the big question was obesity, not just in America but across the western world. Arun Gupta's 2010 article, 'How TV superchef Jamie Oliver's *Food Revolution* flunked out', lists the systemic issues as follows: 'widespread poverty, sedentary lifestyles, junk-food advertising, a lack of health care, corporate control of the food system, the prevalence of cheap fast food, food designed to be addictive, and subsidies and policies that make meats and sugars cheaper than whole fruits and vegetables'. It left nutritionists frustrated and Oliver in tears.

Heather Nunn is among the many academics who accuse him of having 'shamed the poor white trash culture of food' in *Jamie's American Food Revolution*: 'He was coming out as a missionary', she told me in 2017. 'It's one of the areas that people were very pleased to see him not succeed. Even though Jamie has a huge warmth and I always want him to win, at the same time, he's staking a claim in a political setting. You look at *Dream School*, which I wanted to like but I couldn't get over the obstacle of him fixing a few people in that setting, in the context of our educational landscape. If he's going to hit big, people are going to judge him as the context. They're probably not interested in whether he cares about the people in the programme. They're interested in the bigger claims he's making politically.'

Nick Piper's 2015 article, 'Jamie Oliver and cultural intermediation' makes a similar point: 'So-called "ordinary experts" such as Jamie Oliver need to be understood in the context of their varied social reception in order to assess whether people really do accept their authority as taste makers and domestic pedagogues. For one thing, this might cause academics to reconsider the extent to which a socially differentiated audience regards their particular version of ordinariness or expertise as valuable. There's a real underlying concern in the academic debate about the extent to which celebrity chefs and food media carry the ability to democratise taste. This underlines a key point in the debate about the value of celebrity chefs as cultural intermediaries.'

In her 2012 book, *Food Media: Celebrity Chefs and the Politics of Everyday Interference*, Signe Rousseau is clear that, for her, Jamie Oliver is categorically not in a position of authority or expertise. The issue is about getting the facts right and acknowledging the enormity of the issue. She criticises Jamie Oliver's mission to 'plant the seeds of change in America in terms of helping a community to cook better, feed their kids better and save money'. She uses de Certeau's 1984 article on 'the Expert' (another archetype) to study his performance at Long Beach, California, where he accepted a TED prize. He told the audience, 'Sadly, in the next 18 minutes when I do our chat, four Americans will be dead from the food they eat.' The figures were wrong, although the message of his address was not.

Rousseau reports accusations of a 'junk science peddled by St Jamie', conflating various statistics from a number of sources and, instead of exaggerating the figures, inadvertently underrepresenting the threat of obesity. 'One of the most memorable scenes at the end of *Food Revolution*', Rousseau told me in 2016, 'is when he's addressing this conference of nutritionists and dieticians and people who work in schools, and lots of them for many years have been trying to do something to improve the school meals situation and of course it's not just that the people in the canteens don't care, it's that there's all sorts of red tape and funding and all of that business. There was a question from someone at the end and he said what makes you so special? You're standing there talking to a group of scientists and people who know about nutrition. What makes you uniquely qualified to tackle the situation? We didn't hear how he answered the question but in the next shot he's standing outside and he's gutted. He couldn't believe that they weren't more receptive to his ideas. It crystallised something for me in terms of what I was trying to argue, and to ask. I really would have liked to have heard what he answered.'

I told Rousseau how John Ingram, Food Systems Programme Leader at the Environmental Change Institute at Oxford University, had asked me to take a message to Jamie Oliver via Zoe Collins. Ingram had delivered a lecture in 2013 on food security and its impact on the environment, and had urged the need for the consumer to play a more important role in changing attitudes towards waste. 'The power vested in the food industry has changed from the grower dictating what we eat to the consumer at the cash till', he said. 'We need to talk about the cultural function of food and ask what its meta-role is. We need to appreciate the motives of why people do what they do and use regulation, coercion, education and personal action to change habits.' He told me that the most important way to bring about this change was to talk to Jamie Oliver.

Rousseau listened as I told her what happened when I took the message to Zoe Collins a week later. She told me how they had tried – and failed – to deal with waste. 'We had an item on *Food Fight Club* [Channel 4, 2012] called Rude Veg', Collins told me, 'and it was exactly that. It was a knobbly veg campaign. We ran it on Instagram for a while with the hashtag #rudeveg and you'll see lots of hilarious knobbly penises and things. It didn't make the show because it was too puerile but it made us laugh a lot because we are all really puerile. We needed to move the narrative on and we just didn't have enough time to produce it very well so it didn't work.'

She, like many other producers I talked to, explained how difficult austerity narratives are, and how hard it is to produce a factual entertainment programme about bad news. 'If you had a show about waste, I could easily see an item on Food Tube about the ugliest thing you've ever seen in your life. It could be really funny getting Aaron Craze to cook the ugliest things that he can find and that's entertaining and informative, but presented by your academic who wants to do it for long-term benefits doesn't work', she said in 2016.

Since this conversation, *Blue Planet* has brought the waste narrative to life by highlighting the devastating impact of plastics on our oceans, and Hugh Fearnley-Whittingstall followed-up with his *War on Waste* series on the BBC in 2015. These are both great examples of how to bring difficult topics to life through emotional and dramatic storytelling.

But seven months after my chat with Collins in 2013, *Jamie's Money Saving Meals* was on Channel 4, with the accompanying Penguin book, *Save with Jamie*, the Christmas Number 1 bestseller that year. Niki Page, then of Freemantle Distribution, told me how it was sold to her: 'It's about thrift. The idea is if restaurants ran their business like we run our homes, they'd go bust. It's not about cheap food, but about key ingredients.' Rousseau remembered the book. 'I thought that the *Save with Jamie* book was great', she told me in 2016. 'You take a recipe and then there are five other things to do with the leftovers.' If Oliver can give an audience tools to buy more carefully, I suggested to her, isn't this the meta-role of food that Ingram wanted to be communicated to the consumer through Factual Entertainment TV? What Jamie Oliver is uniquely able to do, I continued, is to take the message to the masses, to talk to nutritionists and come back with information and put it on television in a way that people will hear and respond. 'I think that's a compelling answer to that question', conceded Rousseau. 'I would say that you're right.' But she pointed out that it was the narrative of the 'crusading lone chef going out and brazenly claiming to be an expert on childhood nutrition' that was the problem in Jamie's *American Food Revolution*. 'Just because you're a chef doesn't make you an expert on childhood nutrition. Now he's got a whole team of nutrition experts on his website who can answer questions about how to manage diabetes and things like that. It's a fairly "dodgy" thing – something that could backfire.'

Zoe Collins told me what she thought hadn't gone so well in America, and like Thirkell, she referred to the fairy-tale narrative: 'When we make those documentary series, we like to see our heroes suffer, to see them fight a losable fight', she told me. 'That's when we care about them. We want to see them up against it and then finally we can step down and love them, and then our hero will eventually win.' But she realised that in America, that doesn't work: 'It's success that they sympathise with', she said. The postman can be the president, as Amanda Murphy, who had to reframe Channel 4's *Supernanny*, reminded us in 'The making of Jamie' (this volume). 'So what worked in the UK, in the US impacted in a much more negative way', Collins explained. 'We used the same arguments that Jamie had with Nora (the school cook in *Jamie's School Dinners*) in the UK, but in West

Virginia it was a much bigger deal and often equated to fat shaming, a topic which at that time had yet to find its voice in the UK. She said the series producer in America was under a lot of pressure: 'People were saying to him, "campaign, campaign, campaign. We've got to do this; we've got to do that." I said to him, all you need to do is make a really good TV show. Because that's your job. The campaign will work if the TV show works. So I'm really clear about what my job is. My job is to make the strongest piece of narrative TV as I possibly can.'

The narrative extended off-screen as British audiences read in the media that Jamie was failing in America. Collins noticed how it strengthened his following in the UK. 'It was, "oh my god, look at all those people saying Jamie's wrong. We must back Jamie." ' Like the bruising of all heroes, the only people who care are their own. 'Jamie wasn't in the club. He had to fight his way in', said Collins. She wondered if America is 'more about your civil rights and your freedom. They defend the right to do what you want to do. We're much more into being told what to do. I think he fell foul of that.'

Television plays an interesting role in conferring expert status on Oliver in a postmodern televisual environment, where we can check figures on a phone while we suspend our disbelief and watch a chef try to change the world. The *performance* of being Jamie Oliver is central to the power of his message. Oliver is open about his severe dyslexia and relies on a team to represent his ideas in his texts, including scripts. Yet we want to believe in the Odyssey narrative, enjoying the audacity of hope which, for many people, underpinned the Obama presidency. Rousseau is concerned that it is too superficial to work: in her 2012 book, she wrote, 'Oliver is proof that celebrity chefs can be both empowering and inspiring in various ways. But the risk that accompanies their victories is that it becomes all too easy to rely on someone else to tell us how to live.' But perhaps this example best illustrates how production companies, presenters and their audiences are equally entranced by Baudrillard's simulacrum of television, the slipping between reality and its representation on-screen. It is the symbiotic relationship between production (and I include the presenter's performance in this) and audience that creates the image, the investment both ways that suspends the disbelief. When that is successfully produced, with a match between instinct and intelligent research, it works. *Jamie's American Food Revolution* was an example of what happens when belief is ruptured by the production team getting it wrong.

Understanding the mindset of an audience is complex, yet Entertainment TV can cross cultures and speak to a wide variety of audiences with enormous effect. Stanford University's Priya Fielding-Singh has researched attitudes towards healthy eating among high and low socio-economic status (SES) groups in America, but her research may chime with researchers in other territories. She suggests that framing theory, which provides a lens through which experience shapes choices, can explain why so many families which value their children's health and understand how to make healthy choices, feel unable to do so. Her interviews with 68 American families in the summer of 2016 revealed how poverty shifts priorities. She found that low SES families operate through a poverty frame which makes them focus more on the present. High SES families function through an abundance frame and are therefore able to plan more efficiently to meet their goals of feeding their children healthy food. Ninety-five per cent of her high SES research group said that they refuse to give in to their children's requests for unhealthy food choices compared with 10 per cent of low SES respondents, despite both groups sharing long-term goals for their children's health. Most revealingly, the low SES group felt that giving their children what they asked for meant saying 'one less no' in the day: being unable to give them the field trips, vacations and treats, which were affordable to the high SES group, meant saying yes to easier demands such as a takeaway burger.

The screen offers viewers a way of changing the story, but can it change the frame? I asked Rousseau if she thought that Jamie Oliver had gathered enough skills now through his Odyssey to make meaningful change. 'Well, I would say he already has done something meaningful', she told me. 'I think there are limits to what he can do, and I don't say that cynically. I think it would be a mistake to think that it's Jamie Oliver who's going to save the obesity problem. It's going to be Jamie Oliver and everyone else who's also working hard on different platforms and everyone has their own reach. He certainly has the opportunity to be a major force in something if there is going to be a revolution in terms of things turning around. You can give people all the tools they want, but if they want to eat shit food, they're going to be able to do that.'

Collins is realistic: 'The audience is always changing', she told me in 2013. 'They don't come to watch him do "good". They come to watch him fail. Only when he had slayed the dragon did we allow ourselves to celebrate his success. He was really miserable in *Food Revolution*. We were shoving the camera in his face.'

Yet only two years later, in an interview with the *Radio Times* about his off-screen school dinners campaign, Oliver was clear that he had learned from the past and seemed to have a renewed energy; he admitted in *The Telegraph* in 2015: 'I haven't succeeded, mainly because I haven't single-mindedly gone for it. In Britain, eating well and feeding your kid right and being aware about food is all considered very posh and middle class, but the reality is that in most of Europe some of the best food comes from the poorest communities.' He was about to take on his biggest challenge yet.

Sugar smart

The journey of the hero is about learning from mistakes, and off-screen, Oliver (and those responsible for Brand Oliver) responded to the criticism. 'Jamie has really immersed himself in the last few years', said the Jamie Oliver Food Foundation's then campaign director, Jo Ralling, when I first met her in 2016 'He talks to nutritionists, he talks to NGOs, he talks to the NHS in a way that I haven't seen him do before. He's even been doing a course in nutrition.' She said it wasn't just about trying to get it right for the audience and the critics: 'I think it was that process of hearing how bad it is – the 7,000 amputations a year in this country due to type 2 diabetes. It's shocking. I didn't know that and I was working for Jamie Oliver.'

Jo Ralling was Head of Operations on Channel 4's *Jamie's Fowl Dinners, Ministry of Food, Jamie's American Road Trip* (2009), *Jamie's Food Escapes* (2011) and *Dream School* (2011), and when I first interviewed her, she was Director of the Sugar Smart Campaign and UK Partnerships at Jamie Oliver Food Foundation. She explained how Jamie got back in the campaign saddle in 2015: 'Jamie had been very successful with the *School Dinners* campaign and we had got the School Food Plan through, but nearly a decade later, we turned around, and the state of the children's health and obesity rates were going through the roof. There was a real feeling of "what's going on? We need to do something big again." ' An idea in television, as we have heard from the gamechangers, is a process, a collision of factors from personal whim, social movements to cultural zeitgeist. 'It was a process over a couple of years', said Ralling. 'We talked to Channel 4 about what they were interested in making, asked Jamie what he wanted to do, and what we felt would work with his book schedule. It was a process. There wasn't a moment.'

There had been an enormous amount of conflicting advice, food scares and disinformation about the food industry, and government and campaigners muscled in for position on sorting out the national diet. As obesity levels rose, attention focussed on statistics, including those of the OECD Obesity Update in 2014, which showed that for the first time in history, children were likely to die before their parents because of what they ate. Despite assurances from Sir Richard Peto, Professor of Medical Statistics at Oxford University in 2014, that the probability of dying before 50 worldwide had halved in 40 years because of better medical care, decreases in smoking, cleaner water and vaccination programmes (Norheim et al. 2014), it was the western obesity epidemic that hit the headlines, obscuring the reports of victims of another drought in Africa. Rousseau's work prods at this assumption, and in 2016 she told me, 'Directing attention at one thing at the expense of another as if it is not more important, is a key (and frustrating) part of framing.'

'There's a huge number of organisations doing things about obesity and how we can tackle it', said Ralling, 'but we wanted to do something that was going to cut through. We knew sugar was going to be a strong message. There's no silver bullet to beating the obesity crisis: Jamie believes that the solutions have to be multi-sectorial. Getting the government to introduce a sugar tax on sugary drinks was one of the things that we put in our own version of the childhood obesity strategy.' The government had been promising to bring out a strategy but they were taking their time. Jamie decided to publish his version of what a good strategy would look like.

'My arguments about interference are pertinent here', Rousseau told me in 2016, 'mainly in the sense of Oliver claiming the authority to do something – made for television – that he clearly doesn't have the expertise to tackle. He could bully government to get on with it, sure, but a sugar tax is a job for economists, not a chef.' But Ralling said that the strategy was intended to do two things: 'It will help the government see what good would look like and it will also give us and the public and the press something to judge it against when the government brings their own out.' Rousseau noted the perception of influence on the part of the production company: 'It's like judging a house designed by an architect versus one designed by someone who likes to draw houses', she said in 2016.

The thinking at Jamie Oliver's production company was that the government strategy was due to be announced at the same time as the documentary *Sugar Rush* (2015). When it then became evident that this wasn't going to happen, the producers decided that *Sugar Rush* should lead to a 'call to action'. 'We decided to go for a sugar tax on sugary drinks', Ralling told me, following the example of France, Mexico, Colombia, Chile and the Caribbean, as reported in *Beverage Daily* in 2017. 'Forty per cent of kids' sugar consumption comes from sugary drinks', she continued, accepting that in order to make the medium the message, it needed to be simplified: 'Sugar is an incredibly complex and difficult thing to tackle. There are hidden sugars in our processed food, for example. But I think what we're really good at, and what Jamie is really good at, is taking complex problems and simplifying them for the audience. We pride ourselves in our factual accuracy. Because, quite often, when you simplify something, you can actually lose context, but we're always incredibly careful not to do that.' Rousseau is not convinced: 'But of course, this is a key problem. As she acknowledges elsewhere, it's much more complicated than that. Simplifying things doesn't always do the cause a favour, as it encourages a simplistic understanding of a complex issue', Rousseau said in 2016.

A production team usually chooses just five or six key points to get their main story across in an hour-long documentary. I asked Ralling how they decided on the most important points in such a complex set of issues. 'When we're structuring the documentary, we describe the problem', she said. 'We look at why this is so important. We would have been looking at global obesity figures, the rise in child obesity rates and then we look at what the solutions could be and give the audience a call to action.' The narrative must take the viewer on an arc through a series of sequences. 'We say, "how are we going to actually illustrate dental health, for example, and how are we going to give people the factually correct information they need, that it's the slow sipping on a sugary drink all day that damages teeth, and also the carbonation?" [We need to say that] a diet drink is as bad for your teeth as a full-sugar Coke. So we have to think very carefully: "how are we going to make this a powerful sequence that people aren't going to forget?" Well, we're going to take Jamie into a hospital and take him into the operating theatre and he's going to witness one of 24,000 children a year who has their teeth pulled out.' Collins explained it further: 'When we talk about what we do with Jamie, we talk about how we have to offer a way out, we have to offer something that is actionable, a way that people can feel moved and do something about it. They can add their voice to the crowd and so in that respect we're really pleased with it.'

In every TV programme, in every news story, in every article, it's all about the human story: without people in your 'top line', it simply won't engage the reader – or so the mantra is repeated by editors. Collins explained how to tread the delicate balance of using real stories to shock audiences out of their complacency: 'Our position right from the start of the show was, "it's not all your fault." To say it's her fault, that she's a bad mother, is really, really over-simplifying it. There's a whole range of really complex issues that are about the environment we live in that makes it really difficult to give a crap. And most parents do give a crap. The drinks that that kid drank were mango juices. It wasn't gallons of Coke. It was West Indian fruit juices.'

Ralling and Fresh One's team of producers were responsible for casting for the individual storylines. These were then passed on to the executive producer, Zoe Collins. 'When the team first talked to me about tooth decay', Collins told me, 'I went, "meh, I feel I have heard this story." And when I saw those rushes, I thought, "how did I not know this? How is this image so alien to us?" And it's the same with type 2 diabetes. You can become so number blind, so blind to the statistics because they're just so massive that they no longer mean anything to you.' Bringing them down to the individual is about turning a macro story into micro narratives that have emotional impact. Collins said that examples of this in *Sugar Rush* are 'some of the scenes that I'm most proud of ever: the dentist being one of them, and the one with the dietician who lays out what looks like a bog-standard day of food that you would feel pretty good about actually if your children ate all of that – that's five times over the average day of a sugar. So there was really important stuff in there'. I asked Collins if Jamie had to be there, whether we could view that 6-year-old child having five teeth extracted under general anaesthetic and have the same response. Does Jamie Oliver have to show us how to react? 'What Jamie does is he brings a lot of emotion to it. He's a father himself, so when he watches a child being put under a local anaesthetic, his presence makes it more powerful. Could we just interview the doctors and then shoot the sequence? Yes, we could. Jamie also delivers a lot of the facts to the audience in a way that they trust.'

The story was mired with an evolving, controversial science. One of the first things they did was to bring in a science producer. 'We got her across all the assumptions we'd made', Collins told me. 'Her job was to drill down and bring back to us the rock solid [facts]. As you start to dig deeper with a science producer, a lot of the stuff tends to fall away. It doesn't mean that it's not true, it's that if we want to err on the side of caution, and we really do when we're with Jamie, then these are our absolute undeniable truths. We talk about these with Jamie: the undeniable truth with *School Dinners* that he can always come back to is that kids at school should eat food that enhances their education; in *Sugar Rush*, it is that too much sugar makes you ill, so let's keep coming back to our undeniable truths. So that's where the stories started off.'

A powerful Jamie narrative is about a journey into the unknown. *Sugar Rush* was a one-off documentary which journeyed through one of the most complex and multi-layered issues affecting societies across the world. It had to be hard-hitting without being simplistic, and confronting without leaving the audience feeling defeated. I reminded Zoe Collins that when she first told me about the prospect of the show in our second meeting in 2015 it was going to be a new *School Dinners*-style series, complete with the 'will he/wont' he succeed?' jeopardy narrative. 'We could have developed more jeopardy or a different actionable narrative for him', she said, 'but a one-off is really a report, a polemic. Even Jay [Hunt, then Chief Creative Officer of Channel 4] calls it a polemic. For a while on the commissioning sheet, it was called Jamie's Polemic'.

Signe Rousseau told me in 2016 that the Jamie Oliver philosophy is quickly accessible: 'everyone knows what Jamie believes in. It's a short cut, a message.'

She compared him to Dr Oz, the Turkish American cardiothoracic surgeon and professor at Columbia University, and author and television personality who has become 'America's doctor'. He is, she says, 'someone they have grown to trust to distil complex information and deliver it in a way that is less intimidating than having to do the work of thinking these things through yourself. But even if you aren't selling nonsense like some of the pseudoscientific stuff that Oz peddles, and even if your intentions are only well-meaning (as I believe Jamie Oliver's are), the other possible consequence of that is – ironically for something designed as a 'call to action' – a particular kind of complacency in the public at large when it comes to political literacy. We need to encourage more difficult thinking about complex subjects, and I worry that Jamie Oliver's model rather promises that someone else will do it for them.'

When I met up with Zoe Collins a couple of weeks after *Sugar Rush* was first screened in the UK and Australia, she was clearly proud of the show. She knows now how to get the best out of Jamie: 'He's good at catchphrases', she laughed. As we talked about the newspaper headlines and the 'noise' on social media following the programme, something had changed since we first spoke three years before. 'It's not about the show, it's about the ripples', she told me. 'I quite like that. We see our role as agitators and I think it's done its job. We hit our targets on the petition and we're in conversation with the government around an obesity strategy which Cameron says he intends to prioritise.' She said that it felt like 'a bit of a legacy piece for [Jamie]': using his considerable influence, the documentary had Oliver talking to 'all the right people' including many in charge of restaurant chains who would join Jamie's Italian in implementing a voluntary sugar tax. Tesco, one of the most powerful British supermarkets, removed some of the sugary drinks from their shelves, while others were considering 'no guilt lanes', stripping out the treats from the checkout. Lucozade-Ribena was the first brand to announce huge sugar reduction as a result of the campaign, with Coca-Cola next in line. Collins was not going to accept responsibility for this shift, but agreed that the programme had created debate and that debate can be a catalyst. 'But other things have to be in place at the same time', she added: 'it has to be timely.'

In 2016, I asked Signe Rousseau if she thought Oliver might see himself as our moral guide: 'He fashions himself as one', she agreed, 'and there are plenty who are willing to confer that status onto him because it lessens the burden of having to be their own moral guide.' But she doesn't deny him that position: 'In terms of these questions about authority and expertise, I don't think that Jamie Oliver should not be involved. It's not so much about Jamie Oliver. It's more about what the success of a campaign like his tells everyone else about the roles we confer upon people. It's a tricky thing because it's easy for me to say on the one hand celebrity chefs shouldn't be interfering with people's everyday choices, where clearly some people benefit very much from external guidance, whether it's from a doctor or a Jamie Oliver. I'm not denying that at all.'

Jo Ralling was with Oliver when he gave evidence to the Health Select Committee in the House of Commons ahead of the surprise decision by then chancellor George Osborne to impose a sugar tax on fizzy drinks. Ralling was moved: 'If you want to see the power of Jamie in action, what he did in that room that day was extraordinary. It was a flawless delivery of the facts, and his passion and his commitment came over. We mocked up some drink bottles and showed them with the teaspoons on [to show how much sugar was in each portion], and you could visibly see change. You could feel it in the room that day.' She said it was remarkable to be part of shifting public opinion: 'I think there was a moment when the dentists, the doctors, the NGOs, Cancer Research, Diabetes UK, were all calling for the same things. They were all going, "we now support a sugar tax, we now support a ban on marketing and promotion of sugary products…" So, we're lining up the opposition. The media were covering it, and I think there was a moment when George Osborne probably realised that this, as taxes go, it probably wasn't going to be too unpopular, that, actually, we'd shifted opinion.' Collins, Ralling and the team were thrilled with the outcome. 'I think we were expecting them to say, "If the food industry doesn't do something, then we will put a sugary drinks tax in"', said Ralling. 'We thought they'd use it as a sort of carrot towards reformulation. But they didn't. They went for it. And it was an amazing day.'

Osborne announced the new tax with an unusually personal explanation (accompanied by an interview with Oliver punching the air): 'I am not prepared to look back at my time here in this Parliament, doing this job, and say to my children's generation: "I'm sorry – we knew there was a problem with sugary drinks. We knew it caused disease. But we ducked the difficult decisions and we did nothing. "' Many Britons didn't even know that Osborne had children. He had adopted the mantle of personal crusader and, for a moment, he looked like a mortal, a father, a Jamie.

The tax would be levied on the volume of sugary drinks produced and exported, and the delay of two years was deliberately designed to give companies enough time to alter their recipes using less sugar. But post-Brexit, the impact is unclear in terms of how it will affect British business. The tax would become enshrined in law in April 2018, but pressure mounted from the food industry: 'The whole thing should be paused', Ian Wright, director general of industry lobby group the Food and Drink Federation (FDF) – whose members include the makers of Coca-Cola, Pepsi and Tango – told *The Guardian* newspaper in July 2016: 'Confidence in the consumer goods market is very fragile and the government has promised not to impose any new burden on industry.' The food and drink sector accounts for 16 per cent of UK manufacturing, and of the 400,000 people employed in UK food and drink manufacturing, one in four are from other EU countries.

Rousseau was sceptical about the tax: 'One of the issues in global debates about sugar taxes is that while it may be tackling one contributor to obesity and diabetes, it also simplifies the issue to make everything about sugar, which it isn't', she said in 2016. 'Demonising sugar in the end may not be as effective as working harder to get people to limit how much [they consume] of everything. Studies continue to confirm that unless you are diabetic and therefore sugar is literally toxic to your system, when it comes to weight-loss, low-carb is not much more effective than calorie restriction. So the sugar story is more of a heuristic for cutting calories than it is a solid scientific necessity.'

Six months after Osborne's announcement of the sugar tax, a survey carried out by Censuswide for the sugar-free drink Hey Like Wow revealed that over a third of the 1,000 people questioned supported it, including nearly half of those aged 16–24 (FoodBevMedia, 2016). Parents of younger children were less in favour, with almost half of the parents of children aged between 14 and 15 and over a third of parents of children aged between 9 and 11 saying that they did not agree with the tax. Ralling says that there's more work to do: she went on to head up the Sugar Smart Campaign in 2016, which aimed to give UK towns a toolkit to engage public services and tens of thousands of locals in becoming 'sugar smart'. Stickers on vending machines in schools and hospitals with information about how much sugar is in each drink, and Jamie Oliver-style cooking classes were available. With leisure centres, the university, several tourist attractions and the local hospital trust buying into the campaign, Brighton was the first Sugar Smart city in the world, and it was rolled out across 55 cities in the UK as the Food Foundation did with Ministry of Food. 'We're witnessing a generation which has lost any close affinity to food and where it's come from', explained Ralling. 'They don't cook anymore. It's all very well saying we want food education back in our primary schools, but the teachers can't cook. The young teachers in their twenties have got no idea how to pick a knife up, chop an onion and cook some mince. These skills have been lost by an entire generation.'

Ralling is very clear about where the fault lies: 'I think it's the responsibility of the food industry. I think the fact that the cheapest foods on our supermarket shelves are the ones that are highest in calories is the responsibility of the food industry.' She believes that while a sugar tax is crucial, a plan of action can't wait: 'Sugar is such a cheap ingredient, and that's where legislation will kick in. But the legislation will take years to kick in and we don't have years. In the next year, 24,000 kids will have their teeth pulled out and 7,000 people will have a limb amputated. We've just hit four million people in this country having type 2 diabetes. They believe there are another six million people who are in a pre-diabetic condition. We can turn the tide, we can reverse their condition. And I absolutely agree, it's the most hard-to-reach populations that we have to get to. That's where Jamie can help.'

But the closing of Jamie Oliver's Food Foundation in 2019, probably due to the falling revenues of his restaurant business, which had injected a crucial sum, meant that Ralling's Sugar Smart Campaign was transferred to Sustain's management. The annual report said that the trustees had decided 'to wind down the activities for JOFF within the next 12 months', adding that 'the charity is considered to have fulfilled its original purpose'.

In her 2012 book, Signe Rousseau says, 'It is the literal and figurative confla-tion of food consumption and economic consumerism that ensures the cultural capital of the chef, who, unlike other public figures with enormous cultural capi-tal and economic influence like film stars and footballers, has the ability to influ-ence the most mundane and necessary of daily tasks.' I asked her if the Odyssey narrative worked, and if so, for whom? 'I'd imagine Jamie would argue that his various missions are precisely about giving people tools to satisfy actual needs (health primarily) in order to fuel stronger "spiritual" satisfaction (happiness, productivity, hope, etc). What Jamie himself gets out of that is perhaps indeed some quest fulfilment – or failure – though I guess that depends on how one interprets his altruism.'

Zoe Collins understands that she and the team are all on a journey with their construction of Jamie. She told me in 2018: 'I think a place we've got to with Jamie these days is we understand that Jamie has a job to do for us. Jamie talks about it – we both do – as a job. We do all of the hard work and bring back the easy solutions for the audience. And nobody wants to know what it took to do it.' She said that it was about offering the viewer 'the easy answers for you to adapt. Certainly, some of our best books have done that'. She added that time, money and health are what they understand as the key drivers for the audience: 'We'd always say that everything that we've ever done is part of a mission of sorts which is how to help people lead a healthier, happier life with food.' She thinks that there is a tension between the 'chop 'n' cook' and the campaigning shows which can make some people feel 'hectored' while others 'feel a lack of complexity or compelling narrative'. She said that she and the team are clear that one is 'a service we're providing and the other is 'definitely the big campaign that we're driving.'

Part Three

Intangible memories

How we lost our food culture is a very British story of class, power, religion and revolution. Read food historian Colin Spencer's 2002 encyclopaedia of British food for the astonishing history of the last thousand years – but in this chapter, we fill in the gaps in our cultural memory. Spencer believes that food culture is born from 'a combination of planned accidents: it absorbs influences from wherever it attracts. English food has already borrowed from every country that Englishmen have visited and enjoyed'. But if we try to unpick the development of post-industrial and pre-millennium food culture, instead of celebrating a rich British heritage fed to monarchs and their courts by traders and adventurers, we focus only on the near past and how 'meat and two veg' has become the norm in the home. Spencer suggests that we look back to before the Reformation of 1534, when Henry VIII divorced Catherine of Aragon to marry Anne Boleyn, becoming the first monarch to leave the Roman Catholic Church, assume total authority and introduce Protestantism as the new state religion.

Before Protestantism, Britain had a very different food culture: for those of a certain class, food wasn't just cooking, it was theatre. Spencer describes the royal feasts of the Anglo-Norman thirteenth and fourteenth centuries as both sculptural and ludic: 'Cooked peacocks were placed back inside their befeathered skins, live birds fluttered out of a cooked pastry shell, acrobats and dwarves leapt out of giant puddings. Great pastry castles were surrounded by green sward with pheasants, partridges and doves, all cooked and edible but painted to look as if alive.' Food was about appearance and show. Interestingly, the size of the portion was directly linked to the social position of those at the table, with the monarch's family eating the best and most at the high table, and guests seated in order of importance. The most expensively spiced dishes were reserved for the monarchy, and the smallest and meanest portion of the feast was served to the lowest of the order.

By the end of the fourteenth century, and after almost 200 years of civil war, the emergence of small landowners spearheaded the kind of rural peasant cuisine that Italy, Spain and France had already developed based around a self-sufficient economy of produce. Even so, family festive feasts were still modelled on the food of the elite, with stories of lavish dishes passed down from those who worked in the royal households.

It was the Enclosures Acts between 1750 and 1850 which most food historians believe were the death knell on Britain's rich history of food. Fields were enclosed with hedges, walls, fences and roads, and woodland disappeared as it was given over to pasture. New technology raised yields and offered new income streams for landowners, as the ruling classes, nobility and new middle class divided up between them most of the land in Britain. Commons once used for the cottager's cattle for grazing and for gathering fuel for the fire were now owned by the landlord, who could charge the cottager for a privilege he had held for centuries.

By the end of the eighteenth century, 80 per cent of Britain's nine million inhabitants were living in the countryside, a quarter of which was owned by nobility. But a new pattern was emerging: without land to grow vegetables or space to graze animals, many of the poorest began to look to the cities and colonies for their future, losing their connection with the food from their own land. Migrants took their rural recipes to the Americas, while the illiterate poor quickly forgot the recipes of their grandmothers who now lived far from their new homes. Work in the new factories of the industrial age was more like slavery, and the average diet was reduced to bread, jam, tea and sugar.

History reveals a surprisingly stable British food culture before the Enclosures Acts, a long period of food from the land and foods and influences from other lands. The great British dinner of meat and two veg has a long history. In the eighteenth century, it would have been meat 'grown' locally, if not on the country estate or land of the cook's husband, and seasoned sharply, according to the recipe books of Mrs Elizabeth Raffald (for example, *The Experienced English Housekeeper* [1769]). By this time, there was a profusion of good produce regularly served with meat and fish, including onions, leeks, garlic and shallots, as well as cardoons and rampion, a radish-like root vegetable eaten raw, providing the kind of flavour we don't usually associate with British cooking. Spencer suggests that this is perhaps because the literature of the day did not fully describe the detail of the ingredients: 'if pork sausages are mentioned', he wrote, 'we are not told that they were flavoured with spinach, rosemary, sage, oysters, shallots, onions, cloves and mace.' The equivalent in Italian, Spanish and French literary culture of the time, however, would certainly have done so. The question is why.

Spencer suggests that the tension between Roman Catholicism and Protestantism is central to understanding Britain's relationship with French cooking, which has, arguably, dominated haute cuisine up until the last ten years. It would be some time before we began to idolize Italian cooking in the same way, but perhaps the longing comes from the same root: Rome and Catholicism represented all that we might have been had the Reformation not ruptured our culinary culture. Post-Reformation, Protestant food writers like Hannah Glasse were vehemently anti-French (read 'anti-Catholic'). Spencer explains: 'The Englishness [...] represented values of freedom, an elected Parliament, an English Church free of foreign domination, food without taint, fresh from the English soil, while food in the French manner was something quite insidious, almost, she makes us feel, a contamination, a creeping infection, to be much feared and halted if at all possible.'

Street food was for peasants and the working class. The Victorian high street was packed with travelling traders in anything from sheep's trotters, baked potatoes, pies and hot peas to cordials, coffee, tarts and cakes and, from the 1830s, the first sandwiches: a former coffee stall owner found that selling loaves filled with ham and mustard outside a theatre in Westminster was a much better business proposition and gave rise to a new industry of post-concert hawkers in London's West End.

The relationship between the food of the land, the table and the family had broken down in many households by the Victorian urbanization period, and the social observer and journalist of the time, Henry Mayhew, is a useful witness to how this affected eating habits among the classes. He interviewed street sweepers who had never seen a wheat field and had no idea of its connection with the bread that was now an everyday side order for most of the urban poor. Spencer describes the daily diet of a Manchester operative in 1832, who would rise at 5 am and head to the mill, go home again at 8 am for a breakfast of tea and bread and then work again until dinner at noon: a high-fat, high-carb diet of potatoes with melted lard or butter poured over them, and perhaps a bit of bacon if he was lucky. Work then continued until 7 pm when he would go home for bread and tea before bed. This subsistence diet was by 1867 typical of the daily intake of 24,100,000 working-class people in Britain, and the shop keepers, foremen and supervisors who were slightly more skilled than those whose work they oversaw. Malnutrition, needless to say, was rife.

By the mid-twentieth century, the British palate had become used to the limits of the time, with home-grown meat and vegetables providing the staples of the Second World War and post-war diet. Unlike the Mediterraneans, whose food had been part of a stable, unchanging food culture for thousands of years, Britain's cold climate and geography meant that living off the land was dull but hearty, with heavy meats and big, thick sauces to keep off the chill. By the 1970s, the devastating combination of European efficiency directives on farmers, which destroyed many habitats and countryside features, and the introduction of fast food in supermarkets and high streets almost wiped out any remaining interest in food culture in the average household.

But the depth of our culinary culture and our history of helping ourselves to foods we fancy lingers on in the national psyche. 'People always mention the influence of Elizabeth David from the 1950s onward', Spencer told me. 'But we have always loved spicy dishes: ginger became a firm favourite early on.' He explained how we were heavily influenced by the Persian cuisine (sweet and sour, and the use of flowers in cooked dishes) from that time, unlike Paris who eschewed such foreign influences. 'Our national culture is one that has always borrowed from other cultures and then anglicised the influences. British India from 1700 on brought in ketchups and curries, and just about every cookery book must have recipes for them thereafter. Some cultures that came here tended to be insular, but that's because of persecution. If the English decided they liked a flavour they took it over and made it their own.' Thorogood agrees: 'Clearly, it's about an immigrant population and how spices can travel and how we can flavour meat.'

Sharing the memories

The story of British, American and Australian food in particular, is the story of immigration. London is, by 2020, a centre of culinary excellence, with 67 Michelin-starred restaurants and 35 awarded the Bib Gourmand, a sign of more imaginative excellence without the constrains of the award's starrier brother. It is the capital's diversity that has put it on the global map, along with its commitment to excellence and ethics in its produce. But outside the capital, British towns and cities have responded in various ways to their small ethnic communities, moulding to change and embracing the rich and diverse opportunities, or resisting their influences and pushing them to the edge of the town where the poorer immigrant communities can be found. What binds each ethnic community is the food of the old country and this is what attracts or repels their indigenous neighbours.

This is not new: around 3,700 Italians came to South Wales from the poorest areas of Italy during the wave of immigration to the Welsh coalfields between 1851 and 1911, more than to any other area in Britain. Though Italians had also been settling in London, Manchester and Liverpool, they had a profound impact on this more parochial area of Britain. The Italian coffee shops of Swansea and Llanelli became unlikely pockets of sophistication in Britain: my mother and my aunt would tell me how, as post-war teenagers, they would sport voluminous skirts, which they made themselves from newly available materials, and sling-backs seen only in Sofia Loren movies, and head out to share a sundae in downtown Llanelli. 'I'd have a knickerbocker glory', my aunt Eirwen Williams remembered. The Italian ice creams and coffee were the tastes and smells that the Italian coal miners brought from home, while for the local teenagers in 1950s Llanelli, it was the desire for 'cool', which an association with this more stable food culture could confer, that prompted their engagement. Seventy years later, the Italians are winning awards for Wales: the Conti family, who arrived in the nearby town of Lampeter from Bardi in the Northern Italian hills above Parma in 1946, won the top prize in the dairy section of the 2016 *delicious.* magazine Produce Awards. The judges said that their ice cream, made using local organic milk and cream, and sweetened with organic raw cane sugar, was 'straight-up, plain, "traditional". It's flavoured with nothing at all, not even vanilla'.

While Italian ice cream has become part of how Wales sells itself to the increasing number of food tourists who are interested in the produce that this tiny country now boasts, Lukasz Swiatek from the University of Sydney says that dumplings have become part of how Poland sells itself to its own people, as it attempts to lure them home. Born in Poland, Swiatek is one of the millions of Poles who have left their country as economic migrants. He told me in 2017 that he has witnessed a fascinating rise in dumpling restaurants in the old country: 'It's not that they have authentically or nationally Polish food, like goulash, but that the designs are Polish, the colours are Polish, the décor. Even some of the waitresses wear national costume! I think that some food can be complemented with the creation of texts that accompany these foods.' I asked him if these restaurants were created for tourists, but he believes that they play a much more important role in reinforcing the Polish sense of self at a time of mass migration and instability. 'All Poles like dumplings', he told me, 'but they are also genuinely concerned about national identity, and that their cultural memory transmitted through food might be in jeopardy.'

Food is much more than the melange of flavours and textures we put in our mouths. For TV chef Ken Hom, it is about who you are and where you come from, and it is stored in the heart. 'Food memory is what your mum made you', he told me, 'and what your earliest taste buds and smells are. And for me, it's always going home from school, and as soon as I walk in the door, my mum would throw ginger, garlic and spring onion into the hot wok. And that smell is incredible. I mean, until the day I die I will always remember that smell as home-cooked food, and love.' Television understands this and plays with its meta-language to pull an endless progression of ideas for food programmes out of the bag.

The late TV chef, Anthony Bourdain, explained that this was what drove the massive audiences to Food Network's endless stream of 'food porn'. He told Ron Rosenbaum in the *Smithsonian Magazine* in 2014: 'There are huge populations of people who move from the country to the city who, for them, I guess Food Network is nesting. It's evoking a family life, a kitchen table that they probably never had, or maybe only had briefly. I think that's an international thing. But now I don't know because people don't really cook on TV anymore. There're very few shows where they actually dump and stir. Now it's doing stuff like having contests and [...] even the ones where they're actually cooking, it's more about interpersonal drama, like a reality show.'

Nick Thorogood explained how food memory can make what Barthes called 'mythological treasures' into a ratings winner, like Food Network's 2012 *Bake with Anna Olson*, and talked me through an episode in which Olson begins by making ladyfingers: 'It's a level of patisserie or baking that you think, "I've never baked those, but I get it". And in the next segment, she takes the same batter mixture and makes them into Madeleines. And I know what they are. But finally, she ends up making a cheesecake by using the original ladyfingers and lining the tin. Now this is really fascinating. I'm almost certainly never going to make ladyfingers. I hate those. I always fail on my meringues. But because I've eaten boudoir biscuits and trifle sponge fingers, I can imagine what they'll be like. I probably won't make them, but I'll probably think about buying the cake from the supermarket.'

Thorogood believes that the growth of a food culture is directly related to the development of cultural memory, which can only happen over time. He said that the instructional cookery shows of the 1950s in Australia and Britain were limited by how much they could reference: 'It's one of the reasons I believe that wine programming has never worked', he told me. 'If I put a slice of chocolate cake, lemon cake, and coffee cake on the screen and say, "mmm, that's the best coffee cake I've ever tasted!" your food memory would allow you to understand what the presenter was doing and imagine that flavour. Whereas if I said, "and I've got a Merlot, and a Shiraz, and a Cabernet", you're just sitting there thinking, "It's just red wine. I can't tell the difference." You don't have that nuance. And I think part of that is what's happened with television programmes.' He added that memory has to have some imagination too: 'it's about how quickly we learn to understand whether we like those tastes and then [how] we expect to see them reflected in our culture.' The success of television or any other medium looking to engage its audience is in tapping into that food memory. 'I've done food programming for major terrestrial broadcasters', Thorogood told me, 'and the research comes back in the same way: it is the vicarious experience. It's the food porn.'

This hunger to look is unlikely to translate into cooking, yet Bourdieu would still call it an amassing of cultural capital: 'Take *The Barefoot Contessa* [Food Network, 2002–present] a show that is a more entertaining version of Delia', said Thorogood. 'Ina [Garten] teaches you how to cook, but it's all dressed up in this fabulous Hamptons lifestyle. So you watch from an entertainment perspective, thinking. "I could have a bit of that." '

Media academic Louise Fitzgerald doesn't agree: 'I don't think it is as easy as this', she told me when I showed her Thorogood's theory. 'It is still about aspiration which is connected to consumption which is also tied to good citizenship. Aspiration is aligned with morality and cultural capital, all of which is bound up with the idea of entertainment in this instance. Cookery shows used to be instructional, with a familiar instructor telling the audience how to make food. The move away from this format from instructional to aspirational happened at the same time that consumption was seen as an integral factor for the formation of identity and the rise of leisure time for the middle classes. As food became a marker of cultural capital, so the formats of the programmes changed.'

She noted that as the status of food as a sanctioned mainstream pursuit and a marker of class mobility grew in the late 1990s, commentators pointed to an accompanying shift in food media: 'There was a conspicuous move towards higher production values within the programmes (including soft focus close-ups of sumptuous ingredients), and an inclusion of a stylish revision of the overall look of the channel and brand', she told me. 'Programming was punctuated by a common "stamp", a slow-motion sequence that featured an enticingly ripe and glistening cherry falling languidly through a spray of water into an awaiting glass bowl. And a cohort of younger, attractive presenters for whom food preparation was not only a leisure activity but an explicitly sensual bodily pleasure – Nigella Lawson epitomises this shift.'

The Food TV audience is vast now and crosses the class divide. But at Food Network, it is largely a blue-collar, C2D audience, and I asked Thorogood if the explosion in ratings is because this demographic simply watches more TV. He agreed, but told me why he thought food was such a popular choice of viewing rather than any other lifestyle subject: 'There are some universal themes that seem to really resonate with everyone – burgers, barbequing, beef, that's something we all get.' I asked him whether a shared cultural memory could be about anything; at Food Network, he told me, it was cupcakes that attracted the audience: 'For us, they are absolutely ludicrously huge.' He says it's because everyone eats cake. 'We've all had a little cake, whether it was a fairy cake if you're British, or a cupcake if you're American. Something more *chichi* for France or Italy, *natas* in Portugal… There are some really strong universal things.' Who would have known that the humble cupcake could be so full of meaning that it could attract such enormous Food Network audiences and yet divide the academic community?

Fitzgerald said that there was a 'massive backlash against the cupcake', and referred me to Hunt and Phillipoy, who suggest in ' "Nanna style": The countercultural politics of retro femininities' (2014), that the cupcake phenomenon was a nod to 'retro fashions referencing 1940s and 1950s femininity' [and] 'the growing popularisation of crafting and cooking'. 'Many of the 'old-fashioned' practices of domesticity that had been critiqued and rejected by second-wave feminism', said Fitzgerald, 'are being re-imagined as simultaneously nostalgic and politically progressive choices for women (and, sometimes, for men).

The complexity about Food TV is the layering of aspiration, entertainment and the shared memories of the audience. 'It's very aspirational but it's also fantasy, and that's where it ties in with food memories', Thorogood told me. 'So, when Ina or Nigella makes the most beautiful pavlova laden with cream and fruit and drizzled with raspberry liqueur and chocolate shavings, or whatever it might be, you remember it. You've had a meringue or you've had a pavlova. It may not taste as good as this but your experience and your thrill and your aspiration and vicarious enjoyment is heightened because a little bit of you can remember how nice it was when you had it.' Thorogood has proved that working with food memories means moving food across class and gender: 'Something like *Man v. Food* or *Diners, Drive-ins and Dives* [Food Network, 2006–present] is just indulgent entertainment fun, but when he bites into his burger and says, "this is the best burger ever" and it's the size of his head, the truth is that you might be sitting there with some cheese on toast but you can remember that flavour and that feeling.'

As 'delight' has driven the storytelling of British TV food, the experience for the viewer has become more immersive or *haptic*, as if we could taste the food ourselves. The smell of Jamie's lamb has us salivating in our own sitting rooms as we consume the powerful message that cooking a piece of well-sourced meat slowly, fragrantly, with fresh rosemary, will deliver us not just delicious tasting food but a better lifestyle.

But delight is also about the freshness of flavours, colourful foodstuffs, exotic peoples and an escape to somewhere better. From the comfort of our sitting rooms, we can not only travel to places we had only dreamed of, but also gather cultural capital about those places through their food culture. We can broaden our minds through food programmes on India, Thailand, Mexico and learn about different cultures through the way they eat. Food TV is now about much more than just how to cook pasta: it is about the people, the country and the culture. Food TV is no longer the chop 'n' cook format we saw with Fanny and Jonny and *The Galloping Gourmet* (BBC One, 1968–71): with *Jamie's Great Italian Escape* (Channel 4, 2005) and *Nigellissima* (BBC Two, 2012), we have become anthropologists, cooks and cultural experts at the click of a remote.

What we learn about the world is often mediated by the filters of colonial rhetoric that British television finds it so hard to avoid, and by the representation as 'exotic' of different cultures in a way that obscures the hardship and the relations of production. Alison Leitch calls the trend to romanticise the past 'Tuscanopia' in her 2013 chapter in Carole Counihan and Penny Van Esterik's *Food and Culture: A Reader*, in which peasant cuisine and picturesque rurality have become 'key fantasy spaces of modern alienation'. She is writing about the Slow Food movement and critiques the imperialist nostalgia that 'sentimentalises peasant traditions within and outside Europe', comparing the movement to the 'European civilising mission of the nineteenth century'. Ottolenghi, Ken Hom, Madhur Jaffrey and, most recently, Nadiya Hussein, the *Bake Off* winner who travelled to her parents' homeland of Bangladesh in *Chronicles of Nadiya*, have all looked to the street food cultures of Israel, Hong Kong, India and Bangladesh to find their identities, romanticising and often obscuring, as Leitch says, the realities of the life that their families left behind.

Paula Trafford was Ken Hom's producer on the 2012 BBC Two show *Exploring China: A Culinary Adventure*, as well as the More4 series in the same year, *Ottolenghi's Mediterranean Feast*. I asked her in 2013 how television negotiates the problematic relationship with real life in travelogues which almost always feature peasant food and working conditions. She answered by explaining the process of getting *Victoria Wood's A Nice Cup of Tea* commissioned the following year for BBC One: 'The process started with a proposal to the broadcaster who suggested themes that we might include', she said. 'We talked about layers: one would be history and one would be popular culture about how tea had infused our culture. Of course, Victoria Wood was a perfect example of that: Mrs Overalls was always carrying a tray of something. Tea features in her comedy in *Acorn Antiques*, *Dinner Ladies* – in all her sketches.' The programme was commissioned and assigned a budget which then had to be pared down to find what Trafford called 'key elements'. They decided that they had to go to China and India. 'We wanted to go to one of the places where tea was first grown and discovered. We talked about India and the British occupation of India, and how tea and the opium wars were intertwined, so history was an important part of it. But with BBC One, it's got to be history-light so it's not too heavy. So you think about those layers.' She knew that she wanted to include Calcutta 'because it's the thirstiest city in India', she told me. 'All those things we decided we wanted to do we identified in our research period. It was a small team – me as exec, an archivist who mainly worked on the British film, a PD [producer-director], an AP [assistant producer], a China-based AP and an India based fixer.' Getting access to tell stories about people in different countries means going local, and producers will hire 'fixers', local people who not only know how to get access, but also what the foreign producer is looking for. 'I hired an Indian fixer who got access for us to film with the Singhpo tribe in Assam because it was their opium that helped crack the tea trade in the opium wars', Trafford told me.

In consultation with the broadcaster, they worked out 'the most interesting things to follow'. I asked whether those conversations included discussions about how to avoid romanticising nostalgia or imposing an idea that might be more about the audience's fantasy. I suggested that with Ottolenghi, her team had romanticised Israeli street food, constructing a story about who modern Israelis are through the way they eat. 'When we discussed the idea of *Tea* or *Ottolenghi*, there was a layer of cultural exchange in all of these programmes', Trafford told me. 'When Victoria goes to the tea plantation, she picks tea with ladies in Assam and there's a cultural exchange of sorts. She said, "how long can you work in these plantations before they put you out to grass?" and the guy said, "58." And she said, "oh god! I'm 59. I wouldn't be able to get a job here." It's not right on the nose', admitted Trafford. 'When you pitch an idea and discuss the layers that you expect to find in that programme, that's the point at which you have a discussion about whether you're going to access communities. One of the questions we did discuss was, how do we define our Britishness? How do we explain that? What does it mean to be British? How do you explain that in a TV programme? It's quite hard. But one of the ways you do that is by making a cup of tea. It was something that for some reason said something about who we are in Britain. We're not very good at talking in Britain, so we put the kettle on in a crisis. It's a short hand for offering some kind of communication. If you want a gossip, it'll be over a cup of tea. If someone dies, it's, "let's have a nice cup of tea." As Victoria Wood says in the programme, "you never say, let's have a horrible cup of tea." It's ridiculous, really. We use it as a way of not having to say too much. It's a device to let us have a gossip or a cry or a bitch. All these things are easier to do over tea. It's seeped into our society in a way that's quite extraordinary. So those are the kind of conversations we were having about how we translate that into a TV programme.'

The representation of other countries and their cultures is secondary to most of the TV chefs who use them as their backdrop; Jamie Oliver's explorations of Italy, America and Mexico are a metaphor for his personal challenges: his success at home led him first to go to his spiritual home of Italy, to give thanks and to meditate on the meaning of his life before ramping it up for the campaigning years. After Channel 4's *Jamie's School Dinners*, he had to go West, to try his Jamie-ness in the bigger pond of the US, and in Mexico, he found the Holy Grail of the sugar tax, which he could bring home to save the UK from the giants of the food and drink industry. For Nigella, it is Italy where she becomes a better, more Italian version of her domestic goddess-self, the person she dreamed of being as a student of Italian literature. In Italy, she is Nigellissima. But rarely do we find our TV chefs dining at the Michelin-starred restaurants or their equivalents: our tour guides know where to find the best street food in town – any town. Real food is about the food of the people, and access is by them alone.

Perhaps the most enduring fetishization of street food is evidenced most spectacularly in Italy, home to what researchers have proved to be the healthi-est food in the world, with its mix of culture and blend of nutrients. Professor Lorenzo Donini and his team from La Sapienza University in Rome recently concluded a thirty-year study on the components of the Mediterranean diet, drawing up a five-tiered pyramid made up of the ideal combination of food groups, locally sourced and eaten together. The conclusion is that it's culture, civilisation and company that is good for the heart: it's the stuff of Dolmio advertisements, but, like the food that the Dolmio Mamma makes, it is a story which calls upon a nostalgia that obscures the reality of life in modern-day Italy.

The late New York chef, Anthony Bourdain, suggested that what he called the Old World had finally embedded the essence of its food culture in the unstable New World: 'We're just catching on', he told Ron Rosenbaum in the *Smithsonian Magazine* in 2014. 'We are changing societally, and our values are changing, so that we are becoming more like Italians and Chinese and Thais and Spaniards, where we actually think about what we're eating, what we ate last night, and what we're considering eating tomorrow. When I grew up in the '60s, we'd go to see a movie, then we would go to a restaurant. And we would talk about the movie we just saw. Now, you go right to dinner and you talk about the dinner you had last week and the dinner you're going to have next week, while you're taking pictures of the dinner you're having now. That's a very Italian thing. A lot of the sort of hypocrisy and silliness and affectation of current American food culture is just fits and starts, awkwardly and foolishly growing into a place where a lot of older cultures have been for quite some time.'

Meanwhile, in the Old World, the post-millennium generation has recast Mamma as Nonna, as women become more career focussed. As the mother leaves the home, Nonna has added to her skillset arbiter of taste, guardian of the family recipes and keeper of the family values. Eating with Nonna means freshly made pasta in measures that will keep the weight regulated, and family meals that keep the youngest in check and the eldest cared for. The culture will be passed down through the generations as memories are made around a shared experience. Yet obesity among the young, especially in Southern Italy, home of the Mediterranean diet, has become a watchword for junk culture, not just in terms of food, but also in terms of lost family values and a breakdown in civil behaviour.

At Gustolab Food Institute in the centre of Rome, Dr Sonia Massari is in charge of the food studies programmes for international students, mostly from American universities, who come to study the Mediterranean diet. Over the four-week course in cookery, media and nutrition, students are immersed in Italian culture, with trips around the country, interviews with chefs and food producers, as well as long evenings in Roman restaurants to explore for themselves the local food and wine. While the standard tourist trail around Rome's famous monuments is still serving (mostly) excellent pizza slices and home-made gelato, from boho Monti with its superfood cafés and beer and food bars, to Trastevere's Glass Hostaleria – where Michelin-starred chef, Cristina Bowerman has a cool new take on the famous Mediterranean diet – Rome is trying to tell new stories about its food. They come here for the real deal, the heart of food civilisation, but 'authenticity' is not a word Massari will use with her students. 'It doesn't have any meaning for me', she told me in 2017. 'Authenticity has more to do with pride about your origins. For me, it's more about personalized food – it's coming from me, my stories, my world.' She encourages her students to become aware of the storytelling around Italian food, the collective and institutional memory that Italian culture perpetuates, particularly in the interest of the tourist industry and the cultural capital that the oldest, largely unchanged diet in the world can accrue. 'I'm trying to destroy the myth', she said.

I was in Rome to talk to Massari about the message-making about Italian food by British TV chefs. I showed her a 30-second trailer of *Nigellissima*, the BBC series presented by Nigella Lawson. In it, Nigella talks to camera as she picks fruit from a market stall to a Mantovani-style soundtrack. 'Escape with me', Nigella coos. Massari laughs: 'This is about the beauty of Italy. People are really happy there. This is what I think she wants to explain through pasta, through family.' But Massari doesn't recognise the countryside. 'It's like seeing a postcard. I'm not seeing Italy there. I couldn't even recognise the place. For me, it could be Spain. It's just the song that reminds me of the 1950s. We try to avoid this kind of music which is more about the South of Italy. It conveys a specific idea.' The storytelling of Italy in television food programmes is very often about escaping back to a better time, a nostalgic utopian tale of old stone villages where time is slower and values are different. 'It's not my Italy. It's an old-fashioned idea of Italy', she said. 'If the main purpose is to bring tourists, it's very strong. If I'm only a person who wants to know about Italy, it's not what I want to watch.'

Massari believes that it's hard to integrate the reality of the everyday life of Romans with the experience of the tourists: 'Because of the difficult infrastructure of the city, you have a mess. Florence is much worse than Rome. If you get to the centre of the city, you can't survive as a Tuscan person. There's no bridge between the two types of life.' But in a city which relies on tourism for its main source of income, the storytelling has to work. 'If people don't see that romantic image, they won't want to stay in Rome', she said.

As we watched *Jamie's Great Italian Escape*, the myth was further perpetuated. Jamie in a beaten-up old campervan is cruising along the winding corniches of the Amalfi Coast, weaving through mountains towering high above the Tyrrhenian Sea. We see an ancient stone cottage among the hills, wood smoke curling from the chimney and Jamie in the kitchen, sweating over a dish of *linguine con cozze*. The idea that there is always somewhere we can escape to is a powerful aspirational dream. We can leave our world through food, but the space to which we escape does not have to be real: it just has to be better. And even within these spaces, we fantasise about the Italian way of living and eating.

Nonno's house clearly exists because we see it, but it is a place that Sonia Massari told me would be hard to find. 'This is reconstructed for the tourists', she told me. 'It's a myth. If you find this, I want to go there for a vacation! It's very picturesque, but it reinforces the idea of Italy just being about the country-side where people are slow and where the grandmothers and grandfathers live. I don't know why we need to make these postcards.' This romantic representation of poverty grates: 'Most places in Italy were very poor', she reminded me. 'My grandma always says that if we had to go back to the past, it would be so hard. We have so much more now than we had. The storytelling of the past is different to the real past. After the Second World War, it was not so happy.'

Oliver has been much criticised for fetishizing peasant food, or *cucina povera*: 'This phenomenon of Italianisation, which is also evident in Germany, Switzerland, Belgium and the Netherlands, is striking and therefore has drawn considerable interest in food research, particularly in connection with the exam-ination of the nation state, migration and globalisation', writes Thoms, who attempts to trace the outlines of the 'career of Italian cuisine' in Europe in his 2011 article. Thoms concludes that it is this active interference and stereotyping of Italy's regional peasant food which has made it a 'product of the circulation of people, information and goods that fundamentally changed the cooking styles of various European countries.'

Massari is frustrated that Italy is not allowed to be what it really is: 'Italy as the place with the best food in the world is just a package.' She suggested that it is the media storytelling which makes the choices for most tourists. 'Yes, we have artistic monuments in Rome that no one else has in the world. Everywhere you go there's a masterpiece right in front of you! We're very lucky. But the countryside of Rome is beautiful too.' The Amalfi Coast, she said, is sold to the tourists, but towns like Cetara just outside Amalfi, which produces the best anchovies in the country, are ignored. Her students have a list of places that they want to visit, which she questions: 'I say why Cinque-terra? I've been there once in my life. It's an amazing place but there are so many other places to visit. People want to see this fairy-tale place. I can tell you that real life is not like this.'

I asked Massari if perhaps this form of cultural mediation ruptures the idea of authenticity, exposing it for the storytelling that it is, a narrativised utopian dream of a city or countryside that cannot possibly be shared. For Massari, it's about the subjectivity of the personal experience: 'There's one thing that we can touch and feel, and another is the storytelling of it. Cultural mediation will define your approach. From when I'm born to the day I die, I change my food culture because of my environment. The micro-genetic action that you do when you're in a bar is about choices that the manager has already made. Who's making those decisions and why? The most important thing is to look at the cognitive deci-sions. That for me is what authenticity is all about.'

Nutritionists have been studying the effects of the Mediterranean diet in Italy since the American professor Ancel Keys led the Seven Countries Study in the 1950s to assess the relationship between local diet and disease. His ground-breaking work, which helped to establish the epidemiological link between cholesterol and cardiovascular disease, is contested, and he has been accused of cherry picking the seven of the 22 countries in the original study to fit his hypothesis that too much animal fat can lead to heart disease. But his work concluded that the remarkable examples of good health in extreme old age in parts of the Southern Mediterranean could be attributed to a combination of lifestyle and eating a largely vegetarian diet, high in fibre with olive oil, red wine and buffalo mozzarella. In 2016, the diet was again heralded as the best in the world, with researchers at San Diego University returning to the village with Keys and Anna Ferro-Luzzi from Rome's Institute of Nutrition.

UNESCO has rubber-stamped the Mediterranean diet as an example of intan-gible cultural heritage, but Southern Italy where much of the most impressive results were found, has one of the fastest-growing obesity rates among its chil-dren in the world. When the British government decided that the Mediterranean diet would save the NHS from buckling under the weight of rising obesity rates back in 1992, I was working on *Food File* for Channel 4, and producer, Rowena Goldman; presenter, Drew Smith; and our camera crew and I headed for Acciar-oli in Campania, and the village that the experts had concluded was the healthiest in the world. It was simple: the people who lived in this hilltop village pressed their own olive oil, made their own red wine and ate the fit chickens which had spent their happy lives running up and down the hillside. Olive farming was better for the physique than any yoga class, and the long tables set for the community of 300 were the stuff of Jamie Oliver's dreams. Cooking from scratch ingredients that you grew yourself and eating together, preferably under a balmy evening sky, has been proved again and again to reduce the likelihood of demen-tia, heart disease and most cancers.

Twenty-three years on, Campania is still on the Gustolab students' itinerary, and Acciaroli is still telling the story of the Mediterranean diet. It's 'the Italian town where residents live to 100 – and scientists want to know why', according to *The Independent* in 2017. Using the same press release, the *Daily Mail* asked in 2017, 'Could a HERB be the secret to living to 100? Diet rich in rosemary linked to good health and long-life expectancy in Italian village.' 'If you want to live forever, move to this Italian town', said the *New York Post* in 2017.

Massari introduced me to Professor Donini of La Sapienza University in Rome who headed up the thirty-year study. His conclusions were that it was not just the nutritional value of the food and wine, but the conviviality of eating together that had a positive effect on health. But Massari and Donini agree that the long tables of communal family eating are less a part of everyday life now, for Italians and other Mediterraneans. ' "The Mediterranean diet" is a myth in the north of Italy, where meat and dairy are key components of the diet', said Massari. In the poorer south, the famous diet's heartland, the rise in obesity is the starkest in the country. Ancel Keys's diet, Massari told me, was one in which people were able to exchange food from the sea with food from the land: 'They were going back and forth from the sea to the countryside to the mountains. They survived by bartering', she said. 'They were able to get what they needed through hard work. People were preparing their cheese in their bedrooms. Show documentaries [about this] to the tourists and they'll have a totally different idea of the Mediterranean diet. They were able to eat better than rich people in Naples. Rich people were eating more meat, but these people in the south were eating better because they were eating fish, vegetables. Ancel Keys noticed that these people had fewer diseases, but it wasn't that they were better cooks.'

Local produce, artisan-made slow food, and eating and cooking with friends – these are the key messages which represent the new food culture on British television. From Jamie Oliver to Ottolenghi, real food comes from the streets. But Massari told me that this is not the message that American Food TV pumps. Her students are largely from America and as I tested out some of the theses of this book with them at Gustolab in the heart of Rome, I noted that there was an anxiety around food in the classroom. I asked what cooking well meant to them: 'You can be cool. You can impress friends', were the most common answers, although when I asked why some didn't cook, they admitted to a fear of failure – particularly in front of parents. Food is packed with cultural capital for them, and, for them, fear and aspiration were two sides of the same coin. Massari captures their feedback when they leave and told me that overwhelmingly it is not the food that counts most. 'They learn to appreciate wine and how to order it here. And I realise that our students are of the age when they start their first job back in the US. They need a status symbol. The fact that they can buy wine in front of other people, that they can get in front of their boss and say, "I was in Italy, I know how to buy wine," is really important to them.'

A Hungarian food revolution

Budapest: surely one of the most beautiful cities in central Europe with its fairy-tale castles peeking from the Buda hills across the Danube towards Pest, where wide, tree-lined avenues parade designer stores and chic cafés. The Hungarian capital has come a long way since the years of austerity between 1945 and 1989, when the Communist regime with its secret police and bread queues dictated new norms and behaviours in everything from eating to clothing. Budapest's rebirth as a culinary centre, a city break sold increasingly on its food culture, is a story of narratology, intangible food memories and national identity which is largely untold. This chapter explores ideas of authenticity explicit in the romanticised narratives of food and shows how a nation's identity, its sense of self, is re-imagined and re-articulated through culinary culture.

As the Iron Curtain shut out the glitz of western ideology from 1945, Hungary was on its own among the Eastern Bloc to resist the harsh Soviet principles. Although socialism was a way of reaching the utopian goal of an equal society, it struck at the tables of the middle classes whose fine food and manners were seen as bourgeois and therefore anti-party. Perpetuating a nostalgic ideal of family recipes and ancestral identity did not fit with the socialist egalitarian mission to reduce food back to its most basic of functions. One of its first tasks was to limit the distribution of the kind of ingredients which reminded Hungarians of who they had been before 1945. It was a culinary brainwashing programme, and stories are still told of the regular dinners of bread and lard.

After the 1956 Hungarian Revolution against Communist occupation, the government became more lenient and a new era known as Goulash Communism offered a way out of the harsher socialist principles of the past decades. But the collective food memory was already waning as the industrial working-class more than doubled between 1945 and 1960, and the number of agricultural workers decreased. Self-service restaurants became the new normal in eating out, serving basic but bland food such as *spatzle* with salad leaves in a sugar-water-vinegar dressing, potato paprikash with sausage, *fozelek* (a vegetable dish, like Indian dahl made with roux or other flour-based thickeners).

Many stories from the dissenters are preserved in the House of Terror, Budapest's museum to the socialist era housed in the old headquarters of communist Hungary's secret police, where thousands were detained, tried and executed. But Zsuzsanna Clark, author of 'Goulash and solidarity' (2002) who grew up in rural Hungary, says that it wasn't all bad: 'What I remember most was the overriding sense of community and solidarity, a spirit I find totally lacking in my adopted Britain and indeed whenever I go back to Hungary today. With minimal differences in income and material goods, people really were judged on what they were like as individuals and not on what they owned.'

Although fine foods were considered bourgeois, Clark remembers that the government opened up 'cultural houses' in every town and village, 'so that provincially based working-class people, like my parents, could have easy access to the arts'. But since the end of the regime in 1989, she says that even television has dumbed down. As a teenager, 'Saturday night prime time meant a Jules Verne adventure, a poetry recital and a Chekhov drama: now it means the same dreary diet of game shows and American action movies as in Britain.'

The state-endorsed cultural education stopped with food. Food was seen as sustenance, an earthy essential rather than a delicious experience. Clark's earliest memories of living at home are of the animals her parents kept on their smallholding. 'Rearing animals was something most people did, as well as growing vegetables. Outside Budapest and the big towns, we were a nation of Tom and Barbara Goods. My parents had about fifty chickens, pigs, rabbits, ducks, pigeons and geese. We kept the animals not just to feed our family but also to sell meat to our friends. We used the goose feathers to make pillows and duvets', writes Clark. Hungarian food writer, Sara Horvat, agrees. She told me that her grandmother, or *nagymama*, still uses margarine in baking and lard in cooking. 'Basically, nothing at all is healthy in their cooking but everything is tasty and heavy.'

What happened in Hungary is a fascinating example of a country deliberately stripped of its culinary identity and rebuilt through the control of its food. It is about the space that is left when what has previously defined it has gone. If food is about cooking and eating, but also about sitting with family and friends in various spaces, from the home to restaurants, then it is an embodied experience, one which, when stripped by state control and redesigned to display a different set of values, prods at the very nature of identity. As we consider narratology, and the process and power of storytelling, the construction of identity is at its core.

Stuart Hall (who left the Communist Party of Great Britain after the Soviet invasion of Hungary in 1956), was talking about his own sense of self as a member of the Windrush generation, who came to Britain from the Caribbean in 1948, when he wrote in 1987: 'Identity is formed at the unstable point where the "unspeakable" stories of subjectivity meet the narratives of history, of a culture.'

Sue Thornham writes in her 2007 book, *Women, Feminism and Media*, that these stories amount to 'the narratives of the unconscious which are expressed [...] in more public narratives [...] which serve to stabilise and constrain our self-understandings'. In Hungary, the socialist regime was actively recreating public narratives about almost every aspect of experience, stabilising and constraining the Hungarian sense of self.

For Thornham and Hall, it is the resistance to or acceptance of a constructed identity that results in a more acute sense of self. It was the Hungarian resistance to Soviet control that ushered in the era of Goulash Communism following the 1956 Revolution, but it did not save its culinary tradition. Even the term 'goulash' came to represent the worst of Hungarian food identity. Hungarian journalist Sara Horvat believes it has nothing to do with national pride: 'For most people, goulash is made from the worst meat you can imagine. It shouldn't be bad just because it has to be made from cheap cuts of meat: the longer you cook obviously, the more flavour and the more softness and tenderness it gets. But it's not even that. It begins at your average butcher's where there is no quality meat, and ends at the table where no one cares what they eat', she told me. She wonders if the demise of Hungary's national food culture was simply due to the rupture of revolution: 'We always say that socialism is the reason that everything went bad in this country. But Italy had their share of bad history and still they cling to their healthy and fresh ingredients, their pasta and their San Marzano tomatoes.'

Generations of socialist-trained Hungarians emerged into the 1990s with no idea of the richness of their culinary heritage. Food was about survival: L. P. Fischer, in his 2010 article, 'Turkey backbones and chicken gizzards: Women's food roles in post-socialist Hungary', describes how during the socialist period, 'women endured frustrations of long lines and scarce resources. In the post-socialist era, their heroic clout as food providers is diminished by the introduction of a market economy. Nevertheless, the survival skills learned in the socialist era allow them to adapt to the new era of high inflation and high unemployment', now that the state-subsidized rents, transport, sport, culture, utilities and food prices, and free health care have all gone.

Using as a case study the soup making of Ica Néni, a Hungarian widow born in 1933 whom she has followed since 1993, Fischer found that the Soviet regime taught the pensioner many coping skills: 'Elderly women struggle to live on a small income in this new, more expensive market economy. Meat can be expensive: however, Ica Néni can afford to buy poultry backbones from the butcher to make soup. She will take advantage of a free cabbage leaf found on the floor. Her food preparation takes on new challenges and difficulties presented by a post-socialist society. Coping strategies she learned during the socialist period prove useful during the post-socialist period.'

Compared with the world that Marcell Lissak, Budapest restaurateur and former channel chief of Paprika TV grew up in, tales like Ica Néni's are heartbreaking. 'Communism destroyed the gastronomy', he told me in 2014. 'Our food was influenced by Slavs, Turks and Croatians. It was a beautiful mixture. Under the socialist era, the Party People come from the lower classes and hated the food of others. It was a rejection of the bourgeois café culture of Vienna in the communist time. That was the reason we had only goulash and Wiener schnitzel. They only knew these dishes. My grandmother once invited a doctor for dinner and when she made a soufflé, he didn't know what it was. He asked if it was polenta. People quickly forgot bourgeois standards.'

Lissak described the changing foodscape in Budapest, as stories from the West – and just as importantly, the first McDonald's in 1989 – flooded into the post-communist capital: 'The people had forgotten how to eat', he told me. 'After 1989, when the change came, then everything was very fashionable. The whole western culture was about eating everything: Chinese food became so popular, there were queues around the block. There was pizza and pasta. You could also buy Thai noodles. It was very American. It was America that influenced the 1990s.'

Sara Horvat was 15 when the regime ended and she doesn't share the traumatic memories of the rupture in food culture that Lissak described: 'By the end, it was really soft socialism', she said. 'It was nothing. You didn't feel anything. Everyone was happy, and there were no black cars anymore taking the good guys to dungeons. That passed already in the 1980s.' She was one of the lucky ones: her father is a renowned TV journalist who won a scholarship to Columbia University in New York in 1989 when the regime change came. 'I saw the world', she told me. 'I saw that there are people of all colours, that you can go into a supermarket and there aren't empty shelves, that you can buy stuff. People my age travel a lot now. You have your own money to travel the world, to have Internet at home, to be curious about the world, to be curious about everything.'

As people began to travel and bring home new tastes, Lissak spotted the opportunity to prise open a window onto this new world. He launched his own food channel, Paprika TV, in 2004, with the intention of teaching the nation to cook again. Paprika TV would specialise in food, tapping directly into Hungary's intangible food memories: 'We had to find our heritage', he told me wistfully. 'We had to find ourselves.'

Consciously copying the narratives from the British originals, Paprika TV broadcast a series of 'chop 'n' cook' shows based on the themes and format of BBC Two's *The Naked Chef*. The presenters, young male chefs like Magos Zoltan, Bede Robert and Jeney Zoltan, made a variety of different dishes using simple and accessible ideas and ingredients from Italy, France and the Hungarian countryside. Zsolt Serényi became one of Hungary's most popular TV chefs. 'That was a huge influence on the whole country', said Lissak, who was the executive producer. 'The audience could see what Nigella and other French and Italian chefs were doing, but Jamie Oliver was the biggest. Everyone understood how easy it could be.' Lissak is talking about food, but it was also the culture that goes with the ability and aspiration to cook good food that seemed to be so effortless in the Jamie Oliver-style shows. 'People felt that they could be like him', said Lissak.

It wasn't just the TV series: a hardback book, *Piknik* (2013), borrowed the look of a Jamie book. Its author, the chef Viktor Segal, is pictured on the cover riding a bicycle whose basket is overflowing with home-grown vegetables. His white T-shirt, jeans and blue denim shirt flowing in the breeze give an air of a slightly dishevelled but happy lifestyle. Lissak was clear about the reason for its success: 'The copying of Jamie was the most important. They tried to copy Gordon too but that wasn't so successful. You can copy the design and the content but you can't copy the person. We copied the food and the values.'

The series was an enormous success, bringing new audiences to cooking but also kick-starting a wave of social media around food, a new movement of the people which challenged the oppressive ideas of the previous era. Lissak said that the difference between the traditional arbiters of taste and the word from the street was behind a brand-new revolution, this time in food. 'Part of the press hated us because we were not chefs and we had no gastronomic background. It was very snobby in Hungary then. Just the Michelin star restaurants were important. It's not a normal way. It came from the ground, this TV. The Michelin star scene was not part of that.'

Within months, other television channels began to feature cookery programmes and to buy format shows from other territories. Lissak was selling the Jamie Oliver-style shows at MIPTV Media Market at Cannes, across Asia and, ironically, into Russia. He explained that it wasn't about selling Hungary to the world but about the quality of the series: 'The programmes were beautiful, and so they bought them.'

Across Budapest, an artisan food industry began to emerge, with locally sourced ingredients appearing in new farmers' markets catering to audiences suddenly interested in good food. Lissak said that it was a simple recipe for success: 'Food binds people. We made a lot of programmes about this.' I asked him if it was his intention to create food tribes as has happened in Britain: Jamie for the lads, Gordon for the wannabes, Nigella for the sophisticated. 'Yes', he replied. 'This is the goal of the TV people. You are using the role models.'

Zsigmond Gabor, editor of the channel's media partner, *Paprika Magazin*, explained how the magazine continues to fill the vacuum left by the Communist regime in 2014: 'It's about how to enjoy life, the whole of life. You don't have to go to foreign countries; you don't have to travel. You can bring the world into your home with this.' *Paprika Magazin*'s demographics give a snapshot of its readership: its average reader is 45, female and, surprisingly, lives in the countryside rather than the larger cities, although Zsigmond is sceptical about these statistics: 'When we did our Internet survey, it was clear they are in the countryside, but maybe they just have [more] time.' Sales figures show that the magazine does well in Budapest too, but it is the surveys that provide details of lifestyle. For journalist Sara Horvat, one of the more depressing statistics revealed that Hungarian people cook just 12 kinds of food at home.

Led by the influential Food Network, which arrived on Magyar Telecom in 2015, as well as food bloggers' sharp restaurant reviews of hip food finds and delicious recipes, Budapest is raising its game: alongside the shabby cellars of the *romkocsmas* or 'ruin pubs', an ironic nod to the Communist era, the soup bars such as BorsGasztroBar are the place to eat goulash. Locals and tourists pop into the Jewish bistro Macesz Bisztro for *flodni*, a Jewish apple, walnut and poppy seed layered pastry, or find the latest venue for Kavehaz Zsigmond, a chic secret dining club featuring Viktor Segal in the kitchen. Backed by President Viktor Orban, gastronomy has become cool. 'New little restaurants and bistros are opening and ethnic food is becoming an everyday meal for city dwellers', said Horvat.

Horvat added that although Budapest is a 'foodie' city, it still has some way to go. 'It's about wanting and needing that quality of food. And it's not just the quality – it's the surroundings, the plating, everything. But a lot of people still don't need that. A lot of people still want to eat their sausage and white bread and bacon, and that's all they care about.' In the last two years, as the influence of the food blogger has fanned the fire started by Paprika TV, Horvat has noticed an enormous change, and not just in the capital: 'Until recently, people just wanted their goulash which has its limits on your taste. People in Hungary weren't open, but now countryside restaurants are beginning to gain momentum with locally sourced ingredients.'

I asked Zsigmond and Horvat if, as I suggest has happened in Britain, an unstable food culture has been rewritten and a population hungry for change prefers the new story enough to buy into it. 'It's very interesting', said Zsigmond. 'We used to get letters from the readers asking where they can buy *rucola* in the countryside. That was about ten years ago. I think you can buy this now.' A Hungarian-language version of *Good Food Magazine* also reflects the changing interests in food, but Zsigmond suggested that this was more about aspiration and social mobility than a genuine interest in the food itself. The BBC brand represents a Britishness that Budapest, if not the more rural readers, is keen to borrow. 'It's fancy and it's got a nice English name – *Good Food* – which people like.'

Fifty years after the socialist government controlled Hungarian taste through placing limits on distribution, the availability of ingredients is still the deal breaker in the new culinary norm. Horvat explained how the editorial decisions at *Paprika Magazin* were defined by the accessibility of the ideas. 'Every month, we would say, "shall we do this?" "No, I don't think they can buy the lemongrass or whatever." They're not going to buy lemongrass in the countryside, they don't know where to get it, or they won't understand the recipe. This won't suit their taste. So we did recipes for the masses and then there were a few for the people who would try to find the lemongrass wherever. So we had an article about ingredients and the food, and maybe we would do lemongrass one day. We were teaching them.'

Lissak believes that television and its social media entourage have proved an enormous capacity for change in Hungary, and with the country still in crisis, it has work to do. 'The country is weak and small, and politicians organise everything. There is corruption. The media is run by politics. Seven hundred thousand have left the country in two years, which in a small country is devastating. It's very important to entertain the people.'

'You have Jamie', said Horvat. 'We don't have a leader for this whole idea. There are bloggers, there are restaurant owners who tell the story, but Jamie is on a mission: he's on a mission in the States, he's on a mission in the UK. We don't have anyone on a mission.' A new media and foodscape of bloggers and new restaurateurs, including President Orban's daughter Rachel has ruffled the feathers of the traditional newspaper food reviewers, but Horvat says that there is a clear divide between the old and the new. 'They're too snobbish', she said, referring to the voices from the newspaper. 'They're all about three Michelin stars. We don't care about that: we care about good food. And a lot of people care about that, so a lot of people don't consider them opinion leaders, because they're just a couple of old guys. The way they look, the way they write and the way they speak – and what they speak (about) – is just not for the masses. It's for the selected few.'

In 2016, Jamie Oliver came to Budapest (the restaurant not the chef). And unlike the chef, it is not in town to change food culture, but to celebrate it. In a bizarre twist of televisual storytelling, a copycat *Naked Chef* brought culinary pleasure back to Budapest and sparked a revolution. But did its stories reawaken a buried food memory or bring a genuine new interest to a much more exciting world of food? Is Hungary's taste for food more about joining a global movement or developing a taste that was once considered bourgeois? Sara Horvat pondered on the difference between simply enjoying food and good taste. 'I think at first it was about the look, all the fancy (ideas) that "new" food brought with it. Now it has more meaning to it: it's about finding the roots, and yes, aspiring to be better at presenting good quality nourishment. I am more optimistic as ingredients are easier to access and people are more open. It is trendy now to serve good, nice looking food and it's not snobbish anymore to serve something on a chopping board. If Jamie does it, you can do it – although I always laugh at Buzzfeed's hipster restaurant lists about "wtf plating". There should be a balance.'

As with Britain and Australia, it was the instability of Hungary's food culture that allowed storytellers to impose a new narrative; it was the blankness of its canvas which enabled new pictures to emerge. With whispers of food memories tugging at the national sub-conscious, clever businesses and passionate food-ies brought ideas from around the world to Budapest, to *Paprika Magazin* and to the growing number of TV food channels, and Hungary is finally filling its plate. When I caught up with her in 2017, Sara Horvat was optimistic: 'Gourmet Festival is THE place to be in May. The "little people" are also taking over. IGEN (meaning YES) is the only place here with a traditional oven from Naples, and even though it's only about four metres square, there are always long lines despite the hefty price. Babel is another really popular restaurant which was set up by two chefs who are into the whole foraging trend. They do desserts without sugar, sweetened rather by carrots and celery root, and food flavoured with hay and edible flowers.'

By 2019, Budapest has arrived. It is now a foodie destination with gourmet restaurants, cool bistros and food trucks providing a culinary joyride for the tourists flocking into the city, and for the locals finding their way back to a genuinely excellent food culture. IGEN, the pizza restaurant that Horvat referred to, has moved from the Jewish quarter to Grand Boulevard (Nagykörút) as a result of its astonishing success. The city's food hall, Hold Utca, is packed with independent shops and stalls not unlike Rome's Mercato Centrale or Miami's Time Out.

Horvat believes that its success is to do with entrepreneurs like Karoly Gerendai who owns Costes, one of Budapest's six Michelin-starred restaurants, and whose Sziget Gourmet Festival is about to celebrate its 25th anniversary. 'They were always interested in food', she told me. 'But they are creating or rather recreating the culture of the family table. They are reaching back to ingredients of the Austro-Hungarian Empire, the distinct tastes of Transylvania, the Ottoman influence of neighbouring ex-Yugoslavia, and the Slavic culture of the Ukraine. Everything that is just exciting.'

Prime Minister Viktor Orban's nationalist politics may cast a dark cloud over Europe, but at home, his government actively promotes a culture of good food, and not just for the tourists. It supports the city's culinary competition, the Bocuse d'Or, and Orban's wife Aniko Levai is the editor-in-chief of the leading culinary magazine, *Magyar Konyha*. Their daughter Rachel, as Horvat has already told us, is one of the leading influencers in the city's food scene. Can this diet of conspicuous consumption and cultural capital, based on nostalgia and taste, Bourdieu-style, feed Hungary's soul? In Orban's Hungary, it may appear so; regeneration is a nationalist strategy. But the exodus of its younger generation paints another picture; as Gábor Sarnyai writes in *Hungary Today* (2018), 'massive out-migration' is still the most popular political issue. Filling its spiritual belly is clearly not sustaining enough to keep its young people at home.

How to build a food culture

'Fusion': the process or result of joining two or more things together to form a single entity (Lexicon.com). It's a term used to describe Australian cuisine that refuses to go away despite the antipathy many Australian chefs feel about it, suggesting as it does a melting pot rather than a nuanced response to identity in a country built on immigration. 'I think we believe in ourselves here and we develop our own flavours', Neil Perry, one of Australia's most famous chefs told me in an interview for my book *Australia: New Food for the New World* at his restaurant, Wokpool, in 1998, when Sydney was seen as having one of the most successful modern cuisines in the world. 'I don't think we're afraid of developing our own ideas. Australian people don't rip ideas off: they allow themselves to be inspired.'

This chapter explores how a country can develop a cuisine over just 60 years that celebrates the sum of its parts and the integrity of the culinary cultures which contribute to its whole. It is a story of narratives which work, of storytelling that is about a sense of home and a passion for keeping a culture intact as roots are pulled away from the old country and placed elsewhere. But it's also about ignoring a much longer and much more stable food culture that preceded it, and a country where food racism is part of the language among some of the most respected and otherwise politically correct and inclusive food commentators in the world.

The parallels between the post-war construction of Australian and British food identity through television are a fascinating way of assessing the role of storytelling. Both are characterised by the domination of an imperial food ideology, and both are against the rise in material prosperity that swelled the middle class, as aspiration created a taste for a 'better' life. 'Unlike other societies with a dominant agrarian history', writes Michael Symons in *Australian Geographic*, 'we have inherited no cuisine in the traditional sense. Australia's food history has instead been dynamic, urban, industrial, science-based and capitalist-driven.' As middle-class women moved back into the home after their contribution in munitions factories and on the land as part of the war effort, their new role was to grow a nation fed on dreams of that better life. Daytime TV was the instruction manual: as Isabelle de Solier wrote in her 2005 article, 'TV dinners: Culinary television, education and distinction': 'The new medium of television provided a form of company for housewives at home during the day, even taking on some domestic tasks such as babysitting children, a role which earned it the affectionate nickname 'Aunty', signalling its incorporation into the family unit.'

Screened during what Rachel Moseley referred to in 2016 as the feminised viewing time of Daytime TV, Food TV was not only aimed at an audience of housewives, but it was also involved in the construction of this social identity. The 15-minute cooking demonstrations broadcast between 1956 and 1966 featured female hosts who were represented as 'ordinary housewives', both reflecting the audience of the segments as well as providing that audience with models of behaviour to follow. On Australian television, this identity was epitomised in the figure of Margaret Fulton, whose face came to symbolise the Anglo-Australian middle-class suburban housewife, as Delia Smith did in Britain and Julia Child did in the United States.

Australian academic, Isabelle de Solier, examines how in post-industrial society the self is formed by our relationship with the way we consume material cultures or things, including food. She argues that we make 'our meaningful and moral selves through both the consumption and production of material culture – we make them at work and consume them at play, leading to "meaningless" modern lives.' But this is a recent malaise: Australia offers a particularly fascinating tapestry of imperialist and immigrant cultural society over its relatively short history on which to examine de Solier's argument. Against an ascetic British food culture built on a marketing campaign to drive empire goods into the home and the soul, post-war Australia had an almost empty palate on which to paint the national cuisine, which was by the early 1990s, one of the most interesting, diverse and healthy in the world.

Dr Susan Chant is Academic Manager for Le Cordon Bleu in Adelaide, Australia, and in her 2015 article, she argues that Australia's early colonial food history was constructed around the Empire ideology: 'From the 1800s, definitions ranged from state-based references of regional specialties to national branding, evidenced by trademarks referencing the word "Australia" or using Australian symbolism to promote their products.' The move was designed to create a market for goods from the colonies and form a cohesive colonial society. She found that marketing reflected the 'social and moral values of the eras, in particular nationalist and imperial sentiment'. Chant's work looks at how a series of stunning posters commissioned by the Empire Marketing Board (1926–33) were used to promote empire foods as local in Australia, romanticising empire foods and using them as modern public relations and consumer marketing campaigns. The campaign reflected 'popular cultural themes like austerity, refinement, food security, patriotism, nationalism and independence. Campaigns promoting locally produced foods also encouraged Australians to view eating certain products as their moral duty'.

The construction of Australian food culture in the early twentieth century offers interesting parallels here, and illustrates a history of talented and effective British storytelling designed to change consumption patterns. 'One of these campaigns was what was known as the Great White Train, launched in 1924 by the Australian Made Preference League, to promote Australian made food products by appealing to patriotism', writes Chant. 'The League's aim was to counter the popularity of imported goods at the time and promote the demand for locally made products, creating employment and encouraging a class of skilled artisans. A multitude of effective slogans were employed by the campaign which were widely distributed. In general, local industry was encouraged to produce goods that were new, original and reflective of the culture at the time.' In this way, fruit from Australia, lamb from New Zealand and tea from India were all branded 'local', and offered the dual purpose of supporting colonial trade and embedding the notion of ethical consumption. 'Thus consumers were supporting their fellow empire producers by "doing the right thing". Australia's primary produce, namely apples, pears and dried fruits, were targeted as major British imports, signalled by elaborate displays in the retail sphere [...] Empire was idealised as a potentially self-sufficient, reciprocal system of trade, a competitor to the emerging powers of the United States and Germany.'

By the 1950s, Australia had a strong sense of self, although the food was what Christine Manfield, chef, food writer and *MasterChef Australia* guest judge, described as 'Presbyterian Anglo-Saxon'. Her interest in cooking as a young adult came as a reaction against it: 'It wasn't a hedonistic celebration while I was growing up. It wasn't a sensual experience at all', she told me for my book, *Australia: New Food from the New World*. Like many of the Australian chefs who reworked the country's food cultures into one of the most varied and imaginative in the world by the 1990s, her ideas came from growing up among the Mediterranean and Asian immigrants who came to the country from the 1950s onwards and grew the food from 'the old country', actively making meaning of their new selves. Australia quickly showed an extraordinary new confidence in food, leaving Britain behind as its own Italian, Indian, Pakistani, Bangladeshi and Chinese immigrants added ketchup to their tomato sauce and cream to their curries, pleasing their imperial hosts. Australia's Italians, Greeks, Turks and Vietnamese, just as rich with inherited culinary identities but much further from home, would spearhead a new movement in the kitchens of Melbourne and Sydney, Adelaide and Perth. To understand how it happened, we need to revisit Australia's recent history.

White Australia's bland post-war British Australians smelled the basil and spit-roast lamb on the winds as waves of immigrants came from Italy, Greece and Turkey in the 1950s and 1960s, and from Vietnam in the 1970s. The tastes of more vibrant, more stable food cultures would bring delight to native Australians who were only too eager for change. 'The only thing we were happy to throw out was the white food our mothers were cooking for us', David Thompson told me in an interview for my book, *Australia* at his original restaurant Darley Street Thai. The Michelin-starred chef and cookery writer, who was given a lifetime achievement award by the World's 50 Best Restaurants for changing the face and global reputation of Thai food, through his restaurants in London and Bangkok (Nahm), and Singapore, Perth and Sydney (Long Chim), was born in Australia. Thompson believes that it was the instability of British food culture which failed to influence the stronger food cultures which arrived in Australia with the Italians: 'When Australia started to change after the war and began to drift away from its Anglo-Celtic heritage, it wasn't sufficiently entrenched to impose its culture on the newcomers', he told me. The impact was enormous and, as the isolation of the New World led to a curiosity for the young and a nostalgia for the old country, Anglo-Australians became more adventurous, if only in terms of eating out, than their families back home; Michael Symons wrote in his 2014 article, 'Australia's cuisine culture: A history of our food': 'Taking ocean voyages to Europe in the 1950s and 1960s, many Australians had begun to discover the joys of French, Italian, Greek and other traditional cooking. Recipe books of all kinds began to be published in great numbers. The number of restaurants increased by 12–14 per cent each year.'

Like Manfield and Thompson, New Zealander Peter Gordon was from migrant stock. 'My parents were Scottish and Mauri', he told me in 2016, 'so I didn't come from a really rich culinary background. For me to go and just do whatever I wanted to was very easy because no one was telling me I couldn't, except at college and college which was controlled by French, English and German tutors.' Gordon, who went to catering college in Melbourne and was one of a handful of Antipodean chefs who brought exciting new ideas from the other side of the world to London in the 1980s, said that it was a conflation of influence and opportunity that led to what became known as 'fusion food': 'All I learned at catering school was how to do French and English and German food', he told me. 'In Britain it seemed that everyone would bow down to the French kitchen which never grabbed me. It just wasn't my thing. I'm drawn to ingredients rather than cuisines.' He went through catering school with John Torode, who would go on to present *MasterChef* UK, and they would battle with the incongruity of learning traditional culinary techniques in such a diverse and vibrant food culture. 'I would go and eat in all these lovely little ethnic restaurants on my nights off', said Gordon. 'I'd have Japanese food or Moroccan food or northern Italian or something, but we weren't taught any of that at college, and for me it was crazy. There was this amazing world of food and ingredients out there.'

He explained how the tension between the food on the streets in Melbourne and Old World gastronomy created something so fresh and vibrant that it entranced the world. 'A lot of young New Zealanders and Australians were like myself: they might have had a very formal training but actually they had access to ingredients that in New Zealand and Australia were probably easier to get hold of than here in Britain.' The OE (Overseas Experience), was the Antipodean pre-cursor to the European Gap Year and an essential part of growing up for most young Australians and New Zealanders. Asia was the corridor to the West and introduced chefs like Peter Gordon to a whole new way of cooking: 'I spent a year in Asia hitch-hiking around and I was far more excited about some air-dried squid that was dipped in chili sugar syrup and barbequed and served with sticky rice than a buttery sauce served on poached meat', he told me.

Like many Australians and New Zealanders, their OE led to the kitchens of Britain and the restaurants of Notting Hill and Conran: Peter Gordon was one of the first, and brought his own New Zealand restaurant, the Sugar Club, to London's Notting Hill in 1995 and to Soho in 1998. In 1996, the Notting Hill restaurant won a Time Out award for Best Modern British Restaurant, and its accompanying cookbook was published in 1998. Gordon would appear on Nigel Slater's first TV series, *Nigel Slater's Real Food Show*, by the end of 1990s, while John Torode was the chef on ITV's *This Morning* from 1996 to 2000. Torode worked for Conran in London at Pont de la Tour; at Quaglino's with fellow Australian, Martin Webb; and at Mezzo, the 700-seater in Soho where he also wrote his first book of the same name, fusing ideas from Asia and the West such as Fried Crab with Garlic and Chilli, Roast Marinated Lamb with Sweet Potato Mash, Aubergine Ravioli with Black Butter and Capers and Lemon Mascarpone Cake. But it wasn't the taste of home that these young chefs were bringing to Britain, but a cool new concept of eating that fitted with our taste for the new.

Was it authentic? Postmodernism tells us that it is the consumer who is involved in producing authenticity, a moment of a meeting of minds that produces the magic. What was happening in Australia at the same time offers us a fascinating insight into the production of authenticity. The imposition of the stable immigrant food cultures onto the shifting sands and ambivalent taste buds of Anglo/Celtic-Australian food culture hit a bullseye in Australia. And it was an early clash with the dominant controlling cultures that catapulted it into something more than food.

Steve Manfredi was a boy at the Bonegilla migrant camp, home to many of the 20,000 Italian young men invited by the Australian government to fill farm-worker jobs in the 1950s and 1960s. He told me that he still remembered the smell: 'It was clean, but you couldn't smell anything other than Pine-o-Clean. The staff wore starched white uniforms and rubber gloves to handle the food.' In his 1993 book, *Fresh from Italy*, he describes the journey from the stable food culture of Italy to the unstable food culture of a 1950s Australian migrant camp, and its impact on his sense of self. He remembered it for my book, *Australia: New Food from the New World*: 'We had left behind more than a country when we got off the boat from Italy and went to live in that migrant hotel: we'd left behind an entire culture. And in daily life, that culture was expressed in the preparation and eating of our food. It was a feeling, touching and smelling culture.'

Lukasz Swiatek of the University of Sydney suggested that it is a resistance to the imposition of identity that releases the flavour: '[the more] a cultural memory tries to lock in a social identity that's questioned or widespread and not necessarily universal, the more it's going to encounter resistance, the more that there's going to be trouble in uptake', he told me. In 1952, Bonegilla was the scene of a riot in which 3,000 migrants protested about the lack of work opportunity. But one of the protestors, Fernando Donnini, said it was more than that; he told John Newton in his 1996 book, *Wogfood: An Oral History with Recipes*: 'There were 200 Italians in Block 9. In the whole camp there were 3000 young Italian men, all unemployed. They put in charge of the kitchen three Russians who put on top of the pasta one kilo of sugar. You can imagine – sugar on the pasta is for us like poison!'

By 1961, the number of economic migrants passing through Bonegilla's doors had swollen to a million since it first opened in 1947. German-born Italian, Bill Marchetti, whose restaurant The Latin was one of the most successful in Melbourne, was also at Bonegilla as a teenager in 1968. He told me for my book *Australia* how he watched the faces of the Italians on the train to the camp: 'They were thinking, "we're going to have to make our life in the country." Four, five hours on the train where you never saw a blade of grass. And you could see the faces on the old people thinking, "this is it: we're going to die here." '

Planting their own tomatoes and basil at the camp helped to remind them of the old country. Putting down roots was as symbolic as it was practical: 'Cultural embeddedness seems to offer stability and coherence to an identity that might otherwise seem fractured and unstable', writes Sue Thornham, in her 2007 book, *Women, Feminism and Media*. Gordon Ramsay protégée and Food Network presenter Judy Joo's parents did the same when they settled in America from Korea: 'I grew up in the middle of nowhere, New Jersey', she told Libby Purves on BBC Radio 4's *Midweek* in 2015, 'so my mother had to cook from scratch to get that taste of home. Our garden was teeming with vegetables that you would never find in an American grocery store. There was seaweed drying in a garage, there were fermenting things in the laundry room, kimchi on the back porch. It was a gastronomic adventure!'

As Europe shape-shifts both in terms of its union and its people, refugees are bringing new smells and flavours from the Middle East to Germany, France and Britain for the same reason as did Australia's economic migrants. Food is integral to a sense of home, particularly if home is a temporary space. I interviewed Dr Linda Morrice from Sussex University for my 2016 series for Radio Reverb, *Jaibli Salaam* which explored the memories of food and music among Brighton's new Syrian community. She said that food is central to a feeling of community and identity. 'One of the most interesting definitions of communities is Benedict Anderson's definition of "imagined community", that we create an imagined community and a sense of belonging.' I asked her if Anderson meant that it was more like a feeling, a warmth. 'Yes', she said. 'In terms of the migrant communities I've worked with, food is incredibly important (in creating that). There was a long struggle to get the Black and Minority Ethnic Communities building up and running. It was so important to be able to get together and cater and share food. That was a landmark achievement. It's such an important part of everyday life and having space to prepare food the way you want it.'

The term 'fusion' may better describe the conflation of immigrants' sense of longing for the food from the old country, and the warmth and sense of belonging that comes from Anderson's 'imagined community' when uprooted, and a resistance to the instability of Anglo-Celtic post-war food culture. But it is also the diversity of climate that allows Australia to grow the selection of foods from its immigrant communities that sets it apart from the magpie culture of London's culinary scene. David Thompson described how it felt to watch a movement emerge from the waves of immigration: 'What was happening was that people were coming to Australia with an incredible interest in food', he told me. 'Plus, you had this remarkable climate in which to grow the ingredients that they were bringing with them. With sufficient enough migration, there has consistently been enough demand for those ingredients to become available. On top of which, Australians were travelling so much more and for so much longer than anyone else. They'd come back with new ideas and higher expectations.'

The joy of cooking for the family, the visual delight of growing ingredients from the old country, and the smells across the garden fences as various groups of migrants spit-roast their Sunday lamb is the stuff of British television producers' dreams. But breaking free of an oppressive culinary narrative is what Marchetti thinks makes Australians such unusual cooks: 'Without a culture of their own, they're a bit like a blank page', he told me. 'It's great fun putting things on the menu and they taste it and say, "wow! What was that?" You do that in Italy and they'll lynch you. If I had a restaurant in Milan, I'd be cooking Milanese food. If I used Sicilian style for some dishes, they'd say, "hey, what do you think you're doing?" '

While the ingredients of Italy and Greece were becoming increasingly available at markets, Australian TV was also teaching a nation how to cook. Food was the glitter glue of this new nation, and television bosses were quick to spot it. While Britain was playing with a food culture based on the conspicuous consumerism of Thatcher's Britain, the 1990s saw a boom in 'lifestyle' programming on Australian television screens, moving from the information-focussed cookery progammes of the post-war/White Australia period to programmes which celebrated the consumption of it. Eating was delicious rather than cool.

Borrowing the storytelling of British cooks and chefs, 'culinary television was also transformed by the foregrounding of style and fashionability characteristic of lifestyle programming. This new style of cooking show originated in British programmes imported by ABC, such as BBC Two's *The Naked Chef* and Channel 4's *Nigella Bites* (1999), however, it was soon mimicked by local programmes such as ABC's *Kylie Kwong* (2003) and Lifestyle's *Bill's Food* (2004).

Australia was emerging from an extraordinary makeover, transforming its bland Anglo-Celtic nation fed on a diet of meat and two veg into the most exciting culinary culture in the world. Like modern Britain, modern Australia's identity was carved by its relationship with food, and Lifestyle TV was both metaphor and manufacturer with its cookery programmes reflecting the process *and* telling its story. What is interesting about what happened in Australia is how the stories, and what Isabelle de Solier in 2005 called the 'endless flows of fashionable food images that decorate our world [which] contribute to the aestheticisation of everyday life in post-modern consumer culture' were absorbed. They were more than instructional or aspirational, whether or not they originated in Britain or America. Programmes like *MasterChef*, as we have seen in 'Selling Britain to the world' (this volume) became so popular because the audience really could cook. Instead of relying on intangible memories of dishes created on-screen that they could only dream about, the Australian food viewer is more likely to try it out.

Lukasz Swiatek has watched the food scene in Australia grow in the last couple of decades, not just with the astonishing success of British formats like *MasterChef Australia* and *The Great Australian Bake Off* (Nine Network, 2013–present). The improvement in the quality of the food has met the new demand created by the TV food shows, and there is now a plethora of opportunities to eat out. Swiatek argues that Australian home cooks have become 'more daring and imaginative'. With this new confidence, we have watched a new culinary culture built on unstable ground become quickly embedded in and able to play with social media to deepen it further: 'One of the roles that YouTube plays is that you can look up recipes and model cooking in many different domains form savoury to really complex desserts. It has more space for experimentation', said Swiatek. He calls himself a 'foodie' and enjoys experimenting with ideas from all over the world, but recognises how, as a Pole in Australia, his interest in food and his identity as a 'foodie' are constructs. 'If we think of the self as cultur-ally constructed, it's constantly changed according to context – who we meet, who we copy from.' He argued that all national dishes are constructs, as are the environments in which they are consumed: 'All the texts that accompany them [the dishes] from restaurant décor right through to a particular menu design, they're all constructed, even the strategic ways in which particular elements of culture are highlighted and others are excluded. I think of Irving Goffman's idea of framing and, think [that] the ways in which dishes are constructed, probably subconsciously, are constructed in a way that some things are included and other things are deliberately excluded, so that particular forms of national identity can be foregrounded.'

But this astonishing example of authentic storytelling, which hit a national nerve, obscures a much longer story of indigenous food culture. Anglo-Australian food writer, cook and regenerative farmer, Rebecca Sullivan, and her aboriginal partner, Damien Coulthard, have created a new range of Australian native food products for home cooks – including a kangaroo broth and 'tea bags' made with ants and river mint. Their brand Warndu means to 'feel good' in the traditional Adnyamathanha language of Coulthard's indigenous Australian ancestors, who come from the Flinders Ranges. But it was a response to her horror in realising that after working in food around the world for ten years, she had ignored the food culture in her own country: 'I'd been championing, really championing and understanding local, and understanding seasonal food', she told me in 2016, 'and I never bloody even tasted lemon myrtle, the food from my own back garden. And then I started thinking about things like kangaroo, which is easy to get your hands on these days. It wasn't even made legal until the 1990s in Australia. This is food that has sustained an indigenous, a race, for 60,000-plus years, we don't even know exactly, but we know it's more than that. How can that not be legal? How can we be so disgusting as human beings to think that, "oh, it's not good enough for us?" And I went, "oh my god, I'm a food racist! I've not even tried the local food from my own back garden." And that was my aha! moment.' I asked her how the story was not told to Australians fascinated in and open to food cultures that are not their own in a way that we don't find in many countries. 'It was blanked out!' she said. 'It was completely blanked out. If you read back some of the journals from Settlement, there are actually really great compliments to some of the food. But they're not the ones you see. You see, "these people are hunters and gatherers, they're savages." They weren't just hunter-gatherers, they were farmers. They're the oldest farmers that exist.'

She told me that she had learned about aboriginal culture for just one year at school. I asked her if the awkwardness that she clearly feels is an assumed responsibility for the way that Australia handles its own history? 'I think so', she said. 'It's really quite embarrassing for me to now admit to that, but yes. And I think we all feel it – well, most of us. And it shouldn't even be there in the first place, it shouldn't even be a thing.' She told me that after 'walking on egg-shells for months', she had finally asked Damien's father about the food he had grown up with. 'He was so excited to talk about it', she told me. 'Now every time he comes down from where they live, he'll bring me a kangaroo fillet, or some quandongs when they come into season, or some Myakka, which is bush banana. And he's so excited to share that with us.'

Sullivan is a storyteller and an educator: the author of seven books, including *Like Grandma Used to Make* (2013), she has already created a 'Granny Skills' movement, teaching children in schools how to pickle, preserve and avoid waste, and she writes prolifically about finding 'her inner granny'. She is already taking Australian native ingredients – bush tucker – and their stories into schools and creating the products, but says it will take more than storytelling to get people to really understand how it can become part of Australian food culture: 'So what's happened in the Australian native food industry is they've had three or four spikes in popularity since the 1960s, where it's been really trendy, and on all the menus in the top restaurants in Australia. Amazing chefs have been championing it, farmers have gone out and tried to grow it, but then no one at home knows how to use it. So it hasn't trickled down far enough, and the industry's crashed and farmers have lost money.' She thinks that Australia's food culture is now stable enough to absorb something that is more than a trend: 'We're at this tipping point where there's enough new, I guess, new blood coming into the industry that want to see it grow sustainably, that want to champion it.'

Sullivan and Coulthard have written about their journey in their cookbook, *Warndu Mai: (Good Food) Introducing Native Australian Ingredients to Your Kitchen* (2019), and are working with chefs, distillers and wine makers to create the products, the education and the buzz around indigenous products that will enable them to get into people's homes in a sustainable way. 'We don't want to see this industry crash and burn because it's just been on a restaurant menu', she said. 'Food is the thing that brings people together', she told me. 'It's the thing that can make peace actually happen. If we can create a place where people can come, and they can ask, "oh, what's a finger lime? Oh, what's a desert lime? What's lemon myrtle?" and they can taste it, and then they can get curious about Australian native ingredients, or bush tucker, then maybe they'll ask the next question. Then maybe they'll start asking questions about culture and art and creation stories or dream time. And that might be that thing that gives the people permission to just ask another question. And then, you know, reconciliation is a big word, but I think food can do that. I truly think food can do that.'

She says that they are not alone, that there is a growing movement that is bringing back a forgotten national story to the Australian narrative: 'We have so many incredible people to look up to, like [TV chef and chef proprietor at Billy Kwong in Sydney] Kylie Kwong, like Jock Zonfrillo [chef at Orana in Adelaide]. There are people in Australia who are doing amazing things and who have been working in this industry a hell of a lot longer than us, and we're trying to collaborate with them and learn from them. And learn from Damien's family and not be afraid to ask questions, and who knows what can happen. It could be amazing.'

Part Four

Can storytelling save the world?

This final section reflects on what may be TV's most influential narrative and what we can learn from it to tell what may be the most important story of our lives.

An industry of persuasion

Despite the Odyssey narrative of Jamie Oliver, the delight of British storytelling that has been copied and sold all over the world and the phenomenal numbers of (largely unused) cookbooks which are sold every year, statistics suggest that children are likely to die before their parents from obesity-related diseases. As reported by Fooddive.com in 2015, snack sales in the US alone increased from $34.2 billion in 2005 to $47.5 billion in 2015, and Britain has the highest level of obesity in Western Europe, ahead of countries such as France, Germany, Spain and Sweden. According to a 2019 keynote address to G20 agriculture ministers in Japan by United Nations Food and Agricultural Organization boss, Graziano da Silva, more than two billion people worldwide are overweight. 'Projections suggest that the number of obese people in the world will very soon overtake the number of people suffering from hunger, which accounted for 821 million in 2017. This has already happened in Latin America and the Caribbean.'

The sedentary lifestyle of the computer age and an addictive junk-food culture are to blame but, according to *The Men Who Made Us Fat* – a series made for BBC Two in 2013 by Jamie Oliver's production company, Fresh One – it's not just profit that drives the food industry. In the series, investigative reporter Jacques Peretti reveals a clear route from the White House to the industrialisation of high fructose corn syrup (HFCS), which, in just over 50 years, has come to produce the largest single source of calories in the American diet. Peretti tells the story of how HFCS enabled farmers to turn their corn into gold by making a fortune from surplus. HFCS was former US president Richard Nixon's most powerful legacy, and swept across the globe in the 1960s and 1970s. The moreish ingredient is in everything from fizzy drinks to burgers and was the brainchild of Nixon's Agricultural Secretary, Earl Butz, who encouraged farmers to overproduce corn to create what would become known as 'the devil's candy'. With the US becoming increasingly polarized in its views on Vietnam, and with housewives protesting at the soaring cost of food, Nixon was facing a crisis. With an election looming, he seized upon the potential of a new process of enzymatic processing which could convert some of corn's glucose into fructose, creating a product which was cheaper and sweeter than sugar. In an echo of Australia's Empire marketing campaign, the Nixon administration was behind the creation of the Great American Meal, with beef cattle fed on corn, and bread and soda made with corn syrup. Even the chips were fried in corn oil. As Peretti says, from coleslaw to pizza toppings, corn syrup was everywhere. As farmers bought into the idea that mountains of excess corn could make their fortunes, this new business literally changed the shape of a nation. In 2012, one out of four Americans were obese and 40 per cent were over their ideal weight, with more Americans overweight than undernourished.

Obesity is also one of the biggest problems facing the National Health Service in Britain, as well as the health of our global village. With HFCS in most fast foods across the world, endocrinologist Robert Lustig explains in *The Men Who Made Us Fat* how fructose in both glucose-fructose syrup and table sugar leads to obesity: 'Leptin goes from your fat cells to your brain and tells your brain you've had enough', says Lustig. However, when the liver is overloaded with sugar, he explains, leptin stops working: 'It makes your brain think you're starving and now what you have is a vicious cycle of consumption, disease and addiction.' 'The food industry choreographs temptation', argues Peretti in the series. But how can we demand change from an industry whose business model is based on the opportunity to make a profit from obesity? As Professor Simon Capewell of the University of Liverpool – who served on the Health Secretary's Public Health Commission in opposition – says in the series, 'putting the food industry at the policy table is like putting Dracula in charge of the blood bank.' Governments and industry put the responsibility at the feet of individuals to watch their weight, but as the Cambridge University dietary department found, those individuals are twice as likely to be obese if they live near fast food outlets.

New technologies could provide answers, but again the food industry, buoyed by a competitive culture of innovation, can be frighteningly out of touch as it reaches for the stars. Anna Lappé, author of *Diet for a Hot Planet* (2006), gives an example: 'I remember going to a Food Industry conference where one of the speakers was from a large food corporation, and his opening remark was: "Our goal is to get consumers to think it's as absurd to cook your own food as it would be to sew your own jeans. Our goal is to make it so that no one is cooking from scratch anymore and that we've lost all of that knowledge about how to do that, so that you become then completely dependent on buying pre-packaged, precooked product.' In a keynote address to the 2016 *Food Studies Conference* at Berkeley, California, Lappé painted a picture of a futuristic food industry whose innovative brilliance could be captured in a more effective way. She told delegates about the polarities of innovative food science, where agri-ecological solutions on how to dramatically reduce the consumption of meat and dairy were presented next to in-vitro meat initiatives. As she looked at the display of 3,000 plastic petri dishes that had been used to make one in-vitro meat product, she said the irony was heartbreaking: 'the amount of energy it takes to produce this alternative form of meat protein was off the charts', she said. 'And they were admitting it. They were like, "it's still a design problem we've got to solve. But we can figure it out." '

Much of what we need to know to counter the trend is already in the public domain. A system of traffic lights explains nutritional information through food labelling at least in some supermarkets, and the relationship between food miles, global warming and peak oil has been well publicised. A responsible shopper can now do a weekly shop with some confidence that he or she knows how to cause the least impact on the planet, how to be fair to the producer and how to avoid high sugar and salt content. The founder of Slow Food San Francisco, Lorenzo Scarpone, told me that food shopping should be about food justice: Good, Clean and Fair: 'good to yourself and your family by eating well, clean for the planet by eating organic and fair to the producers so that we can build a responsible and sustainable food system.'

But while exposés and TV that create 'noise' on social media are what broadcasters want, it's the joining up of the dots that makes real change. Anna Lappé told me that in the year after the release of *The Inconvenient Truth* (2006), Davis Guggenheim's hard-hitting film about former US vice president Al Gore's global warming campaign, 2,830 articles were published discussing the content, yet just 2 per cent linked it to food systems. An understanding of the relationship between the food we buy and eat and the way it is produced, and who and what it affects, is still not getting through.

Efforts to make a new discursive framework are finding traction as politicians spot an opportunity for a lasting legacy; in London in 2016, the city's newspaper, the *Evening Standard*, launched a media campaign supported by its new mayor, Sadiq Khan, to feed the capital's hungry with waste food. With an online and newspaper story campaign pumping out headlines such as 'How London can follow Birkenhead's lead in reducing food waste', 'Our food waste charity Felix is given £1 million in one month' and 'Couriers go Uber and above call of duty to feed hungry London', it was the kind of combined storytelling that could change the way the capital understands waste, and, crucially how it buys its food. James Bardrick, head of one of the campaign partners, Citi, in the UK, said: 'Food waste and food poverty are serious issues facing cities around the world, which Citi is already addressing in places such as New York, Madrid and Sao Paolo.' Funding opportunities for innovative start-ups lends London a gold rush narrative for waste, an invitation for good ideas to gain currency and make sustainability cool. 'Uniquely in London', said Bardrick, 'we're investing our time and £200,000 of funding in discovering and supporting pioneering ideas developed by the community for the community.'

All over the world, community groups, charities and activists are quietly making real change, yet we barely hear about them, except perhaps through social media. In some parts of Europe and America, nursery and primary school children are learning through the food they grow and eat in their own dining halls. Healthy food initiatives are everywhere as individuals, groups and even some governments tackle institutions head on. Bee Wilson tells the story, in her book *First Bite: How We Learn to Eat* (2015) of the SAPERE movement. From the Latin which has the multiple meanings 'to be able', 'to taste' and 'to know', SAPERE has, like Alice Waters's Edible School Yard in the US, encouraged children to explore the pleasures of food across schools in Sweden, Denmark, the Netherlands and some parts of Switzerland and France. But it was in Finland that it resulted dramatically in children's weight-loss. The call to action came in the early 2000s with an alarmingly high rise in obesity among its children compared with its neighbours', Sweden and Norway: '9.2 per cent of Finnish boys were obese against 4.2 per cent in Sweden', Waters' notes. According to the World Health Organisation (WHO) in 2009, almost one in five 5-year-olds in the Finnish city of Seinäjoki were overweight or obese. Prompted by nursery staff's observations of how much fizzy drink was packed with children's lunches, all kindergartens in the city of Jyväskylä were given funding to introduce SAPERE-style lessons: 'The goal was to create a positive and natural relationship with food and eating, playing with their food using all their senses', Wilson writes including,'the hard crackle of rye crispbread, the soft fuzz of a peach, the puckering sourness of raw cranberries.' As 10,000 kindergarten, healthcare and catering staff were trained in applying SAPERE-food education during 2009–14, they noticed that children were losing weight and were more likely to eat vegetables if they were allowed to pick them up with their fingers. Wilson reports that their parents noticed that 'instead of being disgusted by beetroot, they were now fascinated by the question of how it turned the cooking water purple'. Wilson cites WHO conclusion that since the experiment, 'the municipality's health department has worked with the childcare, education, nutrition, recreation and urban planning departments to ensure all day care centres and schools provide the same quality of services. As a result, the proportion of 5-year-olds who are overweight or obese has been halved'.

America's James Beard Foundation celebrates the legacy of one of its very first TV chefs by joining the dots along the food chain and exploring the way that food enriches lives. It references Brillat-Savarin in its mission statement: 'You are what you eat not only because food is nutrition, but also because food is an integral part of our everyday lives. Food is economics, politics, entertainment, culture, fashion, family, passion [...] and nourishment.' The foundation's 2016 Leadership Awards went to the food activists, including Anna Lappé for her role in founding the Small Planet Institute and Real Food Media. The foundation's president, Susan Ungaro, called them 'gamechangers who have made an impact in improving childhood nutrition, fighting hunger, and promoting justice and equality in our food system'. Civil Eats, one of the awards partners, followed the ceremony with a call to action giving consumers a list of what they can do to change the food system: 'Organize. Connect. Speak up', said Anna Lappé, a Civil Eats spokesperson. 'We are more than just eaters. We can also all advocate for a more equitable food system – and there has never been a better time to do so.'

Lappé told me about American chef Tom Colicchio's work: 'He's a really successful restaurateur but also a really powerful advocate. His wife produced a powerful film – documentary – about hunger in America, called *A Place at the Table* [2012], and has tried to use this platform that he has as a public figure to really push on food policy.' Colicchio's initiative, Food Policy Action, encourages candidates to think about how they can use their position as elected officials to support policy that's good for food, farming and sustainability. Lappé thinks that there's a 'huge role for media' and that chefs have a part to play: 'They have become such superstars in our culture. I remember, about ten years ago, the new president of the James Beard Foundation came to me for advice and said she had this vision of really adding a level and a layer of programming at the James Beard Foundation, not just to honour the biggest and brightest chefs, but to really think about how they can use the position of the James Beard Foundation to educate their chefs about sustainability, to encourage their chefs to see that they have this powerful educational role, to honour those chefs that are doing that kind of educational work. To have a conference that brings those people together and this many years later they've really done that. And I think that chefs and media combined can play that really.'

Who controls the media is an issue: 'You've seen the same kind of consolidation that you see in the food sector happening in the media industry', said Lappé, 'where now you have about five companies that control pretty much everything we see, hear and read.' And power is also about what she calls the 'narrowing of messages. You have the kind of filter-bubble phenomenon of people getting so much of their media now filtered through a platform like Facebook, so you see what you expect to see'. Lappé's Real Food Media, an online resource for anyone interested in food, is a response to the media landscape she describes: 'I was trying to figure out some creative ways to do the kind of storytelling I think is so important, and get those messages out', she told me. 'What's our kind of work around?' An international film contest, was one of her answers, as well as an online book club 'to bring conversations together around the table around books, to highlight who are the leading authors we think people should be reading'. Independent documentaries which bypass the commissioning process of the broadcasters, mean an opportunity to work with the kind of people who might not find their way into the corridors of power or the talent pool which Nick Thorogood describes in 'Man vs food' (this volume). 'We partnered with a group called Story Core that does incredible interpersonal storytelling', said Lappé. 'We get food workers across the food chain to share their story with each other and then show those publicly.' Real Food Media is a response to the 'limitations to what we can get from the media industry' and a way to empower new ways of storytelling. 'We can think of ourselves, all of us, as media makers, and storytellers', she told me.

A Channel 4 executive told me that what the broadcaster, which advertises itself as 'born risky', wants is something new. Always. 'We've done campaigns', she said. 'We've done *Fish Fight*; we've done Jamie Oliver. We want something else because it's boring after a while. Everyone else is doing it. We should do, "why there are no visionaries", "what's wrong with politics", "why private school networks create nucleuses of power which are not dynamic." It's all about the chess game of power. If we did something with Simon Cowell about where are the visionaries, if we used TV as a vehicle to discuss that, I get that, but it has to be done in a different way. Everything has to come from the bedrock of lifting back the covers off society and saying something.'

I asked TV producer Nick Thorogood, and former TV producer and now Senior Teaching Fellow in Media Arts at Royal Holloway University Amanda Murphy, to spin up a series to change the world. It would be based on a real food story that had a strong implicit message about sustainability and food heritage, linking food systems with obesity and sedentary lifestyles. I could have chosen any number of ideas, from my visit to *Food Studies Conference* in California 2016, to the nose-to-tail competitive festival, Cochon 555, which is sweeping across America, to the sci-fi meat technologies witnessed by Anna Lappé. I chose Warndu, the story described in the previous chapter about Australian food writer, Rebecca Sullivan, and her aboriginal partner, Damian Coulthard, and their 'Native Food Revolution providing Australia with sustainable and nutritious food'. I gave a brief summary, deliberately using buzz words so often used in TV proposals: white Australian food writer with a good social media following, along with her cool aboriginal partner revisit a food history which has been obscured in Australia. Foraging for indigenous foods, cooking and chatting to aboriginal families about the link between their foods and dreamtime bring together Sullivan's and Coulthard's real-life business, but could its lessons on everything from sustainable food systems to food heritage reach a global audience? I wondered if Damien Coulthard could be the new Siba whom Thorogood discovered in a deliberate bid to access South African culture in a way that Food Network hadn't done before.

We talked for no more than 20 minutes, with both producers focussing on the audience they know best. Thorogood was hesitant but could see it working in Australia: 'With Siba, we set out to find somebody who appealed to a very specific sector of the market in a very specific country where we had the channel', he explained. 'So, on Food Network Australia, it may well be that this would be a show that would be welcomed by the audience and be a big success. Siba was targeted for sub-Saharan Africa, very specifically actually for the emerging black middle-class market of South Africa. The people who produced the show for us were the people who had made shows like *Barefoot Contessa* and *Nigella* [Channel 4, 1999] and *Pioneer Woman* [Food Network, 2011–present], so they understood how you take a very specific culture and apply a filter that makes it very accessible. We had a show that absolutely would travel. But we didn't set out to do that, and I think that is quite important.'

Amanda Murphy, whose *Supernanny* on Channel 4 created a new narrative on parenting in the early 2000s, saw a series which could tap into a trend in the link between sustainable and healthy food. 'I think you could absolutely make a series around sustainable food as long it's not preachy', she said. 'As long as it's celebrational and they have interesting characters. I think, with more and more diverse outlets like Amazon and Netflix, there's a whole new scope of where you could take these kinds of programmes and how you can spin these sorts of narratives.' A former executive producer, Murphy is used to referencing existing ideas as short hand for building an idea. 'And you could combine that with fusion food to make fusion-sustainable food in an interesting territory.' She referenced *I'm a Celebrity Get Me Out of Here* and *Bear Grylls*: 'They've made people understand that you can eat something as basic as a bug. And so you can take that further along the line: you can tie in foraging and you can have some really quite glammy *MasterChef* type food. You can absolutely spin a series out of that in a number of ways – possibly front-led because talent-led food shows seem to do better. People connect to them more when someone's actually doing the doing, who is an expert in something. I think there are certain things you could do along the lines of *Jamie's School Dinners* that go back to [being] bit preachy, but you could do them in a different way for a food show. Because it's an issue that's not going to go away, and issues that don't go away just get worse and worse and escalate and TV shows do actually help those issues.'

Murphy had been thinking of a similar idea after chatting to a nutritionist on a plane: 'We ended up having this incredibly interesting conversation about people not connecting somehow to the fact that they're ill because of what they put in their mouths. We won't say, "I'm ill because I ate badly" or "I have Irritable Bowel Syndrome because quite frankly I drink far too much wine and a hell of a lot of coffee and I keep eating far too much acidic stuff." We won't take responsibility. No one has addressed illness.' When I first interviewed a Channel 4 executive for this book in 2013, she told me that she expected this trend would emerge on television: 'Our generation which is so skilled at using TV as a medium is starting to enter a phase where people are getting ill and dying', she told me then. 'Suddenly you get a whole rash of programmes about rainforests and unusual natural remedies.' In 2015, Kew Garden's botanist, James Wong, was listed by the *Sunday Times* as one of the top 20 most influential people in horticulture after his success with BBC Two's *Grow Your Own Drugs* (2009). In 2017 he travelled across four continents with Dr Michael Mosley uncovering how plants and plant science underpin the food we eat in BBC Two's *The Secrets of Your Food*.

Thorogood said that sustainability has already slipped into all sorts of programmes: 'If you were to look at *The Victorian Farm* [BBC Two, 2009], a classic history commission, a huge element of it, obviously, was about food, because farming was about making food. And what was really interesting was that you saw one of the presenters show you how they then use that food from the land: how they had to preserve the food, how they had to cook it and how it tied into their religious festivals. Just as you describe the experience for aboriginal food, *The Victorian Farm* was an experience from the UK that was all about the way that people lived and interacted with the land, their food source. And, what's really fascinating was it was about cooking things that you would look at and think, "there's no way I'd eat that, because they're boiling lambs' heads and whatever." ' He said Warndu could be framed in a similar way but would fit with 'something like Channel 4', which would mix and explore food history and current food trends. 'The discussions that happen in the corridors of big broadcasters are often driven by the culture of their company', he said. 'So, somewhere like Channel 4 that's trying to push its "born risky" agenda is trying to say we're not just populist. Maybe they are a little more *Daily Mail* and a little less *Sun*, although they might not like to see themselves in that way. And yet, if you look at the kinds of programmes they commission, they would very much reflect what you will see in Femail. So you talk about "eat yourself out of cancer": that is an article you would have seen in the *Daily Mail* almost every day for the last ten years.'

But he couldn't see the idea on Food Network: 'You can't move backwards', he said. 'However much we think it's interesting to revisit different ideas of food culture in that way, it's almost like a novelty experience. Unfortunately, a lot of people watch Food TV for the pure vicarious thrill of seeing someone else cook and create something they're not going to do themselves. They buy cookbooks to use as food porn. They sit there and literally paw the pages as they turn them, not intending to cook the recipes – or maybe they think they will but they never do. You know, the research is very clear on this.'

I told Thorogood what Anna Lappé had said about the response to *The Inconvenient Truth* and the link with food systems. He wasn't surprised: 'You know, people wanted to watch it to be shocked in a way, and to be angry. But how many people watched it and did nothing as a result? You know, how easy would it have been to sign an online petition, or to send an email to your MP or to write a physical letter? And yet, how many people vote each week on the *X Factor*?' He said that audiences want the path of least of resistance: 'You think about eating strawberries out of season. It used to be something you wouldn't dream of: it would be the fancy West End delicatessens that would have berries flown in from halfway round the world. Now you buy them for less than a pound in your supermarket. And you think of the food miles attached to a South African blueberry or a South American. It is extraordinary. And yet we expect that to be cheap.' He is pessimistic about how that message can be effective in television: 'I don't think you're going to get the consumers to take that level of engagement. They love a good story, they love to be entertained, they love to watch the shows, but do they take the next step?'

If television can (and does) create a new narrative, Thorogood reminded me that it's 'just entertainment'. It's also a business. 'We can do anything we like', he said, 'but it is a waste of time unless there is an interest or response from the public. So the idea that Food TV can dictate the response of the public is wrong: there's got to be either an interest in it, or even an interest that isn't even known by the audience, to be found.' With anyone looking for buy-in from the public, from supermarkets to television producers, it's all about the consumer: 'The reality with trying to change the world', he said, 'or improving the things that people want to cook or eat, is that it is driven by price sensitivity, their own personal needs, the supply chain', said Thorogood. He said that the dramatic shifts in the way we eat, such as the influence of Ken Hom who brought Chinese food to BBC Two in 1984, were facilitated by the supermarkets which provided not only the ingredients, but also the ready meals too at a price that made it hard to match the home-cooked recipes. 'So, suddenly, the onus of responsibility shifts from the individual cooking at home to the supply chain in the ready-meal or in the ingredient source', said Thorogood. 'You know, everyone says, "oh, it's dreadful that the farmers can't afford to take pints of milk out of cows and sell it to us," yet we all revel in the fact that we can buy a pint of milk for 40p that's been shipped halfway across the continent rather than buy it from the UK and pay a few pence more. And that is the real challenge.'

Thorogood thinks that we've come a long way in terms of food awareness, not just because of Hugh Fernley-Whittingstall or Channel 4's *Superfoods* (2015–17) or *Food Unwrapped*, but simply because there are more people cooking. 'I think those men who for the first time, back in the late 1990s/early 2000s, watched Jamie cook and suddenly thought, "do you know what, I'll have that a go." This isn't all about women in the kitchen with bowls and whisks, this is about getting your hand in and tearing and mixing and pounding and making. And I think that is crucial. Suddenly we had a whole half the population suddenly going, "yeah, you know what actually, (a) I like it, (b) I'm interested in it, (c) it's cool, and I'm now going to embrace it and know more about it. That doesn't necessarily mean they're going to then go to the next step and say, "right, I'm going to go out and get free-range eggs" or "I'm going to go and get Fair Trade coffee" or whatever it may be.'

Zoe Collins says that food education is at the heart of the solution but that it's a tricky line to negotiate: 'I think a lot about my work in terms of tensions at the moment, and that's a good thing', she told me. 'At one end of this it's about people being better informed and being able to make better decisions, and at the other end what critics would call the nanny state, taking the decisions out of your hands through regulation, government intervention, so that there is no choice. I don't think you have to be in one camp or another. I think it's two philosophies and you have to find a place in the middle of those two things. But it's also interesting to notice that the food industry, when put under scrutiny and pressure, will say it's all about information and people being able to make the right choice. The food industry when put under scrutiny, under pressure, is where they jump towards. I don't think they're wrong, but I don't think that that can be it. I think we're better informed now than at any other time in our lives but we're still making the wrong decisions. So, on its own, TV cannot be the answer.'

These issues are massively complex and take a huge amount of resource and really clever people to think it all through. And what we tend to do as TV producers do is drive a simple and clear story because that's what we are – we're storytellers. Would we have called ourselves that ten years ago? We still are idealistic, but I think we were just in the middle of it and we thought we could change the world. What storytelling requires is complexity and sophistication but also clarity. And so I don't think that I expect our shows to solve everything. I think we hope that our shows will create debate. Jamie actually calls himself an irritant. He keeps going on. You have to keep scratching it and eventually you've got to deal with it. And I think that is what we do.'

For Mark Thompson, one of the original architects of modern Food TV, Jamie Oliver is only part of the story: 'Jamie tried and failed', he told me in 2013 before Oliver's success with *Sugar Rush* (2015). 'Audiences are more sophisticated now. I don't believe that there's one answer to obesity – the causes are so complex, but super-size portions play a role.' He believes that peer pressure is the answer, and paraphrased Max Weber: 'Deferred gratification is a middle-class thing and family discipline is about that. It's about, "do your homework, eat your greens." It's a cultural activity. Healthier food is the middle-class domain – look at how smoking stopped in the middle classes. You'll always get those middle-class people who think it's transgressive to smoke, but most people know it's unhealthy. It took 50–60 years to filter smoking change.'

I asked Jane Root in 2013 whether television can change the story of obesity. 'I don't know', she admitted. 'It's a really big question. But you have to make it human and personal.' I spun the question round to ask why it is so difficult to tackle issues like climate change, obesity and food security on television. 'Because people come to TV for pleasure', she answered. 'They use the Internet for information and that's really affected things. But television occupies a different space and so it has to have personal jeopardy and stakes and human emotion and all those things.' I told her that according to James Purnell, Director of Strategy and Education at the BBC, even though we now watch on a variety of screens, more TVs are being bought than ever before, and that his research shows that the first thing people buy for their own home is a TV. Root agreed that the sofa is a symbol of what 'home' means: 'TV is more sensual and when you're on your sofa, you're after entertainment and pleasure, even if it is getting your goat. But the Internet is about taking information away.'

Root's television production company Nutopia, produced what she called 'this huge thing', the history series *How We Got to Now*. Presented by media theorist and author of *Where Good Ideas Come From* (2010), Steven Johnson, it was broadcast on America's PBS from 2014 and on BBC Two from 2015, with what Root called an 'enormous [online] information hub', *How We Get to Next: A Magazine of the Future*. The series, which is about innovation in the past and the present, explored in entertaining documentaries how concepts such as 'clean', 'dirt', 'glass' and 'heat' became part of the modern world. 'There's a lot of public service stuff in there', said Root. 'It's contemporary, social action oriented. That's how we've ended up – that history is pleasure and narrative, and the website is action. Nutopia is not alone in using this multimedia experience in motivating action: Root referred me to *The Biggest Loser* (NBC, 2004–16), which offers advice, information and a motivational app to accompany the TV show. 'That's led to a tonne of other material off TV in the US', she told me. She said that MTV's *16 and Pregnant* was another milestone in television and suggested that it had led to a substantial decrease in teenage pregnancies. 'What's interesting about *16 and Pregnant* is that nobody says, "I'm being told a social message here." The idea that being 16 and having a baby is an attractive thing or that life is easy is actually how damn tough it is instead. It's interesting but it's really smuggled in there and targeted at the audience that it's trying to get to.' She said that her original BBC philosophy of 'delight' is what works with audiences across the world: 'Jamie, Two Fat Ladies, Sophie [Dahl], Delia', she said, 'they're all grounded in pleasure. *Teen Mom* (MTV) is grounded in the pleasure of looking at girls' lives, and then the other stuff is all around it.'

Food Unwrapped follows in the footsteps of Channel 4's *Food File*, the channel's first series about the stories behind the way food is produced, which Pat Llewellyn and I both worked on in the early 1990s and which has done much to make a mainstream audience think about its consumption behaviour. Its presenter since 2013, Matt Tebbutt, told me for the *delicious.* podcast in 2019 that it had opened *his* eyes to issues that he had taken for granted: 'I've been in food for 25 years now, and I didn't question why, in a slice of ham, there's no hole. You just presume, "oh, it's a slice of ham." But then you see how that slice of ham gets in a packet and it's like, "oh wow." It blows your mind. Animal welfare, all sorts of issues get raised.' Yet he says the BBC One show he also presents, *Saturday Kitchen* is *not* the place to 'preach', that weekend morning television plays a different role: 'Some people have it on in the background, some people dip in and out depending on what's going on. So many kids are going to kids' clubs', he told me. 'But food is for everyone. I'm absolutely not into standing up and going, "yes you have to have free range; yes, you have to have organic," because people can't afford it. Not everyone can afford it. It's not the platform to start spouting your personal views. It's a platform to entertain, to celebrate food and to showcase people.'

I asked him if there was an assumption among the producers of what the national conversation of the day is. 'Absolutely', he told me. He gave me an example: '*Saturday Kitchen* has decided it's gone completely single-use plastic free, which is throwing up challenges, especially with dairy, things like that. If your chef wants to roll something in clingfilm and poach it, he can't. You have to work something out. And initially, you throw your hands in the air and you go, "oh my god, what am I going to do," but you can soon think round it.'

For Zoe Collins, it is about keeping that delight in mind while understanding the needs of her audiences: 'On the one hand, there's the audience that loves the campaigning Jamie', she told me in 2018, 'and then at the other end, there's the audience that just wants Jamie to give them fantastic and tasty and gorgeous food. I don't think everyone wants campaigning Jamie all the time.' I asked her how she manages those expectations with trickier messages, and reminded her that when we first talked in 2013, she told me that Jamie Oliver was looking for something to get his teeth into. I told her then about John Ingram's message that food must be taken to the consumer as meta-value, that is, as the stories that food represents, if we are to affect change. We had talked about waste and silly-shaped vegetables, and she had told me how difficult it was to make a compelling story out of austerity issues. Not even a year later, I reminded her, *Jamie's Money Saving Meals* (Channel 4, 2013) was on TV, based around a single idea of running a domestic kitchen with the same business sensibility that a chef might adopt to run a restaurant-kitchen. I suggested that it was a brilliant way of dealing with waste. 'You'd obviously talked about that [with Jamie] and come up with a plan', I said. 'Exactly right, yeah', she replied, telling me that *Save with Jamie*, the accompanying book published in 2013, dealt with 'a very specific need', but for Fresh One, it wasn't about waste: 'I think we understand that Jamie has a job to do for us. Jamie talks about it – we both do – as a job: we do all of the hard work and bring back the easy solutions for the audience. And nobody wants to know what it took to do it. It's, "here's the easy answers for you to adapt." Certainly, some of our best books have done that – time, money and health being the three that we talk about. We'd call those chop 'n' chat. We wouldn't call those campaigning. So we'd always say that everything that we've ever done is part of a mission of sorts, which is how to help people lead a healthier, happier life with food.' I asked her how she measures impact, whether that message got through: 'We can measure book sales and we can measure the reach of our content. And these days, we can have a direct dialogue with our audiences across social', she said. 'In 2010, *Jamie's 30-Minute Meals* sold 735,000 copies in ten weeks, our most successful book ever, closely followed by 2017's *5 Ingredients*. But', Collins added, 'our *15-Minute Meals* [2012] is our most successful book ever.'

Impact is an interesting issue in television, where overnights (ratings) and 'noise' on social media and newspaper headlines are the measure of success and the key to the next commission despite viewing habits changing all the time as platforms multiply. 'The closest analysis I will get is the TweetDeck that Sara Ramsden [Channel 4 commissioning editor, *Sugar Rush*] sen[ds] me, and then we look at what the peaks relate to', said Collins after *Sugar Rush*. I asked what kind of peaks she had noticed in the documentary. 'I think there were some around the mother and the child, loads around the day's worth of food – that really engaged people – and then loads around Mexico, particularly around the mother breastfeeding the baby and then giving him Coke. There were 'Outrage tweets.' I asked her if this extra layer of information and feedback from social media had affected her 'gut' in storytelling. 'It's a really interesting question', she said. 'I've never worked with a marketing team before and now we get analyses which I find a combination of irritating and interesting. And where I find it irritating is when they tell me things that I can't do that I want to do (I do them anyway) and what I find interesting is when they give me analysis that backs up my theories!' She told me that she would never put Jamie into a position where he would be vulnerable, but added that he wouldn't allow himself to be compromised either and has a very strong opinion on what he will and won't do: 'He's got a very clever, manipulative way. If you make him do something that he doesn't want to do, he screws it up so it's unworkable. He does it in a very subtle way so you get into the edit and it doesn't quite work.'

In 2018 Collins was intrigued that I should think of Jamie Oliver as a full-time campaigner: 'Is it Jamie's job to campaign on our behalf? Does he always have to stay in that space, or is it his choice? I don't think we think he does. I think we think he does it when he is moved to and when he has something new to say.' 'Like a real person then?' I said. She laughed. 'Yes, like a real person.'

In 2018, Jamie announced that he was on a mission to halve childhood obesity in the UK by 2030, and that his entire business would be helping to deliver that goal – from cooking shows to products deals. Jamie himself says that campaigning is something he finds increasingly difficult. 'If I'm honest with you, it's a huge burden', he told me for the *delicious.* podcast in 2017. 'I'd love to [live without it]. I haven't got a choice. If you're a half-decent person who has a platform, and I have an unusual platform, when you're shown things, when you've been there and you've seen that, you're changed.' I asked him what he thought he had achieved through his television programmes. 'If I look back across 20 years, by luck or chance in the early days, and then what I've done by intention over the last 13 years, then in the last three years, being much more rigorous and ninjaed and structured, we've got campaigning departments and people that specialise in writing and communications and all sorts. I don't know if it's my dyslexia, but you have to have the capacity to be very nuanced about the minutiae, but also go ultra-galactic.'

I asked him about the impact of *The Naked Chef,* and, although Pat Llewellyn had denied any intention to target young men specifically, Oliver was clear about what he had set out to do. 'We wanted to get men cooking. Twenty years ago, they weren't, in any real numbers. And that was paralleling women going to work. So you get a couple both putting a 12-hour day in and getting back and around the country, quite old-fashionedly, men would be going, "what's for dinner, love?" So, of course, as we both know, it ain't just about the food, it ain't just about the cooking. It's interconnected with so many other things – equal opportunities for men and women, going to work in large numbers, socially how the household and therefore how the (family) changes because of that.'

I asked him what drives him now. 'One of the problems that I have', he told me, 'and I can only look you in the eyes and tell you that this is the truth, is that the reason that I get up and work (and plan to for the next 12 years) is the gap between advantage and disadvantage in society. If you're a poor kid in Britain today, it's tough. So our sights are primarily about getting more real food to the poorest communities.'

Jamie Oliver says that the job is multi-faceted, and his layers of storytelling over the past 20 years now allow him to smuggle, Jane Root-style, the most important messages into his programmes and campaigns. He hosts off-TV campaigning events which barely make the news, such as the UK Harvest CEO Cook Off organised by the Jamie Oliver Food Foundation in 2017 in which he paired corporate bosses, including CEOs from Mars, Lucozade and McDonald's' Paul Pomroy, with celebrity chefs to cook for the inaugural charity banquet, UK Harvest, which redistributes quality restaurant waste that would have gone to landfill to people in need. McDonald's UK was given a Good Farm Animal Welfare Good Dairy commendation in 2017 from Compassion in World Farming (CIWF) for its use of organic milk. McDonald's UK has already won Good Egg Awards (2008 and 2015), a Good Sow Commendation (2013) and a Best Marketing Award (2016) from CIWF.

Pomroy says he's on a mission to 're-image' the UK business. He told *CEO Magazine* that McDonald's now uses 100 per cent British potatoes and beef, RSPCA-assured pork and has 17,500 UK farmers in its supply chain. The company has around £1 billion of investment in the region's economy. 'McDonald's has also implemented its Progressive Young Farmer programme, designed to support new agricultural talent in the pipeline and offer career opportunities', he told the magazine.

Pomroy was partnered with top chef, Mark Hix, at the CEO Cook Off, and told me that they share the same interest in provenance. 'We look after our farmers' said Pomroy. 'We source 100 per cent British beef.' Commitment to reducing waste is Pomroy's next project at McDonald's. 'There's a huge amount of food waste that goes out from the back doors of restaurants. We've been involved in British farming and agriculture and it's a natural step for us.'

Peter Harding of Lucozade-Ribena, who cooked with Oliver at the banquet, told me that the company had realised 'that we'd been on the wrong side of the argument for quite some time. We realised it was time for a change. We had an opportunity to lead the soft drinks industry, and we've undergone a massive reformulation of our drinks to cut 50 per cent of the sugar.' I suggested that Lucozade-Ribena must have known about the impact of sugar on our health before Jamie Oliver made a TV programme about it. 'I think Jamie's been an inspiration for us', he told me. 'He had a point. I care about the health of the kids in the UK and now I have a thousand people working here in the UK punching the air, shouting and cheering as new products come off our line.' He said that the drinks still have glucose and 'taste wonderful, and that makes them proud to be part of our company. They then become advocates for what we're doing. I'm excited that I can stand beside people like Jamie Oliver and beside Action on Sugar and say what we're doing is the right thing to do.'

Working with the CEOs, lending them Oliver's 'cool', his national treasure status, is arguably more persuasive than any television programme. But it couldn't have happened without *The Naked Chef.* Harding told me for the *delicious.* podcast that his colleagues preferred it to 'being told what to do'. For Oliver, it's a no-brainer: 'They have a huge reach', he told me. 'They have a huge power in terms of procurement and connections with businesses like agriculture and of course acknowledging things like waste. When you're working with the bosses, it means that you've got an amazing opportunity to inspire and empower and make a big impact.' He said that Peter Harding had openly thanked him for promoting the sugary drinks tax. 'Who would ever have thought that that would happen?' he said.

'The Jamie Oliver business now – and even me as a person – is like an onion', he told me. 'It depends which button you want to press. Most people know me as jazz hands, having a laugh and going on an adventure, and I'll happily do that and that is me as a mainstreamer, that is, quick and easy, five ingredient food. But behind the scenes, it's like a duck under water: there's these little legs paddling away.'

Are we there yet?

When I started the research for this book in 2013 as a senior lecturer in Broadcast Media and Broadcast Journalism at the University of Brighton, I was interested in getting under the skin of storytelling, not to change the world myself, but to encourage the next generation of storytellers to do so. I saw an opportunity to inspire through teaching, to empower through leadership. Academic analysis of my experience in television production and journalism could, I thought, leave a legacy, the untold story of the thinking behind the camera.

But as I encouraged the producers to pick apart their process with the help of academics and their books, I began to feel the tug of envy... and guilt. As I interviewed people from all over the world who were telling and creating stories to change the way we think about food, I began to feel uncomfortable. What started as an academic auto-ethnography was not just reflecting on my own journey through television and media, connecting my conclusions to wider cultural, political and social meanings, but it was also offering me a mirror to reflect back to me my own *inactivity*. This was the inertia that the television industry I was unpacking through academic analysis and personal memory was working so hard to move in its audiences.

In the summer of 2016, I left academia to return to food journalism, specialising in producing and presenting food podcasts that could tell the story of the people who are changing food culture. My portfolio now includes the *delicious.* podcast, which tells the stories of food from the small producers to the best chefs in the world, including the big issues in health, food waste and sustainability, *How to Eat to Save the Planet*, a brand new podcast series for the 'naturally fast food' company, Leon, *Cooking the Books* and *The Borough Market* podcast, which celebrates the stories of the people behind the stalls in London's most famous food market. I produce *Stop the Machine* and *The Big Table*, which are CEO Philip Lymbery's campaigning podcasts for Compassion in World Farming (CIWF), and *Right2Food*, a Food Foundation podcast series on food poverty hosted by children living every day with food insecurity and introduced by its ambassador, Emma Thompson DBE. Supported by their various teams, I have access to the chefs, writers, artisan producers and campaigners who help to change our thinking about food. I can overtly challenge or gently smuggle, as Jane Root describes it in the previous chapter, a vision of sustainability and responsible sourcing into the very fabric of food media.

What I've found in this buzzing society is a vibrant new food culture of activism, hard work and passion closing the circle of food consumption, carbon emissions, intensive food production, mass distribution and thoughtless over-consumption of energy, land and water. Responsible sourcing is the bottom line in many artisanal foods and restaurants, which have become safe spaces to rely on good provenance. Food markets and cookbooks encourage new trends, while immersive eating experiences use food as theatre, attracting new 'audiences' to food. Supper clubs such as the Conflict Café, a pop-up in London's Waterloo, raise awareness while breaking bread with strangers; the Café brings stories of war from Lebanon to Sri Lanka to the shared tables of (largely) Millennials looking to taste the food from these lands while listening to speakers about the cultures behind the headlines. Food and food production have become the medium through which culture is explored, eyes are opened and assumptions are challenged.

delicious. magazine, the most mainstream, entertainment-oriented medium in my portfolio, has led readers interested in cooking to become more aware of the issues behind food production, reflecting the growing number of readers whose fascination and love of food have become culturally and politically engaged. Editor Karen Barnes told me there is 'a big purpose behind *delicious.* and that is to shout about the wonderful produce in this country. Food only tastes really good if all the ingredients you're using come from a good place. We constantly advise readers to use high-welfare produce, and everything interlinks together. I see this approach as the heartland of *delicious.*' The *delicious.* podcast was nominated in its first year for a Fortnum & Mason Food and Drink award for best food programme, the only podcast to be included in a shortlist of BBC radio programmes, including Radio 4's *The Food Programme*, and it has topped the iTunes food charts several times.

It's a small part to play in the greater plan to change the national conversation, yet a steady weekly diet of chats with A-lister chefs and pioneering farmers drip feeds the kind of new information that is needed to stimulate debate. A Guild of Food Writers' panel discussion held in October 2019, in which senior commissioning editor at Quadrille books, Celine Hughes; editor of *Waitrose* magazine, Jessica Gunn; and John Farrand of the Guild of Fine Food were asked to predict the Next Big Thing, concluded that #sustainability is the next subject *du jour*. Early adopters include the *delicious.* podcast: over the past year alone, it has covered natural, organic and biodynamic wine, mob-grazing, sustainable tea, the Food Foundation's #vegpower campaign, vertical farming and rewilding. It's asked if #veganism can save the planet, it's made gin from waste grapes, it's visited Raymond Blanc's bee garden and it has featured some of the most influential food writers and YouTube celebrities in the land, who are pushing vegan recipes into the mainstream.

In the podcasts that I have produced for CIWF's CEO, Philip Lymbery, he calls for no less than a UN Convention on food and farming to secure food for future generations. His books, *Farmageddon: The True Cost of Cheap Meat* (2014) and *Dead Zone: Where the Wild Things Were* (2018), were the first to make the link between the cost of cheap meat and the decimation of rainforest and plains, and the impact on wild animals now facing extinction. Ahead of CIWF's 2017 *Extinction and Livestock* conference, which was the first to look at the impact of food production on the planet, Lymbery said, 'We need a total rethink of our food and farming systems before it's too late. Intensive livestock systems are at the heart of so many problems affecting health, food security, biodiversity, the environment and animal welfare. Unless we have a UN Convention to specifically tackle the wide-ranging impacts of food and farming, the targets on climate change won't be achieved and our world will continue to be ravaged by our broken food systems.' Lymbery claims, in his chapter in D'Silva and McKenna's book of the conference, *Farming, Food and Nature* (2018), that we could have more than enough food to feed the population of 9.6 billion projected to be on the planet by 2050 (according to the UN *World Population Prospects* report published in 2019). 'Without factory farming', writes Lymbery, 'we could feed everyone with better quality food using less farmland, not more. Leaving room for nature. Allowing the planet to breathe. Preserving fresh air, clean water and soils for future generations.'

While critics, and vegans in particular, argue that methane emissions from livestock are responsible for the greatest threat to the global environment, as well as the major cause of deforestation, loss of biodiversity and desertification, Philip Lymbery is keen to underline the difference between intensive and extensive farming. It is the intensive mega farms or *factory* farms, in which 74 billion animals are reared and slaughtered every year for food, which we need to boycott, rather than high-welfare, pasture-fed cattle farms. He encourages people to eat less but better high-welfare meat because of its role in countering climate change. 'Extensive farming provides animals the scope to lead more natural lives in ways that enhance that life-support system, being more beneficial for essentials like soil health and farmland biodiversity', he writes in his August 2019 blog post, 'Why our planet needs less meat and more extensive farming'. 'It uses less oil-based fertilisers and water, all big pluses in the sustainability stakes.' To balance the argument for veganism, he finds persuasive evidence for environmental transformation, as we create spaces for 'regenerative, agroeco-logical forms of farming'. Grazing animals, he writes, 're-engage the age-old nitrogen cycle where sunlight pushes up plants, eaten by animals whose drop-pings return nourishment to the soil. They can express their natural behaviours – running, flapping, grazing – making for happier animals with better immunity, cutting down on the need for veterinary antibiotics and reducing risk of disease'.

Changing the narrative, according to MEP Florent Marchesi, is the most important priority. Marchesi was one of the speakers at a round table discussion on the impact of food production on the planet, along with Philip Lymbery, at the European Parliament to promote Lymbery's book, *Dead Zone*. Marchesi argued that we must change the way we think about meat and reduce our consumption by 80 per cent, choosing only high-welfare, extensively farmed products. But he said that statistics are not powerful enough to change behaviour: 'we don't change people with numbers. You have to prove the possibility of a new model – agroecology – with less meat and more plant-based proteins. But to get to this point, you have to change the narrative, you have to change the way we think. We have to think that the good thing, the *cool* thing, is to have less meat, or at least, not to waste meat. We have to change the emotion of the people, the heart of the people', he said.

In 2012, as press officer at People for the Ethical Treatment of Animals (PETA) in London, Ben Williamson led the campaign to raise the profile of veganism, before heading up campaigns as PETA's senior international media director in Los Angeles from 2015. He told me in 2019 how hard it was at first to get vegan-ism into the national conversation: 'Every week, I was banging on the door of TV and radio shows trying to get veganism on the air', he said. 'I remember writing to *Sunday Brunch* numerous times suggesting different vegan celebs to come on the show and being ignored week after week.' He believes the tipping point came in March 2015, when the *Evening Standard* put Veganism on the cover. The article, 'Green is the new black: How veganism became sexy in London' by Rosamund Urwin listed the coolest vegan places to eat in the capital, and used the time-honoured media tradition of calling it the Next Big Thing. While the daily press had a new song to sing, Williamson says that the cooking shows were late to embrace it. 'Hugh [Fearnley-Whittingstall] was still doing his high-welfare thing, and Jamie would do plant-based occasionally', he told me. 'Gordon has always been a lost cause to us.'

He believes that it was Netflix that propelled veganism into pop culture, despite his own 2015 winning performance on ITV's *Take Me Out* as the 'vegan guy making you purr!' 'Netflix got the vegan message to get into people's homes with documentaries like *Cowspiracy, Forks Over Knives* [2011], and more recently *What the Health* [2017]', he told me. 'We started to see an uptake in Vegan Starter

Kit requests after these films launched on Netflix. *Okja* [2017] was also another big one for us', he said, referring to the Korean–American action adventure film about a girl who raises a genetically modified superpig. He thinks he understands why: 'These cooking shows only have half or an hour to fill, so why devote a part of it to a diet that's only embraced by 3 per cent of the population?' Netflix, he says, fanned the flame already lit by the increasing availability of good-tasting technologically innovative vegan foods, and the rise of reducetarianism or flex-itarianism diets, in which meat is not always included in a dish as standard, and plant-based is no longer a binary choice. 'Weekly studies showing the benefits of plant-based diets, the rise of grime and the vegan rappers who came with it, and Veggie Pret appearing on the high street' contributed to an inexorable rise, he says. 'I don't think there was any one thing that caused the mainstreaming of veganism in the UK in recent years', he continued. 'It's all about giving people options and meeting them where they are and not forcing people into categories.'

By 2018, the rise of 75,000 people signing up for Veganuary in just one year did not inspire TV to respond, despite a glut of vegan cookbooks appearing on the market in 2017 and 2018. Waitrose reported a five-fold increase in searches for vegan food on their website in the days running up to New Year 2018, and shares in Greggs, the high street bakery, jumped more than 13 per cent after the success of its sell-out Quorn-filled vegan sausage roll. Yet there is still no vegan TV chef, despite the enormous success of vegan chefs Bosh!, and Gaz Oakley's delightful YouTube channels. Oakley told me in 2018 that there 'have been talks', yet nothing has materialised. But why chase terrestrial TV when the audiences are looking to the smaller screen? Ian Theasby and Henry Firth are the former entrepreneurs who became social media sensations when they set up their own Bosh! TV channels in 2016. Their first recipe book was the highest-selling debut cookbook of 2018 and the highest-selling vegan cookbook of all time, and with 28 million views of their daily videos, they hardly need more exposure. But they told me for the *delicious.* podcast in 2019 that they would love a TV show of their own: 'Telly has a different value', said Firth. Theasby agreed: 'Having a TV show would be a significant marker in time, not just for us but for vegan food.' They explained that, however large their presence was on social media, it was about getting to 'the grown-ups of Normal England', as Firth said. 'It would be massive… a real honour', said Theasby. Firth winked. 'Watch this space.' As this book goes to press, they tell me that their dream has come true, and that *Living on the Veg* will be coming to ITV in early 2020.

So what does this mean for food storytelling and the vital role it plays in changing consumption habits? What can it offer the various tribes that the viewing experience – still known as 'television' – has created, even as it continually fragments? The old chop 'n' cook shows feel old-fashioned now, as food lays its cultural pedigrees, its back- or origin stories and its impact on the kitchen table. Through personal journey narratives, Netflix original series, such as *The Chef's Table* (2015–19), have brought high gastronomy into our hearts. Netflix's 2018 documentary, *The Game Changers*, harnessed the mighty influence of Arnold Schwarzenegger, Jackie Chan and Lewis Hamilton to encourage teenage boys set on pumping iron to think again about the place of meat in their protein-rich diets.

A collision of media platforms is speeding up the message-making, with narratives dovetailing across social media, reverberating around the echo chambers and onto people's plates. A shocking investigation in 2017 by CIWF into Parmesan production in Italy's Po Valley revealed that cows there are forced to live in barns, with no access to the outdoors, and in their own waste, unable to express their natural behaviours. The report and video went viral before television could respond.

In a multimedia age, what we can conclude as we devise ever newer forms of storytelling for change, is that persuasive narratives are triangulated online, offline and in real life. In a Borough Market podcast capturing the Market's Borough Talks series, the panellists, who were made up of an Instagram influencer, a food writer and a TV producer, discuss how the media can help your food business: 'It's empowering', said the panel's chair, broadcaster and food writer Sybil Kapoor. 'You can put forward seeds of ideas and opportunities for people to discover new things and think about things in a new way. Writer and blogger Milly Kenny-Ryder, whose online food, culture and fashion magazine *Thoroughly Modern Milly* has made her an Instagram 'influencer', says that social media 'spreads the word. It gives food a platform to shine, visually, and it allows people to interact. I see a post going up and then a few comments down, I see friends chatting about [it]'. Fellow panellist, Pete Lawrence, is former head of in-house features at the BBC and chief creator at Hungry Gap Productions in Bristol, and he has produced Nigel Slater, the Hairy Bikers, Nigella Lawson, Lorraine Pascale and Rachel Khoo. I asked him if the rise of Instagram storytelling could reduce the impact of the power of television. 'I think that unlike a lot of social media where everything is instant, TV has the opportunity to unfold a story over a period of time. I think that television will change a lot over the next few years because of social media, but it's going to be all about the story. You can shoot things beautifully (on social media) but there is something about the skill of the storyteller that makes the end product good or bad.'

And good television still has the power to transform attitudes: in 2017, David Attenborough's *Blue Planet II* on BBC One did more to raise awareness of the impact of plastic waste than any number of campaigns. As Attenborough accepted the Impact trophy at the 2018 National Television Awards for *Blue*

Planet II, he said, 'If our television programmes have helped stir the conscious-ness of people around the world, and we are going to do something to protect our beautiful world, then all of us will be very pleased.'

Attenborough was asked what he wanted to see in people's behaviours as a result of the show, and he said, 'Think of the consequences of what they do, of what they throw away and what they eat and how they organise their lives. And, in the end, who they vote for.' The then British chancellor Philip Hammond responded by telling the House of Commons that he and then environment secretary, Michael Gove, would investigate how the tax system and charges on single-use plastic items could be used to reduce waste. 'Audiences across the country, glued to *Blue Planet II*, have been starkly reminded of the problems of plastic pollution' said Hammond. 'And I want us now to become a world leader in tackling the scourge of plastic littering our planet and our oceans.'

Attenborough, who was keen to point out that he only wrote and voiced the narration in *Blue Planet*, and that it was the production team who deserved the Impact Award, illustrates that the most powerful messages are delivered by the (very few) television personalities whom we trust, whose authenticity blows all other message-making out of the water.

Attenborough's documentary, *Climate Change: The Facts* (BBC One, 2019), in which he said that 'global warming was our greatest threat in thousands of years', was critically praised: *The Guardian* called it 'a rousing call to arms'. The documentary was aired seven days after Extinction Rebellion's first 'disruption' in London over ten days in Easter 2019. The timing was TV gold. While Atten-borough at 92 pulled no punches in the documentary, silencing critics who had accused him – and the BBC – of previously failing to address the political and economic solutions necessary to stop climate change, his audience was moved. His message was clear: fossil fuels are at the heart of the problem; deforestation must stop and the link must be made clear with our meat-intensive diets; and climate change is here and already devastating many of the world's most vulner-able communities.

The dovetailing of Extinction Rebellion and Attenborough's *Climate Change* documentary was given the storytelling trump card in May 2019, when *Time* magazine featured the Swedish teenage climate activist, Greta Thunberg, on its cover. It was a thrilling triangulation: our 92-year-old national treasure was fighting for *our* survival in the winter of his life, while thousands of respectable, largely middle-class rebels were resurrecting the spirit of the Suffragettes by chaining and gluing themselves to railings and getting arrested for their beliefs. And for a nation that loves an underdog, the story of a 16-year-old girl with Asperger's, stoically travelling from leader to leader across the globe to deliver the simplest of messages, 'our house is on fire', changed the world. As I finish this book, she graces the cover of British *Vogue*, guest-edited by self-styled ambassador for the fight against climate change, former A-list Hollywood actress (and now former Royal), Meghan, Duchess of Sussex. The magazine came out during London Fashion Week, where Extinction Rebellion's demands for an end to mindless consumption made every headline.

Will it work in time to reduce the biodiversity loss and reduce greenhouse-gas emissions to net-zero by 2025, as Extinction Rebellion urges? Will the government respond to the deliberately disruptive campaigning tactics of the movement and go beyond declaring a #climateemergency to take control of the reins, as the four horsemen of the apocalypse ride out of control (as predicted by Ashcroft's 2012 documentary *Four Horsemen*): Famine, War, Conquest and Death already appear in our headlines as the threats of food insecurity, social unrest, fascism and extinction. Will our penchant for fetishizing food be remembered by history as the decadence that precipitates the fall of an empire in our Age of Consequence, as Ashcroft calls it? He quotes Sir John Bagot Glubb's 1978 essay, *The Fate of Empires*, in recognising the remarkable similarities between the life cycle of empires: 'From the early pioneers to the final conspicuous consumers who become a burden on the state', narrates Ashcroft, the common features of its decline include 'conspicuous displays of wealth; massive disparity between rich and poor; and obsession with sex'. In each empire lasting around 250 years, Glubb and Ashcroft point out that the Age of Affluence moves into the Age of Intellect, ending with 'bread and circuses in the Age of Decadence'. Ashcroft uses images in his film of the orgiastic feasts of the last days of the Roman Empire to make his point. A scroll through the Instagram images on any account would deliver a twenty-first-century equivalent of food porn and body fetish, a visual feast to distract from the realities of climate change already affecting our world. Susie Orbach, British psychoanalyst and social critic, writes in the Extinction Rebellion handbook, *This Is Not a Drill* (2019), that the way to persuade people to confront the terrifyingly real challenges of climate change is by the telling the tough stories and touching the emotions: 'If we look at how moved and concerned children are when they hear about endangered bears, we see a tap for political action. That tap root should be part of the toolkit for activists.' She believes that we need to provoke conversations and touch hearts. 'In doing so, we will build a movement that can handle the horrors we are facing, without the secondary issue of internal denial. We will be more, not less, robust. More, not less, effective. More, not less, compelling.'

Even if most people refuse to change their consumption habits for what they see as just an existential threat rather than a real emergency, there is still hope. As communication theorist Everett Rogers explains in his book, *Diffusion of Innovations* (2003), we only need 15–18 per cent of take up for any message to be adopted for real change to be made. Simon Sinek of Innovation Bell Curve explains Rogers' theory in a 2016 Ted Talk on the market's response to the latest version of the iPhone, the early-twenty-first-century premium in cultural capital, but it is a vital lesson for storytellers. Sinek says that the first 2.5 per cent of the market are the innovators, and 13.5 per cent are the early adopters, with the early majority and the late majority at 34 per cent each, and the 'laggards' trailing behind at 16 per cent. 'If you want mass market acceptance of an idea', he says, 'you cannot have it until you achieve a tipping point of 15–18 per cent market penetration.' Peer pressure among the innovators and early adopters is the key to real change, but is it lasting? Mark Thompson told us earlier in this book that healthier food is the middle-class domain, but that it would, he believed, trickle down to the rest of society, as has the decrease in smoking.

Tim Mead of Yeo Valley, who has been pioneering organic dairy farming in Somerset for 25 years, believes so too. To increase the 4.5 per cent of organic dairy that consumers currently in the UK to 10 per cent of the total market, Mead told me that it would take four million people to put three organic dairy products in their shopping basket every week. He says that there is a revolution in farming on the way. He believes that because intensive farming over the last 75 years has left the soil so depleted of minerals, it has to change, and that despite their methane emissions, grazing animals are a vital part of that mix, making grassland valuable to the farmer and contributing to carbon capture. 'The top metre of the world's soils contains three times as much carbon as the entire atmosphere, making it a major carbon sink alongside forests and oceans', Mead told me. 'Soils play a key role in the carbon cycle by soaking up carbon from dead plant matter. Plants absorb CO_2 from the atmosphere through photosynthesis, and pass carbon to the ground when dead roots and leaves decompose.'

More and more farmers, including Mead, are looking at sustainable options such as 'mob-grazing', the movement of animals across the same pasture, leaving a trail of natural fertilisers behind. Philip Lymbery, whose next book has the working title 'Sixty Harvests Left', calls it the 'reappearing act', as cows are followed by sheep, which are followed by pigs which are followed by chickens and then crops, bringing back a rotational system first pioneered in the late 1700s by agricultural reformer Thomas Coke. And with the bugs and insects that love a cow pat comes the reappearance of the wildlife, such as barn owls and songbirds, which have been lost as the domino effect of factory farming brought down their homes.

With this explosion of stories, will we see a reprise of the great values of British storytelling that set off such an extraordinary mind-bomb 25 years ago? Will these stories remind us of the wealth of this green and pleasant land, and of the resilient spirit of its people before it's too late? Will an echo of Pat Llewellyn's warm pastiche of Britishness stir our national spirit just in time? Or has the glass shattered, scattering its influence onto a myriad different platforms, rupturing the national conversation and leaving us to chat among ourselves?

Food is complicated; it's about quality, health, the environment and the economy, and is an essential part of our social and cultural fabric. It's also about governance, about who makes the rules, and why. As this book leaves my laptop, we are in the most divisive period in modern history, with Trump, Brexit and the rise of populism dominating timelines and news media, and the most important story of all time, climate change, still being obscured by squabbling politicians. But it also morphs from manuscript into book with the news that *Spitting Image*, that perfect satirical storytelling that united a nation in the 1980s and 1990s, is returning to terrestrial television. Let's hope that the joy of a good laugh can change the story, poke fun at our junk-food culture and make sense of our world again.

References

ABC News (2014), 'Nigella Lawson speaks out about fraud trial', http://abcnews. go.com/GMA/video/nigella-lawson-speaks-calls-fraud-trial-mortifying-21396875. Accessed 2 December 2014.

Allinson, K. and Featherstone, K. (2019), *A Pinch of Nom,* London: Bluebird.

Andersen, K. and Kuhn, K. (2014), *Cowspiracy: The Sustainability Secret,* USA: Appian Way.

Arthurs, J. (2004), *Television and Sexuality: Regulation and the Politics of Taste,* London: Open University Press.

Arvidsson, A. (2005), *Brands: Meaning and Value in Media Culture*, London: Routledge.

Ashcroft, R. (2012), *Four Horsemen*, USA: Renegade.

Barthes, R. (1957), *Mythologies,* Editions du Seuil, Paris (translation) and London: Jonathan Cape.

Barnes, K. (2017), in-person interview by Gilly Smith.

Baudrillard, J. (1994), *Simulacra and Simulation (The Body in Theory: Histories of Cultural Materialism)*, Ann Arbor, MI: University of Michigan Press.

Bazalgette, P. (2016), in-person interview by Gilly Smith.

Beeton, I. (1861), *Mrs Beeton's Book of Household Management*, London: S. O. Beeton Publishing,

BBC News (2000), 'Delia's [sic] cooks up a commotion', http://news.bbc.co.uk/1/hi/ entertainment/597387.stm. Accessed 23 June 2016.

Bilmes, A. (2001), 'Say what you like about Nigella Lawson', *GQ*, January, http://www. nigella.com/nigella/detail.asp?article=35&area=10. Accessed 2 December 2005.

Biressi, A. (2017), in-person interview by Gilly Smith.

Biressi, A. and Nunn, H. (2013), *Class and Contemporary British Culture*, Basingstoke: Palgrave Macmillan.

Blumler, J. and Katz, F. (eds) (1975), *The Uses of Mass Communications: Current Perspectives on Gratifications Research*, Beverley Hills: Sage.

Bordo, S. (1998), 'Hunger as ideology', in R. Scapp and B. Seitz (eds), *Eating Culture*, Albany, NY: State University of New York Press, pp. 11–35.

——(2003), *Unbearable Weight: Feminism, Western Culture, and the Body*, Berkeley: University of California Press.

The Borough Market Podcast (2017), 'How the Media can Help your Food Business', 24 May, https://play.acast.com/s/theboroughmarketpodcast/19080da7-274d-47b5-8561-d9fa52d5f71e. Accessed 26 May 2020.

Bourdain, A. (2005), *Kitchen Confidential*, London: Bloomsbury.

Bourdieu, P. (1984), *Distinction: A Social Critique of the Judgement of Taste*, London: Routledge.

Brillat-Savarin, J. (1970), *The Physiology of Taste*, (trans. A. Drayton), London: Penguin.

Brownlie, D. and Hewer, P. (2005), 'Culinary tourism: An exploratory reading of contemporary representations of cooking', *Consumption, Markets and Culture*, 8:1, pp. 7–26.

——(2011), '(Re),covering the spectacular domestic: Culinary cultures, the feminine mundane, and brand Nigella', *Advertising and Society Review*, 12, pp. 7–26.

Brunsdon, C. (2005), 'Feminism, postfeminism, Martha, Martha and Nigella', *Cinema Journal*, 44, pp. 110–16.

Brunsdon, C. and Spigel, L. (1997), *Feminist Television Criticism: A Reader*, London: Open University Press.

Buckley, R. (2008), 'Glamour and the Italian female film stars of the 1950s', *Historical Journal of Film, Radio and Television*, 28, pp. 267–89.

Butland, B., Jebb, S., Kopelman, P., McPherson, K., Thomas, S., Mardell, J. and Parry, V. (2007), 'Tackling obesities: Future choices – project report', Department of Innovation Universities and Skills, https://assets.publishing.service.gov.uk/government/uploads/system/uploads/attachment_data/file/287937/07-1184x-tackling-obesities-future-choices-report.pdf Accessed May 2016.

CEO Magazine (2016), 'Paul Pomroy', https://www.theceomagazine.com/executive-interviews/food-beverage/paul-pomroy/. Accessed 8 August 2018.

Chant, S. M. (2015), 'A history of local food in Australia 1788–2015', Ph.D. thesis, Adelaide: University of Adelaide.

Clare, C. (2017), telephone interview by Gilly Smith.

Clark, Z. (2002), 'Goulash and solidarity', *The Guardian*, 2 September, https://www.theguardian.com/comment/story/0,,824560,00.html. Accessed 1 April 2016.

Clarke, S. (2014), 'Masterchef's secret sauce', TBI Vision, https://tbivision.com/2014/10/29/masterchefs-secret-sauce/. Accessed 3 June 2016.

Climate Change: The Facts, (2019, UK: BBC One).

Cohen, D. (2016), 'Food for London: Sadiq Khan and Sainsbury's support our campaign on food waste', *Evening Standard*, 22 September, http://www.standard.co.uk/news/foodforlondon/food-for-london-sadiq-khan-and-sainsburys-support-our-campaign-on-food-waste-a3351466.html. Accessed 29 September 2016.

Collins, Z. (2013, 2015, 2018), in-person interview by Gilly Smith.

Comolli, J. (1980), 'Machines of the visible', in T. De Laurentis and S. Heath (eds), *The Cinematic Apparatus*, New York: St. Martin's Press, pp. 120–42.

Corkery, C. (2016), 'Mary Berry's husband speaks out about her *Great British Bake Off future*', *The Mail Online*, https://www.express.co.uk/showbiz/tv-radio/710606/Mary-Berry-The-Great-British-Bake-Off-Paul-Hunnings-Paul-Hollywood-Sue-Perkins-Mel. Accessed 30 April 2017.

Counihan, C. and Van Esterik, P. (2013), *Food and Culture: A Reader*, New York: Routledge.

Cowdrey, K. (2016), 'Jamie Oliver to release two cookbooks in 2016', *The Bookseller*, https://www.thebookseller.com/news/mj-strikes-gift-deal-publish-two-new-jamie-olivers-year-322901. Accessed 3 August 2017.

Dimond, G. (2008), 'Forty years of eating and drinking in London', *Time Out*, 24 September, http://www.timeout.com/london/restaurants/forty-years-of-eating-and-drinking-in-london. Accessed 23 June 2016.

D'Silva, J. and McKenna, C. (2018), *Farming, Food and Nature*, London: Routledge.

Ellis-Peterson, H. (2016), '*Great British Bake Off* moves to Channel 4 as BBC negotiations collapse over fee', *The Guardian*, https://www.theguardian.com/tv-and-radio/2016/sep/12/bbc-loses-great-british-bake-off. Accessed 13 September 2016.

Elkington, S. (2016), in-person interview by Gilly Smith.

Extinction Rebellion (2019), *This Is Not a Drill: An Extinction Rebellion Handbook*, London: Penguin.

FAO (2019), 'FAO chief warns of the "globalization of obesity", urges G20 to ensure healthy diets through regulation', http://www.fao.org/news/story/en/item/1193594/icode/. Accessed 9 September 2019.

Fielding-Singh, P. (2017), 'A taste of inequality: Food's symbolic value across the socioeconomic spectrum', Sociological Science, https://www.sociologicalscience.com/download/vol-4/august/SocSci_v4_424to448.pdf. Accessed 2 March 2020.

Fitzgerald, L. (2016, 2017), in-person interview by Gilly Smith.

Flanagan, J. C. (1954), 'The critical incident technique', *Psychological Bulletin*, 51, pp. 327–58.

Flego, A., Herbert, J., Waters, E., Gibbs, L., Swinburn B., Reynolds, J. and Moodie, M. (2014), 'Jamie's Ministry of Food: Quasi-experimental evaluation of immediate and sustained impacts of a cooking skills program in Australia', *PLoS ONE*, 9:12, p. e114673.

Flett, K. (2001), '1987 and all that', *The Observer*, 14 October, https://www.theguardian.com/lifeandstyle/2001/oct/14/foodanddrink.features4. Accessed 12 July 2016.

——(2005), 'Where the fashion world eats', *The Guardian*, 16 January, https://www.theguardian.com/lifeandstyle/2005/jan/16/foodanddrink.features5. Accessed 23 July 2016.

FoodBevMedia (2016), 'Hey like wow adds "revolutionary sugar-free vitamin water range"', https://www.foodbev.com/news/hey-like-wow-launches-revolutionary-sugar-free-vitamin-water-range/. Accessed 3 September 2017.

Food Foundation (2019), *Children's Future Food Inquiry*, https://foodfoundation.org.uk/wp-content/uploads/2019/04/Childrens-Future-Food-Inquiry-report.pdf. Accessed 2 March 2020.

Foulkes, N. (2002), '192's number is finally up', *Evening Standard*, https://www.standard.co.uk/go/london/restaurants/192s-number-is-finally-up-6326513.html. Accessed 16 May 2016.

Freedman, D. (2016), 'The Great British Bake Off sell off is a sign of the TV time', *The Conversation*, 14 September, https://theconversation.com/the-great-british-bake-off-sell-off-is-a-sign-of-the-tv-times-65346. Accessed 15 September 2016.

Friedan, B. (1963), *The Feminine Mystique*, New York: W.W. Norton &Company.

Friedman, A. (2018), *Chefs, Drugs and Rock & Roll*, New York: Harper Collins.

Furness, H. (2015), 'Jamie Oliver admits school dinners campaign failed because eating well is a middle class preserve', *The Telegraph*, 24 August, http://www.telegraph.co.uk/news/celebritynews/11821747/Jamie-Oliver-admits-school-dinners-campaign-failed-because-eating-well-is-a-middle-class-preserve.html. Accessed 23 March 2016.

'Fusion' (2020), Lexico.com, https://www.lexico.com/en/definition/fusion. Accessed 2 March 2020.

Geoghegan, S. (2016), in-person interview by Gilly Smith.

Godwin, R. (2015), 'Queen of the restaurant scene turns 70', *The Evening Standard*, https://www.standard.co.uk/go/london/restaurants/queen-of-the-restaurant-scene-fay-maschler-turns-70-10396913.html. Accessed 5 July 2017.

Gordon, P. (2016), in-person interview by Gilly Smith.

Grenfell, M. (2012), *Pierre Bourdieu (Key Concepts)*, London: Routledge.

Grosz, E. A. (1994), *Volatile Bodies: Towards a Corporeal Feminism*, Bloomington, IN: Indiana University Press.

Gupta, A. (2010), 'How TV superchef Jamie Oliver's food revolution flunked out', Alternet, 7 April, http://www.alternet.org/story/146354/how_tv_superchef_jamie_oliver's_'food_revolution'_flunked_out. Accessed 4 April 2016.

Hall, S. (1978), *Policing the Crisis*, London: Palgrave Macmillan.

——(2000), 'Whose heritage? The impact of cultural diversity on Britain's Living Heritage', *National Conference at G-Mex*, London: Arts Council of England.

Hamlyn, M. (1988), *Hannah Woolley, English Cookery of the Seventeenth Century*, Sevenoaks: Kingswood Publishing.

Harding, P. (2017), in-person interview by Gilly Smith.

Hayward, T. (2018), 'Anthony Bourdain obituary', *The Guardian*, 9 June, https://www.theguardian.com/lifeandstyle/2018/jun/09/anthony-bourdain-obituary. Accessed 2 March 2020.

Heneghan, C. (2015), 'Snack attack: How quick eats are revolutionizing the industry', Food Dive, https://www.fooddive.com/news/snack-attack-how-quick-eats-are-revolutionizing-the-industry/403961/. Accessed 3 July 2017.

Hewer, P. and Brownlie, D. (2009), 'Culinary culture, gastrobrands and identity myths: "Nigella", an iconic brand in the baking', in A. L. McGill and S. Shavitt (eds), *Advances in Consumer Research*, vol. 36, Duluth, MN: Association for Consumer Research, pp. 482–87.

Hickman, L. (2002), '192, Notting Hill', *The Guardian*, 12 April, http://www.theguardian.com/lifeandstyle/2002/apr/14/foodanddrink.ethicalliving. Accessed 11 January 2016.

Hill, A. (2005), *Reality TV Audience and Popular Factual Television*, Oxford: Routledge.

Hollows, J. (2000), *Feminism, Femininity and Popular Culture*, Manchester: Manchester University Press.

——(2003), 'Feeling like a domestic goddess', *European Journal of Cultural Studies*, 6, pp. 179–202.

Hom, K. (2016, 2019), in-person interview by Gilly Smith.

Horvat, S. (2015), in-person interview by Gilly Smith.

Hunt, R. and Phillipov, M. (2014), ' "Nanna style": The countercultural politics of retro femininities', *Journal of Media and Culture*, 17:6, http://www.journal.media-culture.org.au/index.php/mcjournal/article/viewArticle/901. Accessed 23 May 2016.

Hussain, N. (2019), in-person interview by Gilly Smith.

Ind, N. (1995), *Terence Conran*, London: Sidgwick and Jackson.

Ingram, J. (2013), in-person interview by Gilly Smith.

Jaine, T. (2016), 'Keith Floyd obituary', *The Guardian*, 15 September, https://www.theguardian.com/global/2009/sep/15/keith-floyd-obituary. Accessed 12 June 2016.

James Beard Foundation, http://overallsandaprons.com/james-beard-foundation/. Accessed 23 July 2017.

Jenkins, H. (2008), *Convergence Culture: Where Old and New Media Collide*, New York: NYU Press.

Joo, J. (2015), interviewed by Libby Purves, *Midweek*, BBC Radio 4, London, 14 January.

Killelea, A. (2014), 'Top TV exports: The British shows which became hits all over the world', *The Mirror*, 20 November, http://www.mirror.co.uk/tv/tv-news/top-tv-exports-british-shows-4663729. Accessed 23 May 2016.

Laneri, R. (2016), 'If you want to live forever, move to this Italian town', *New York Post*, https://nypost.com/2016/04/12/if-you-want-to-live-forever-move-to-this-italian-town/. Accessed 4 July 2017.

Lappe, A. (2006), *Diet for a Hot Planet: The Climate Crisis at the End of Your Fork and What You Can Do about It*, London: Bloomsbury.

Lawson, N. (1999), *How to Eat: The Pleasures and Principles of Good Food*, London: Chatto & Windus.

——(2000), *How to Be a Domestic Goddess: Baking and the Art of Comfort Cooking*, London: Chatto & Windus.

——(2013), 'Nigella Lawson: "Nigellissima"', Talks at Google, http://www.youtube.com/watch?v=3sKwBpEeH90. Accessed 2 March 2020.

——(2017, 2019), in-person interview by Gilly Smith.

Leitch, A. (2009), 'Slow food and the politics of virtuous globalisation', in D. Inglis and D. Gimlin (eds), *The Globalisation of Food*, Oxford: Berg.

——(2013), 'Tuscanopia', in C. Counihan and P. Van Esterik, *Food and Culture: A Reader*, London: Routledge.

Levy, P. (2009), 'Keith Floyd: Television cook who paved the way for the modern generation of celebrity chefs', *The Independent*, 15 September, http://www.independent.co.uk/news/obituaries/keith-floyd-television-cook-who-paved-the-way-for-the-modern-generation-of-celebrity-chefs-1787820.html. Accessed 30 July 2016.

Lewis, M. (2007), 'Marco Pierre White on why he's back behind the stove for TV's *Hell's Kitchen*', *The Caterer*, 25 April, https://www.thecaterer.com/articles/313310/exclusive-marco-pierre-white-on-why-hes-back-behind-the-stove-for-tvs-hells-kitchen. Accessed 21 June 2016.

Lewis, T. (2010), 'Branding, celebritisation and the lifestyle expert', *Cultural Studies*, 24:4, pp. 580–98.

Llewellyn, P. (2005, 2006, 2008, 2013, 2015), in-person interview by Gilly Smith.

Lissak, M. (2015), in-person interview by Gilly Smith.

Lott, E. (2013), *Love & Theft: Blackface Minstrelsy and the American Working Class*, Oxford: Oxford University Press.

Low, S. (2002), 'How the TV chef was cooked up', *Daily Telegraph*, 20 July, http://www.telegraph.co.uk/foodanddrink/foodanddrinknews/3298706/How-the-TV-chef-was-cooked-up.html. Accessed 4 September 2004.

Lymbery, P. (2014), *Farmageddon: The True Cost of Cheap Meat*, London: Bloomsbury.

——(2017), *Dead Zone: Where the Wild Things Were*, London: Bloomsbury.

——(2016, 2017, 2018, 2019), in-person interview by Gilly Smith.

——(2017), 'Keynote speech', *Extinction and Livestock Conference*, https://philiplymbery.com/media-videos/. Accessed 26 May 2020.

——(2017), 'Hard cheese, hard life', Compassion in World Farming, https://www.ciwf.org.uk/philip-lymbery/blog/2017/11/hard-cheese-hard-life. Accessed 23 January 2018.

——(2019), 'Why our planet needs less meat and more extensive farming', 23 August, https://philiplymbery.com/why-our-planet-needs-less-meat/. Accessed 3 October 2019.

Mackie, R. (2019), 'We must change food production to save the world, says leaked report', *The Guardian*, 3 August, https://www.theguardian.com/environment/2019/aug/03/ipcc-land-use-food-production-key-to-climate-crisis-leaked-report. Accessed 25 September 2019.

Magee, R. M. (2007), 'Food puritanism and food pornography: The gourmet semiotics of Martha and Nigella Americana', *Journal of American Popular Culture (1900–present)*, 6:2, http://www.americanpopularculture.com/journal/articles/fall_2007/magee.htm. Accessed 23 April 2013.

Mail Foreign Service (2010), 'Jamie Oliver reduced to tears (and so are the Americans as they reject his healthy eating advice)', *Daily Mail*, 24 March, http://www.dailymail.co.uk/tvshowbiz/article-1260052/Jamie-Oliver-reduced-tears-US-rejects-healthy-eating-advice.html#ixzz4OvvcCK7J. Accessed 2 April 2016.

Manfredi, S. (1993), *Fresh from Italy: Italian Cooking for the Australian Kitchen*, Sydney: Hodder Headline.

Massari, S. (2017), in-person interview by Gilly Smith.

McCracken, G. (2005), *Culture and Consumption II: Markets, Meaning, and Brand Management*, Bloomington: Indiana University Press.

McKie, R. (2019), 'We must change food production to save the world, says leaked report', *The Guardian*, 4 August, https://www.theguardian.com/environment/2019/aug/03/ipcc-land-use-food-production-key-to-climate-crisis-leaked-report. Accessed 22 January 2020.

Mead, T. (2019), in-person interview by Gilly Smith.

Mindock, C. (2020), 'Trump administration announces reversal of Michelle Obama's healthy school food reforms – on her birthday', https://www.independent.co.uk/news/world/americas/us-politics/trump-school-lunches-michelle-obama-birthday-fruits-vegetables-a9289461.html. Accessed 22 January 2020.

Miller, D. and Reilly, J. (1994), *Food 'Scares' in the Media*, Glasgow: Glasgow University Media Group.

Mills, E. (2018), *Deliciously Ella*, London: Yellow Kite.

Millstone, E. (2013), in-person interview by Gilly Smith.

Moody, N. (2013), in-person interview by Gilly Smith.

Moriarty, M. (1991), *Roland Barthes*, Cambridge: Polity Press.

Morley, D. (1992), *Television, Audiences and Cultural Studies*, London: Routledge.

Morreale, J. (2007), 'Faking it and the transformations of identity', in D. Heller (ed.),
    Make-over Television: Realities Remodelled, London: I.B. Tuaris, pp. 95–106.

Moseley, R. (2002), 'Glamorous witchcraft: Gender and magic in teen film and
    television', *Screen*, 43, pp. 403–22.

——(2016), *Television for Women*, London: Routledge.

Mulvey, L. (1989), *Visual and Other Pleasures*, Houndsmill: MacMillan.

Munro, J. (2016), in-person interview by Gilly Smith.

Munt, S. (2000), *Cultural Studies and the Working Class: Subject to Change*,
    London: Continuum.

Muphy, A. (2012), in-person interview by Gilly Smith.

Nathanson, E. (2009), 'As easy as pie: Cooking shows, domestic efficiency, and
    postfeminist temporality', *Television & New Media*, 10:4, pp. 311–30.

Newcomb, H. and Hirsch, P. M. (1983), 'Television as cultural forum', *Quarterly
    Review of Film Studies*, 8, pp. 44–55.

The Naked Chef, (1999–2000, UK: Optomen Productions for BBC Two).

Newton, J. (1996), *Wogfood: An Oral History with Recipes*, Sydney: Random House.

NHS (National Health Service) (2011), 'National Child Measurement Programme –
    England 2011/2012', https://digital.nhs.uk/data-and-information/publications/
    statistical/national-child-measurement-programme/2011-12-school-year.
    Accessed 24 August 2016.

——(2017), *Health Survey for England 2017*, https://digital.nhs.uk/data-and-
    information/publications/statistical/health-survey-for-england/2017. Accessed 23
    June 2019.

Norberg-Hodge, H. (2019), *Local Is Our Future: Steps to an Economic Happiness*,
    Totnes: Local Futures.

Norheim, O. et al., Jha, P., Admasu, K., Godal, T., Hum, R., Kruk, M., Gómez-
    Dantés, O., Mathers, C. D., Pan, H., Sepúlveda, J., Suraweera, W., Verguet, S.,
    Woldemariam, A. T., Yamey, G., Jamison, D. T. and Peto, R. (2014), 'Avoiding 40
    per cent of the premature deaths in each country, 2010–30: review of national
    mortality trends to help quantify the UN Sustainable Development Goal for
    health', *The Lancet*, https://doi.org/10.1016/S0140-6736(14)61591-9.

Nunn, H. (2017), in-person interview by Gilly Smith.

Oakley, G. (2018), in-person interview by Gilly Smith.

Oliver, A. (2013), 'Dazzling picture of innocence: The secret photo-shoot of
    "beautiful and flirtatious" Oxford student Nigella, more than 20 years before her

court ordeal', *Daily Mail*, 22 February, http://www.dailymail.co.uk/news/article-2519928/Secret-photoshoot-Oxford-model-Nigella-Lawson-20-years-court-ordeal.html. Accessed 11 March 2016.

Oliver, J. (2010), *Jamie's Italy*, London: Penguin.

——(2017, 2019), in-person interview by Gilly Smith.

Office for National Statistics (2011), https://www.ons.gov.uk/census/2011census. Accessed 4 June 2019.

Oren, T. (2013), 'On the line: Format, cooking and competition as television values', *Critical Studies in Television*, 8:2, pp. 20–35.

Ouellette, L. and Hay, J. (2008), *Better Living through Reality TV: Television and Post-welfare Citizenship*, Oxford: Blackwell.

'Pabulum' (2020), Lexico.com, https://www.lexico.com/definition/pabulum. Accessed 26 May 2020.

Page, N. (2016), in-person interview by Gilly Smith.

Pearson, A. (2011), 'Why Jamie's *Dream School* is failing', *The Telegraph*, https://www.telegraph.co.uk/comment/columnists/8372110/Why-Jamies-Dream-School-is-failing.html. Accessed 1 June 2015.

Phillipov, M. (2016), 'The new politics of food: Television and the media/food industries', *Media International Australia*, 158:1, pp. 90–98.

The Pioneer Woman (2011–present, USA: Food Network).

Piper, N. (2015), 'Jamie Oliver and cultural intermediation', *Food, Culture and Society*, 18:2, pp. 245–64.

Plunkett, J. (2013), 'Simon Cowell's *Food Glorious Food* is his lowest-rating launch ever', *The Guardian*, https://www.theguardian.com/media/2013/feb/28/simon-cowell-food-glorious-food. Accessed 15 December 2019.

Pomroy, P. (2017), in-person interview by Gilly Smith.

Pope Fischer, L. (2010), 'Turkey backbones and chicken gizzards: Women's food roles in post-socialist Hungary', *Food and Foodways: Explorations in the History and Culture of Human Nourishment*, 18:4, pp. 233–60.

Popham, P. (1995), *Consuming Geographies: We Are Where We Eat*, London: Routledge.

Prince, R. (2014), 'How we're fed 434 hours of TV cookery a week – but the more they show, the less we cook', *Daily Mail*, 27 September, http://www.dailymail.co.uk/tvshowbiz/article-2771553/How-fed-434-hours-TV-cookery-week-cook.html#ixzz4NRZb0Y4Y. Accessed 12 September 2016.

Prince, R. (2005), *The New English Kitchen: Changing the Way You Shop, Cook and Eat*, London: Harper Collins.

Radio Times (2015), 'Jamie Oliver on his new campaign: "We need a sugar tax"', https://www.radiotimes.com/news/2015-09-03/jamie-oliver-on-his-new-campaign-we-need-a-sugar-tax/. Accessed 7 April 2016.

Ralling, J. (2016, 2019), in-person interview by Gilly Smith.

Rogers, E. (2003), *Diffusion of Innovations*, New York: Free Press.

Redden, G. (2010), 'Learning to labour on the reality talent show', *Media International Australia*, 134:1, pp. 131–40.

Richards, D. (1998), 'Big and getting bigger', *Washington Post*, 23 February, https://www.washingtonpost.com/archive/lifestyle/1998/02/23/big-and-getting-bigger/075167a6-9717-4429-89fe-6841d4d73a04/. Accessed 12 July 2016.

Rick, C. (2012), in-person interview by Gilly Smith.

Right2Food (2020), Food Foundation, https://shows.acast.com/right2food/. Accessed 26 May 2020.

Riviere, J. (1929), 'Womanliness as masquerade', *International Journal of Psychoanalysis*, 10, pp. 303–13.

Root, J. (2013), telephone interview by Gilly Smith.

Rosenbaum, R. (2014), 'Anthony Bourdain's theory on the foodie revolution', *Smithsonian Magazine*, https://www.smithsonianmag.com/arts-culture/anthony-bourdains-theory-foodie-revolution-180951848/#1SM5ZWhWPqHUACxY.99. Accessed 2 March 2020.

Rousseau, S. (2012), *Food Media: Celebrity Chefs and the Politics of Everyday Interference*, Oxford: Berg.

——(2016), Skype and email interview by Gilly Smith.

Rumbelow, H. (2016), 'I'm studying for a master's degree. It's changed my life — it's proper geeky', https://www.thetimes.co.uk/article/i-m-studying-for-a-master-s-degree-it-s-changed-my-life-it-s-proper-geeky-v9nnr7q0l. Accessed 7 September 2016.

Saner, E. (2012), 'Are there too many food programmes on TV?', *The Guardian*, 17 August, https://www.theguardian.com/tv-and-radio/2012/aug/17/conversation-food-tv-bake-off. Accessed 19 May 2020.

Sarnyai, G. (2018), 'Hungarian exodus: Examining Europe's falling population from an economic perspective', *Hungary Today*, https://hungarytoday.hu/hungarian-exodus-examining-europes-falling-population-economic-perspective-33519/. Accessed 23 June 2019.

Scarpone, L. (2016), in-person interview by Gilly Smith.

Shildrick, M. (1997), *Leaky Bodies and Boundaries: Feminism, Postmodernism and (Bio) Ethics*, London: Routledge.

Shipley, D. (2017), 'Picture this: Joe Wicks and his Instagram peers are strengthening publishing', 12 January, https://www.theguardian.com/books/booksblog/2017/jan/12/picture-this-joe-wicks-and-his-instagram-peers-are-strengthening-publishing. Accessed 23 November 2018.

Sinek, S. (2015), *Law of Diffusion of Innovation*, https://www.youtube.com/watch?v=VVXuN2drSpg. Accessed 13 November 2019.

Sitwell, W. (2016), *Eggs or Anarchy*, London: Simon & Schuster.

Skeggs, B. (1997), *Formations of Class and Gender: Becoming Respectable*, London: Sage.

Smith, G. (1998), *Australia: New Food from the New World*, London: Andre Deutsch.

——(2005), *Nigella Lawson: A Biography*, London: Andre Deutsch.

——(2008), *The Jamie Oliver Effect: The Man, the Food, the Revolution*, London: Andre Deutsch.

——(2012), 'Barthes on Jamie: Myth and the TV revolutionary', *Journal of Media Practice*, 13:1, pp. 3–17.

——(2016), 'Jaibli Salaam', Radio Reverb, SoundCloud, January, https://soundcloud.com/gilly-smith/sets/jaibli-salaam. Accessed 2 March 2020.

Solier, I. de (2005), 'TV dinners: Culinary television, education and distinction', *Continuum*, 19:4, pp. 465–81.

Spencer, C. (2002), *British Food: An Extraordinary Thousand Years of History*, London: Grub Street.

——(2005), telephone interview by Gilly Smith.

Start the Week (2016), BBC Radio 4, UK, https://www.bbc.co.uk/programmes/b07h69n9. Accessed 5 June 2017.

Steele, C. (2013), *Hungry City: How Food Shapes Our Lives*, London: Penguin.

Stevens, L., Cappellini, B. and Smith, G. (2015), '*Nigellissima*: An exploratory study of glamour, femininity and performativity', *Journal of Marketing Management*, 31:5&6, pp. 1–22.

Sullivan, R. (2016), in-person interview by Gilly Smith.

Sullivan, R. and Coulthard, D. (2019), *Warndu Mai (Good Food): Introducing Native Australian Ingredients to Your Kitchen*, Sydney: Hachette.

Swiatek, L. (2017), telephone interview by Gilly Smith.

Swenson, R. (2009), 'Cooking class: Gender on the Food Network', National Communication Association, 1 April, https://www.natcom.org/CommCurrentsArticle.aspx?id=914. Accessed 14 January 2020.

Symons, M. (2014), 'Australia's cuisine culture: A history of our food', *Australian Geographic*, 27 June, http://www.australiangeographic.com.au/topics/history-culture/2014/06/australias-cuisine-culture-a-history-of-food. Accessed 2 October 2016.

Theasby, I. and Firth, H. (Bosh!) (2019), in-person interview by Gilly Smith.

Thinkbox.tv, (2018), 'Home page', https://www.thinkbox.tv/news-and-opinion/blogs/the-video-world-in-2017/. Accessed 23 June 2018.

——(2019), 'Top programmes report: Week 48, November 25 – December 01', https://www.thinkbox.tv/research/barb-data/top-programmes-report/. Accessed 10 October 2019.

Thirkell, R. (2010), *CONFLICT: An Insider's Guide to Storytelling in Factual/Reality TV and Film*, London: Bloomsbury.

Thompson, M. (2013), telephone interview by Gilly Smith.

Thom, U. (2010), 'From migrant food to lifestyle cooking: The career of Italian cuisine in Europe', European History Online (EGO), http://www.ieg-ego. eu/thomsu-2010-en URN: urn:nbn:de:0159-2011051250 [YYYY-MM-DD]. Accessed 18 May 2010.

Thornham, S. (2007), *Women, Feminism and Media*, Edinburgh: Edinburgh University Press.

Thorogood, N. (2016, 2019), in-person interview by Gilly Smith.

Torode, J. (1997), *The Mezzo Cookbook*, London: Octopus.

——(1998), in-person interview by Gilly Smith.

Trafford, P. (2013), in-person interview by Gilly Smith.

UN.org (n.d.), 'Ending poverty', https://www.un.org/en/sections/issues-depth/ poverty/. Accessed 10 October 2019.

Urwin, R. (2015), 'Green is the new black: How veganism became sexy in London', *Evening Standard*, 4 March, https://www.standard.co.uk/lifestyle/foodanddrink/ green-is-the-new-black-how-veganism-became-sexy-in-london-10083206.html. Accessed 12 September 2019.

Vincent, A. (2016), 'ITV spark *Bake Off* Twitter backlash after promising to reveal new presenters', *The Telegraph*, https://www.telegraph.co.uk/tv/2016/ 09/14/new-great-british-bake-off-presenters-announced-live/. Accessed 2 December 2016.

Vincent, S. (2004), 'Nigella Lawson: Who'd be a goddess?', *The Guardian*, 16 October, http://www.theguardian.com/lifeandstyle/2004/oct/16/foodanddrink.shopping. Accessed 20 January 2014.

Walkerdine, V. (2003), 'Femininities: Reclassifying upward mobility and the neo-liberal subject', *Gender and Education*, 15:3, pp. 237–48.

Wan, L. (2017), 'Sugar taxes: The global picture in 2017', *Beverage Daily*, https://www. beveragedaily.com/Article/2017/12/20/Sugar-taxes-The-global-picture-in-2017. Accessed 10 October 2019.

Warin, M. (2011), 'Foucault's progeny: Jamie Oliver and the art of governing obesity', *Social Theory & Health*, 9:24, pp. 24–40.

White, M. P. (2017, 2019), in-person interview by Gilly Smith.

Wickes, J. (2015), *Lean in 15: The Shift Plan: 15 Minute Meals and Workouts to Keep You Lean and Healthy*, London: Bluebird.

Williams, E. (2015), in-person interview by Gilly Smith.

Willett, W., Rockström, J., Loken, B., Springmann, M., Lang, T., Vermeulen, S., Garnett, T., Tilman, D., DeClerck, F., Wood, A., Jonell, M., Clark, M., Gordon, L. J., Fanzo, J., Hawkes, C., Zurayk, R., Rivera, J. A., De Vries, W., Majele Sibanda, L., Afshin, A., Chaudhary, A., Herrero, M., Agustina, R., Branca, F., Lartey, A., Fan, S., Crona, B., Fox, E., Bignet, V., Troell, M., Lindahl, T., Singh, S., Cornell, S. E.,

Srinath Reddy, K., Narain, S., Nishtar, S. and Murray, C. J. L. (2019), 'Food in the Anthropocene: The EAT-*Lancet* commission on healthy diets from sustainable food systems', *The Lancet*, 16 January, https://www.thelancet.com/commissions/ EAT. Accessed 29 November 2019.

Williams, Z. (2014), 'Quaglino's, London SW1, restaurant review', *The Telegraph*, 12 December, http://www.telegraph.co.uk/foodanddrink/restaurants/ 11285098/Quaglinos-London-SW1-restaurant-review.html. Accessed 2 June 2016.

Williamson, B. (2019), in-person interview by Gilly Smith.

Wilson, B. (2015), *First Bite: How We Learn to Eat*, London: Fourth Estate.

——(2019), *The Way We Eat Now*, London: Fourth Estate.

Wood, Z. (2016), 'Halt sugar tax introduction, urges food and drink industry', *The Guardian*, 10 July, https://www.theguardian.com/business/2016/jul/10/halt-sugar-tax-introduction-urges-food-drink-industry. Accessed 20 August 2016.

Further reading

Aldridge, A. (2003), *Consumption*, London: Polity Press.

Barthes, R. (1977), *Image, Music, Text*, London: Fontana.

——(1987), *Criticism and Truth*, London: Athlone Press.

——(1988), *The Semiotic Challenge*, New York: Hill and Wang.

Benjamin, W. (1983), *Charles Baudelaire: A Lyric Poet in the Era of High Capitalism* (trans. Harry Zohn), London: Verso.

Brown, J. (2009), *Glamour in Six Dimensions: Modernism and the Radiance of Form*, New York: Cornell University Press.

Butler, J. (1989), *Gender Trouble: Feminism and the Subversion of Identity*, New York: Routledge.

——(2011), *Bodies That Matter: On the Discursive Limits of Sex*, New York: Routledge.

Cassell, C. and Symon, G. (2004), *Essential Guide to Qualitative Methods in Organizational Research*, London: Sage.

Castle, T. (1986), *Masquerade and Civilization: The Carnivalesque in Eighteenth-Century English Culture and Fiction*, Stanford: Stanford University Press.

Counihan, C. (1999), *The Anthropology of Food and Body: Gender, Meaning and Power*, New York: Routledge.

Cullen, J. (1976), *Saussure*, London: Fontana.

Deery, J. (2012), *Consuming Reality: The Commercialization of Factual Entertainment*, Basingstoke: Palgrave Macmillan.

Dovey, J. (2000), *Freakshow: First Person Media and Factual Television*, London: Pluto.

Drummond, R. (2009), *Accidental Country Girl* to a *Pioneer Woman Cooks: Food from My Frontier*, London: William Morrow Cookbooks.

——(2011), *Black Heels to Tractor Wheels: A Love Story*, London: William Morrow Cookbooks.

Ewen, S. (1988), *All Consuming Images: The Politics of Style in Contemporary Culture*, New York: Basic.

Hartley, J. (2008), *Television Truths*, Oxford: Blackwell.

Hebdidge, D. (1997), *Subculture: The Meaning of Style*, London: Routledge.

Hetsroni, A. (2010), *Reality Television: Merging the Global and the Local*, New York: Nova Science.

Hoggart, R. (1957), *Uses of Literacy*, London: Penguin.

Huff, R. M. (2006), *Reality Television*, Westport, CT and London: Praeger.

Grosz, E. A. (1995), *Space, Time and Perversion: Essays on the Politics of Bodies*, New York: Routledge.

Gundle, S. (2002), 'Hollywood glamour and mass consumption in postwar Italy', in R. Koshar (ed.), *Histories of Leisure*, Oxford: Berg, pp. 32–51.

——(2008), *Glamour: A History*, Oxford: Oxford University Press.

Gundle, S. and Castelli, C. T. (2006), *The Glamour System*, Basingstoke: Palgrave Macmillan.

Hooks, B. (2014), *Black Looks, Race and Representation*, New York: Routledge.

Jameson, F. (1991), *Postmodernism or the Cultural Logic of Late Capitalism*, London: Verso.

Jermyn, D. and Holmes, S. (2004), *Understanding Reality Television*, Abingdon: Routledge.

Kavka, M. (2012), *Reality TV*, Edinburgh: Edinburgh University Press.

Kieran, M. (ed.) (1998), *Media Ethics*, London: Routledge.

Lupton, D. (1996), *Food, the Body and the Self*, London: Sage.

Mackay, H. (ed.) (1997), *Consumption and Everyday Life*, London: Sage.

McLuhan, M. (1964), *Understanding Media: The Extensions of Man*, New York: McGraw-Hill.

Miller, D. A. (1998), *Theory of Shopping*, Cambridge: Polity Press.

Parker, A. and Sedgwick, E. K. (1995), *Performativity and Performance*, London and New York: Routledge.

Probyn, E. (2000), *Carnal Appetites: FoodSexIdentities*, London and New York: Routledge.

Skeggs, B. and Wood, H. (2012), *Reacting to Reality Television: Performance, Audience and Value*, London: Routledge.

Warde, A. (1997), *Consumption, Food and Taste*, London: Sage.

Wiseman, M. (1989), *The Ecstasies of Roland Barthes*, London: Routledge.

Wood, H. and Skeggs, B. (2011), *Reality Television and Class*, Basingstoke: Palgrave Macmillan.